Household Perspectives on Minority Language Maintenance and Loss

BILINGUAL EDUCATION & BILINGUALISM

Series Editors: Nancy H. Hornberger, *University of Pennsylvania, USA* and Wayne E. Wright, *Purdue University, USA*

Bilingual Education and Bilingualism is an international, multidisciplinary series publishing research on the philosophy, politics, policy, provision and practice of language planning, Indigenous and minority language education, multilingualism, multiculturalism, biliteracy, bilingualism and bilingual education. The series aims to mirror current debates and discussions. New proposals for single-authored, multiple-authored or edited books in the series are warmly welcomed, in any of the following categories or others authors may propose: overview or introductory texts; course readers or general reference texts; focus books on particular multilingual education program types; school-based case studies; national case studies; collected cases with a clear programmatic or conceptual theme; and professional education manuals.

All books in this series are externally peer-reviewed.

Full details of all the books in this series and of all our other publications can be found on http://www.multilingual-matters.com, or by writing to Multilingual Matters, St Nicholas House, 31–34 High Street, Bristol, BS1 2AW, UK.

BILINGUAL EDUCATION & BILINGUALISM: 115

Household Perspectives on Minority Language Maintenance and Loss

Language in the Small Spaces

Isabel Velázquez

MULTILINGUAL MATTERS
Bristol • Jackson

DOI https://doi.org/10.21832/VELAZQ2272
Library of Congress Cataloging in Publication Data
A catalog record for this book is available from the Library of Congress.
Names: Velázquez, Isabel (Maria Isabel) - author.
Title: Household Perspectives on Minority Language Maintenance and Loss: Language in the Small Spaces/Isabel Velázquez.
Description: Bristol; Blue Ridge Summit: Multilingual Matters, [2019] | Series: Bilingual Education & Bilingualism: 115 | Includes bibliographical references and index.
Identifiers: LCCN 2018031322| ISBN 9781788922272 (hbk : alk. paper) | ISBN 9781788922289 (pdf) | ISBN 9781788922296 (epub) | ISBN 9781788922302 (kindle)
Subjects: LCSH: Hispanic Americans—Languages—Case studies. | Bilingualism—United States—Case studies. | Language maintenance—United States—Case studies.
Classification: LCC P40.5.H57 V45 2019 | DDC 306.442/610973—dc23 LC record available at https://lccn.loc.gov/2018031322

British Library Cataloguing in Publication Data
A catalogue entry for this book is available from the British Library.

ISBN-13: 978-1-78892-227-2 (hbk)
ISBN-13: 978-1-78892-868-7 (pbk)

Multilingual Matters
UK: St Nicholas House, 31–34 High Street, Bristol BS1 2AW, UK.
USA: Ingram, Jackson, TN, USA.

Website: www.multilingual-matters.com
Twitter: Multi_Ling_Mat
Facebook: https://www.facebook.com/multilingualmatters
Blog: www.channelviewpublications.wordpress.com

The policy of Multilingual Matters/Channel View Publications is to use papers that are natural, renewable and recyclable products, made from wood grown in sustainable forests. In the manufacturing process of our books, and to further support our policy, preference is given to printers that have FSC and PEFC Chain of Custody certification. The FSC and/or PEFC logos will appear on those books where full certification has been granted to the printer concerned.

Typeset by Nova Techset Private Limited, Bengaluru and Chennai, India.

The world without mysteries is not a demonstrably better world than the world with them, and social science that cannot stand the mysteries that motivate and activate human behaviors is not a better social science than social science that attempts to approach these mysteries without destroying them.

Joshua Fishman (1989) *Language and Ethnicity in Minority Sociolinguistic Perspective*

Contents

Acknowledgements

This book is dedicated to the families whose experience serves as the basis of this project, and to all those whose grit, optimism and determination give life to Latino communities throughout the Midwest. To my husband José Miguel and my son José María, who have grown accustomed to looking for me in coffee houses, and love me nonetheless. To M. Jacobs, T. Catalano, P. McMahon, R. Werum and A. Montes, whose words of encouragement came just when I needed them. They have modelled for me what excellence looks like in research and in life, and I am proud to call them my colleagues and my friends. Lina Reznicek-Parrado, Luz Stella Valencia and Elisa Mateo contributed their work, their talent and their optimism to this project.

Finally, I am deeply grateful and much indebted to Marcus Vinícius Barbosa, whose careful reading and powerful insights taught me to challenge my own assumptions about the social and historical dimensions of linguistic experience. This book is better because of him. All mistakes are my own.

Este esfuerzo y todos: Para mi familia. Para a minha família. For my family. Siempre.

Acknowledgements

Preface: Language Planning in Intimate Household Settings

Every story of language maintenance is, in some way, the story of human resilience. This is not an exception. This book is about language and much more than language. Language is the vehicle for memory – collective and individual. It is the site of practices, ideas and stories that make us a *we*. It is also the site of practices, ideas and stories that make us an *I*. Through language we give form and meaning to the experiences that create the (speech) community. In community we create and give meaning to language. This is a book about language in the small spaces: the language of cursing and laughing, of crying and scolding and asking for the trash to be taken out at night. In other words, it is a book about the language through which the joint experience of a family comes together. This is an analysis of everyday household language dynamics and planning efforts in a group of first-generation Spanish-speaking families in the US Midwest. It is also a comparison of the self-perceptions and attitudes of the mother and one child in each of these households about their family language and its viability in public and private spaces. Most importantly, this is an in-depth examination of the gendered nature of linguistic transmission in immigrant households (Lanza, 2007; Okita, 2002).

Because this is a discussion about language from the perspective of working-class immigrant families, it is a discussion about language planning with no armies, no institutional agendas, no official proclamations, memorandums of understanding or certificates of achievement. On a larger scale, it is also a discussion about the everyday choices that take place in communities and families in every country on the receiving end of global population movements. This book is written at a specific point in the history of Spanish–English contact in the heart of the United States. It is a snapshot, a slice in time, of the experience of US Latinos in a mid-21st century, post-industrial, hyper-globalized Midwest. As such, one of the secondary arguments made here is that states like Nebraska constitute a suitable laboratory in which to study the sociolinguistic aspects of language contact dynamics which have been accelerated in recent decades by global labor movement, international agribusiness markets and post-industrial population shifts.

Language experience takes place along at least five dimensions: the materiality of language and its use; the perception of speakers about these conditions; their beliefs about self and others in the speech community; their emotional responses about language; and their emotional responses about language users. Despite this fact, even though bilingualism at the individual level and language contact at the level of the speech community are, by definition, dynamic, in attempting to describe them most research efforts (this one included) run the risk of framing them as linear processes with an either/or result. And yet, in thinking about language maintenance and language loss, linguists might do well to borrow an insight shared by neuroscientists and students of Buddhism alike: there is no intrinsic identity in anything; when conditions change, reality – and our perception of it, changes (Olendzki, 2012: 81).

In studying language dynamics in these households, how are we to know if we are witnessing the maintenance of Spanish or just a stage in the path toward its loss? Most likely, we may not answer that question without the recourse of time. What then, is the value of studying language use in these households, in this period, under these conditions, if we cannot arrive at a definitive answer? I will argue that this value lies precisely in these small spaces: in that window of time between being and losing, between inhabiting and dissipating; therein lies linguistic – which is to say human – experience.

1 Language Maintenance and Loss in Low Vitality Settings

Carina[1]: My children here and my children over there

So, what types of things do you do in a normal week that help your children develop their Spanish? As a middle-class immigrant who enjoyed the privilege of coming to this country with an intact family, I misunderstand Carina's answer the first time I hear it. Why is she using the plural? I've seen her pick up her son Luisito from kindergarten. He's bright, funny, opinionated – the type of kid that steals your heart the first time you speak with him. I've seen him chat with her as they walk home hand in hand. *The boy, I make him trace the letters, we write little words, like this. He asks me, 'Mom, what does it say here?' I tell him to get out his notebook and we work together. I tell him it's important that he know how to read in Spanish. That he knows how to write. With the girls, well no, they're older, and with them, I can't with them, right?*

Carina grew up in the most rural part of a Mexican state that in 2014 occupied fourth place for the percentage of the population in extreme poverty. Without completing elementary education and with little knowledge of English, she came to the United States five years ago with her husband and her youngest child, leaving her two eldest daughters behind. *It was very risky. I didn't want to put them in danger. Him I had to bring because he was still a baby. How could I leave him with relatives?* Was the sacrifice worth it? Is it even fair to ask this question?

Carina has lived in Lincoln for the past five years. She works in a restaurant kitchen and, with her husband and son, shares a two-bedroom apartment with her sister's family. She is tiny, with long black hair, a perennial smile, and a problem in one eye that she has not had checked because she doesn't have insurance and doesn't want to take time off work. She always amazes me with her energy and her determination to help her son maintain Spanish.

One morning in early April, the mothers in our workshop are talking about the difficulties of making their children speak Spanish at home. Carina joins in and gifts me this powerful insight: That as an immigrant mom, as a learner of English yourself, when you hear your kid using English you get a bittersweet mixture in the center of your heart – pride because he's picking up English, but guilt because he's not using Spanish. That you also feel a tinge of anger, of frustration when you spend four years trying to learn English and your kid picks it up in the playground by mid-summer. That when we feel frustrated, angry, guilty when/if our kids don't use Spanish correctly, our kids feel the same way because they feel they disappoint us. A feeling of falling short, frustration. A mixture of feelings.

Several weeks later, I'm fumbling with my keys, trying to open my front door, and I am surprised by the sound of laughter and Spanish on my street. I turn around just in time to see Luisito and his parents racing past my house on their bikes. In their giddiness, they don't see me. It's a beautiful May afternoon, the sunlight coming through the trees, the wind in their faces. Luisito rides ahead of his parents. He's exhilarated, and also looking back once in a while to make sure they are still there. His parents are encouraging him, telling him to look forward, to mind the road. I make a mental picture of that moment. I don't know what the future will hold. I don't know – have no way of knowing – how that family will face the challenges ahead of them. I don't know if Spanish will be a relevant part of Luisito's life by the time he reaches adulthood. What I do know is that the memory of this afternoon was written in Spanish, and that this afternoon Spanish was the vehicle for the love that I just saw riding by.

This book was written with three types of reader in mind. The first is interested in learning about the social dimensions of the US Latino language experience. The second is interested in finding out what everyday language contact looks like when the second (Spanish) and third (English) most spoken languages in the world (Ethnologue) co-exist in the same space with vastly asymmetrical positions. The third is interested in understanding the role of speaker attitudes and self-perceptions of agency in the intergenerational transmission of a minority language. This effort is dedicated to all of them, together with an invitation to bear in mind that the stories presented throughout these pages are not a vehicle to display linguistic exemplars *in vitro*, but a slice of the lived experience of the three-dimensional women, families and community in this study.

What follows is a brief overview of the main theoretical issues related to Spanish/English contact in New Latino Diaspora communities (Wortham *et al.*, 2002) with low ethnolinguistic vitality (LEV) for Spanish. To illustrate these issues I will use the example of LEV communities in the state of Nebraska, in the US Midwest. The first concept I will address is that of *language vitality*. Ethnolinguistic vitality theory (EVT) is a sociopsychological approach to the study of minority language maintenance. In the last three decades, EVT has been used as a framework in numerous studies on topics as diverse as language attitudes, intergroup relations, intercultural communication, language choice and language revitalization (Yagmur & Ehala, 2011). In very broad terms, the core assumption behind this theory is that language practices function as a marker of ethnolinguistic identity (Kindell & Lewis, 2000). In its original articulation, Giles *et al.* (1977: 308) defined ethnolinguistic vitality as 'That which makes a group likely to behave as a distinctive and active collective entity in intergroup situations'. For Giles *et al.*, a group's relative ethnolinguistic vitality could be assessed by measuring several structural variables, which Miller (2000: 170) organizes into three categories: *status factors* (economic status, social status, sociohistorical prestige, and status of language both within and outside a community), *demographic factors* (number of members, distribution, concentration, proportion, birthrate, and patterns of immigration and emigration), and *institutional support factors* (the extent to which the group receives support for the language in both formal and informal institutions such as home, school, government, church, business, etc.). Under this framework, high vitality groups would be more likely to maintain their language, whereas low vitality groups would be more likely to assimilate to the majority group. Later reformulations of this theory place greater emphasis on speaker perceptions as determiners of maintenance. Bourhis *et al.* (1981) argue that group members' subjective vitality perceptions of each of these structural variables may be as important as the group's 'objective' vitality. Yagmur and Ehala (2011: 103) elaborate on this idea, suggesting that the integrative versus segregative attitudes of one generation influence the language behavior of succeeding generations.

Although widely used, EVT has also been widely criticized, most notably by Husband and Saifullah Khan (1982), who argue that this framework creates the illusion of vitality measures being empirically testable and quantifiable, and by Tollefson (1991), who argues that it does not account for the institutional constraints created by dominant groups to prevent minorities from accessing social and political institutions. Two more recent contestations of EVT are germane to the study of Spanish/English contact in New Latino Diaspora communities. Using the example of Anglo-Nigerian pidgin, Mann (2000) contests the notion that LEV scores should necessarily lead to language shift. He writes that some languages that do not map one-on-one with a specific local, ethnic or social group – such as pidgins and creoles, for example – can still be sociocommunicationally alive despite failing to meet most of the parameters of traditional EV assessment. In light of this argument, he formulates his *sociocommunicational need hypothesis*: 'A language will show good and/ or progressive vitality, in contexts where there is a sociocommunicational need for it, even if it has low status, low demography, and low institutional support' (Mann, 2000: 470).

The second contestation to EVT to be discussed here is that of Karahan (2004). In his study of the ethnolinguistic vitality, attitudes and practices of Bosnian Turks in Sakarya, Turkey, Karahan finds that, while his subjects wished to preserve their Bosnian ethnic and cultural features, they did not necessarily choose the Bosnian language in their everyday life (Karahan, 2004: 88), thus putting into question the perforce relationship between ethnic identity and language practices. An additional drawback of EVT relevant to this study is that it was not intended to account for speech communities that are not spatially bound, but rather are highly mobile and are distributed along transregional/transnational networks which are partly located in larger communities with low overall demographic density. Nonetheless, we refer here to the concept of high ethnolinguistic vitality in order to operationalize its opposite: communities where speakers choose to speak their family language and transmit it to their children, *despite* low status, low demography and low institutional support for Spanish.

What does low ethnolinguistic vitality look like? By definition, Spanish/English bilingual communities in the New Latino Diaspora share all or some of the following features (Velázquez *et al.*, 2015):

- low overall demographic density;
- rapid growth of Latino population as percentage of total population;
- rapid growth of second-generation speakers as percentage of K-12 student population;
- reduced public presence of Spanish;
- reduced institutional support for Spanish;
- contact with speakers of other minority languages;
- majority Mexican and Mexican American dialects, in contact with other varieties;
- disconnect between intra-group and inter-group language ideologies and goals;
- diglossia;
- decoupling of ethnic identity and linguistic skills;
- reduced opportunities for literacy development;
- religious education as vehicle for literacy/maintenance in the second generation;
- language brokering as motor for household maintenance;
- gendered communities of practice as sites for linguistic/cultural maintenance;

- Spanish vested with social capital in local support networks;
- L2 speakers are often evaluators of native speaker competence;
- children have reduced contact with middle-class, upwardly mobile bilinguals.

Another authoritative approach to the study of minority language maintenance and shift is Fishman's reversing language shift theory (RLS). For Fishman (1991), linguistic vitality is determined by intergenerational transmission. Minority languages survive and grow, he explains, 'in the realm of intimacy – home, family, neighborhood, friendship, immediate community – a realm which is difficult to engineer, easy to overlook, since higher functions easily elicit more attention because they are power related, functions to which individuals graduate as they leave the home and go out into life' (Fishman, 2001: 4). Heavily influenced by the RLS model, UNESCO's (2003) report on Language Vitality and Endangerment enumerates seven factors which may be used to assess language vitality: intergenerational transmission; absolute number of speakers; proportion of speakers within the total population; trends in existing language domains; response to new domains and media; availability of materials for language education and literacy; and language attitudes and policies (UNESCO, 2003: 7). Appendix 1 is an adaptation of UNESCO's vitality assessment scales, presented to exemplify the situation of Spanish in LEV communities. Here, the reader is invited to keep in mind that the original scales were designed to assess the vitality of endangered languages, and that they are used here for illustrative purposes only.

Another element of Fishman's work (Fishman, 2001) that we will use here is the following notation for the functional distribution of languages:

$$\frac{P}{n-P} : \frac{Th}{Th}'$$

where P represents the more powerful social functions of language (e.g. employment, higher education, mass media, government, etc.); $n - P$ represents functions related to family, neighborhood, community and some types of community-controlled preschool and community education (Fishman, 2001: 10), and Th represents the threatened language. This equation, then, represents the ideal outcome of many RLS efforts around the world: a speech community where both power and non-power functions are discharged by a previously endangered language (Fishman, 2001: 10). In actuality, explains Fishman, the following situations are more common:

(a) $\frac{P}{n-P} : \frac{n-Th}{Th}$,

(b) $\frac{P}{n-P} : \frac{n-Th/Th}{Th}$,

The notation in (a) describes a situation of diglossia, where the majority language is used to perform all power-related functions. In (b), the majority and minority languages share some of these functions. An additional distribution is possible, of course, in which the public and private functions are shared by both languages. Fishman's notation is useful to illustrate two major pressures faced by minority language communities: on the one hand, the need to elevate Th from $n - P$ to P functions (Fishman, 2001: 11); on the other, the need to arrest the encroachment of the majority language in intimate spaces so that intergenerational transmission can take place successfully.

Trying the reader's patience, I will introduce here a fourth and final notation, (d), which describes the situation of Spanish in LEV communities in the New Latino Diaspora:

$$(d)\ \frac{P}{n-P} : \frac{E/S2}{S1/E}$$

In (d), E represents English, $S1$ represents varieties of Spanish native to the local speech community, and $S2$ represents both varieties of Spanish not native to the community and Spanish as a second language (L2). The reader will note that, in the linguistic situation described in (d), it is possible to have agents of P-functions – e.g. teachers, school administrators, doctors, lawyers, police officers, judges, politicians, etc. – who belong to the same language community as their clients, students, patients, etc., without necessarily belonging to the same speech community.[2]

Language Planning and Language Management in the Context of the Family

The second element of the theoretical structure to be developed here is related to language policy and language planning. In one of the earliest uses of the concept, Fishman (1989: 265) defines language planning as 'consciously organized authoritative efforts to allocate resources (rewards and sanctions) in connection to language'. At the level of the household, King et al. (2008) define family language policy as 'explicit and overt planning in relation to language use within the home among family members' – in other words, all explicit efforts to influence 'how languages are managed, learned, and negotiated within families' (King et al., 2008: 907). For these authors, the core of family language policy consists of decisions and actions taken by parents – or other caretakers – in three areas: *status planning* (whether and when to use one or more of the family languages); *corpus planning* (what language or language variety is used for what types of literacy activities); and *acquisition planning* (deciding how, when and where to teach what language or language variety to which members of the household) (King et al., 2008: 910).

Despite parents' best intentions, however, the results of family language planning are not guaranteed to be successful (Spolsky, 2009). They may or may not have clear, articulated goals (Ricento, 2006), can be explicit or implicit (Wiley, 1995), are not unidirectional, can in fact be conflicting (Lanza, 2007), and result in what Baldauf (1994) and Kaplan and Baldauf (1997) identified as *unplanned language planning*: 'A formal language plan that does not take into account existing unplanned language plans within the social ecosystem' (in Spolsky, 2009: 10). Taking this into consideration, it seems more appropriate here to adopt Spolsky's concept of *family language management*, which the author understands as conscious attempts made by adult speakers 'to control the household sociolinguistic environment by selecting a language to speak with each other or with the children, or give explicit instruction' (Spolsky, 2009: 16). Language management strategies may include attempting to control the home language environment, bringing speakers of the target language into the household, seeking outside support, community activism and/or relocation (Spolsky, 2009: 24). An advantage of Spolsky's model is that it acknowledges the tension between household-internal and household-external forces which impinge on the results of language management:

> Organized language management in the family domain begins when a family member with authority (normally a parent) decides to correct the unsatisfactory language performance or proficiency of another family member [...] and to persuade them to modify their language practices. This stems from a common belief that a parent has responsibility for the language competence of children and further depends on the values assigned to different languages or varieties or variants. These values in turn are derived most probably from experience outside the family domain [...] As participants gain experience outside the family, they bring in new practices and beliefs. [...] The domain-internal pressures are challenged by external pressures, making clear that while it is valuable to analyze domains separately, they are regularly open to influences of the wider sociolinguistic ecology. (Spolsky, 2009: 30)

Another contribution of Spolsky's model is that it highlights the fact that language management is, fundamentally, a social and ideological process. In other words, even as it deals with individual language choice, it is a phenomenon that is grounded in the speech community (Spolsky, 2009: 2). As McGroarty (2008) points out, ideological frameworks determine choice, evaluation and use of language for all speakers and in all language communities. In the specific case of immigrant households, however, parental ideologies about languages, about parenting itself and about their own sense of agency in their children's development perform the double duty of reflecting broader societal attitudes and ideologies (King et al., 2008), and setting the conditions for their children's acquisition – or lack thereof – of the family language(s) (De Houwer, 1999; Durand, 2010; Lanza, 2007; Velázquez, 2014b). In fact, Baker (2005: 215) argues that the absence of strong integrative or instrumental attitudes may be linked to the absence of minority-language reproduction in the home. In very simple terms: ideology fuels parental language choices; these choices result in sustained language practices. Sustained practices result in language socialization, socialization fuels intergenerational transmission, and intergenerational transmission is the sine qua non condition for minority language maintenance (Fishman, 1991).

Two additional elements of Spolsky's language management model will serve us well in attempting to understand household language dynamics in LEV settings. These are the sociolinguistic concepts of *domain* and *speech community*. Spolsky borrows the concept of domain from Fishman (1972), and defines it as a social space in which language choices are determined: by location – and social interpretations of that location; by the relationships between the participants; and by the topic – 'what is appropriate to talk about in the domain' (Spolsky, 2009: 3). Understood in these terms, then, the family household constitutes a domain. 'Essentially', writes Spolsky (2009: 3), 'regular language choices made by an individual are determined by his or her understanding of what is appropriate to the domain'. The second concept of which we shall make use here is that of *speech community* (Gumperz, 1964; Labov, 1974). In constructing his explanatory model of language management, Spolsky distinguishes between a *speech community* – 'those who share a communication network, agreeing more or less on the appropriateness of the use of the multiple varieties used in that community' (Spolsky, 2009: 2), and a *language community* – 'all those who speak a specific variety of a language' (Spolsky, 2009: 2).

Family Language Management in Minority Language Households

Let us pause here to outline how these concepts apply to language management in minority language households in general, and to Midwestern, first-generation Latino households in particular. Language dynamics in immigrant households differ from language majority households in at least four ways. These are related: to participation in different speech communities, as illustrated in Figure 1.1 and Table 1.1; to the physical and social dislocation of household members; to the power imbalances that result from these dislocations; and to differences in the acquisition of and socialization to language(s) and language varieties.

In Figure 1.1 the reader will note the intersecting nature of the different speech communities to which the members of a Midwestern, first-generation Latino household can lay claim. Each area in this diagram represents a distinct social space with location, participants and topic. In other words, this household could also be conceptualized as a space of interaction inhabited by members 'who share a communication network, agreeing more or less on the appropriateness of the use of the multiple

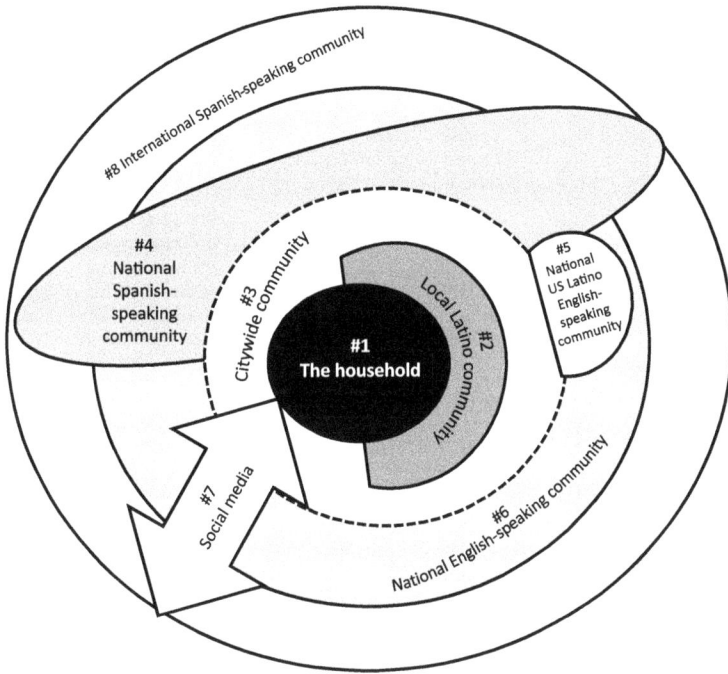

Figure 1.1 Participation in different speech communities

Table 1.1 Participation in different speech communities

Community #1 Family

Language policy Spanish more important	Dominant language Spanish-dominant with code-switching depending on member, generation, topic	Language managers ENDOCENTRIC/EXOCENTRIC Parents, children, other adults
Location Household	Relationship between participants Kinship	Examples Everyday interactions

Community #2 Local, Latino

Language policy Spanish more important	Dominant language Spanish-dominant with some accommodation for non-members and younger speakers	Language managers ENDOCENTRIC
Location Physical (and virtual) Businesses, churches, community organizations, schools, others	Relationship between participants Neighborhood, friendship, workplace, shared communities of practice, consumption	Examples Service encounters, religious services, community events, ethnic festivals, local Spanish-language radio and print media

(Continued)

Table 1.1 (*Continued*)

Community #3 Local, citywide

Language policy English more important	Dominant language English-dominant with some accommodation via translation/interpretation	Language managers ENDOCENTRIC
Location Physical (and virtual) Neighborhood, workplace, schools, churches, businesses, city and state government offices and websites, hospitals, others	Relationship between participants Neighborhood, friendship, workplace, shared communities of practice, consumption	Examples PTA meetings, doctors' appointments, sports matches, service encounters, local and state government websites, register of deeds, local paper, radio

Community #4 National US Latino Spanish-language media

Language policy Spanish more important	Dominant language Spanish-dominant with some code-switching	Language managers ENDOCENTRIC/EXOCENTRIC (e.g. programs produced in Latin America)
Location Virtual	Relationship between participants Consumption, shared communities of practice	Examples Soap operas, soccer broadcasts, Spanish-language artists, *People en español* and *TVyNovelas* magazines, blogs, websites, podcasts, newsfeeds, radio, corporations targeting this market

Community #5 National US Latino English-language media

Language policy Code-switching more important	Dominant language Code-switching, English- dominant	Language managers ENDOCENTRIC
Location Virtual	Relationship between participants Consumption, shared communities of practice. Mostly young bicultural Latinos	Examples *NuvoTV, MTV Tr3s, mun2* TV networks, *Latino, Cosmo, Quinceañera* magazines, blogs, websites, podcasts, newsfeeds, radio, corporations targeting this market

Community #6 National English-speaking

Language policy English more important	Dominant language Standard English with some variation Some accommodation via translation/interpretation	Language managers ENDOCENTRIC
Location Virtual and physical	Relationship between participants Citizenship, consumption, work, shared communities of practice	Examples English-language cultural industries (entertainment, print publishers, radio, internet), court documents, passports, tax documents, mortgages, insurance policies, national

(*Continued*)

Table 1.1 (*Continued*)

		media, entertainment industry, publishing industry, blogs, websites, podcasts, newsfeeds, radio, corporations targeting mainstream markets
Community #7 Social media		
Language policy Depends on personal network	Dominant language Code-switching and standard/non-standard varieties of Spanish and English depending on personal network	Language managers ENDOCENTRIC/EXOCENTRIC Content producers (self and others), user policies
Location Virtual	Relationship between participants Friendship, kinship, work, shared communities of practice	Examples SMS messages, Facebook posts, tweets, Skype, Instagram, Snapchat
Community #8 (a) International Spanish *speech* community		
Language policy Spanish more important	Dominant language Spanish-dominant with some code-switching	Language managers ENDOCENTRIC/EXOCENTRIC
Location Virtual and physical (Family's country of origin; first-generation speakers living in other parts of the United States)	Relationship between participants Friendship, kinship	Examples Personal correspondence, visits, remittances, phone calls, greeting cards
Community #8 (b) International Spanish *language* community		
Language policy Spanish more important	Dominant language Standard Spanish with some variation	Language managers ENDOCENTRIC
Location Virtual	Relationship between participants Consumption, shared communities of practice, and sometimes citizenship	Examples Latin America and Spain-based cultural industries (entertainment, print publishers, radio, internet); textbooks, grammars, schooling systems, language academies and institutes; Latin America and Spain-based corporations targeting US-based Spanish speakers. In some cases, official documents issued by other countries

varieties used in that community' (Spolsky, 2009: 2). To be sure, the members of a hypothetical English monolingual household living on the same street as this hypothetical bilingual household would also belong to different speech communities. There would, however, be two important differences among them. First, and most evident, for the monolingual household, the unmarked choice for participation in all speech communities would be English – as opposed to Spanish, English or code-switching (C/S) for the Latino household. Secondly, for the monolingual household, language authority would be endocentric to each specific community, while for the Latino household it would be both endocentric and exocentric, depending on the speech community.

A second source of power imbalance is present when one or both parents do not know how to speak English or have limited experience in communicating with institutional actors in their new community (e.g. navigating the school system, interacting with service providers). As Spolsky explains:

> In a household that respects authority, there is likely to be accommodation to the desires of the person with most authority, who can become language manager. In immigrant situations, the weak status of the first generation immigrant *vis-à-vis* the new society gives an opening to children to try to dominate language choice. Confirming or conflicting with the effect of personal status, the status of the languages themselves is relevant. The ideological status of each language usually reflects its status in the wider community. (Spolsky, 2009: 29)

Aside from the physical, social and cultural dislocations involved in transnational migration, for many first-generation Latino families in the Midwest physical dislocation often includes a second process of trans-regional displacement: from densely populated metropolitan centers with traditional Latino settlement, such as Los Angeles, Miami or Chicago, to non-metropolitan, rural and semi-rural Midwest localities. In some cases, it also includes the separation of one or both parents from one or more of the children for extended periods of time (Velázquez, 2014). Among many other emotional and developmental impacts, this separation takes a toll on the structure of authority within the household.

Children in all households influence their parents' linguistic choices, of course, but in language minority households instances of child language management may include, for example, exchanges in which the child refuses to use the home language and the adult switches to English for expediency reasons, or instances where children serve as linguistic and cultural brokers for their parents (Faulstich Orellana, 2003; Tse, 1995). In fact, Touminen (1999) argues that in immigrant households it is the children who decide what the home language will be. The result, she adds, is a potential power imbalance that can occur between adults and children. The point made by Touminen is of particular relevance for the purposes of language socialization. Unlike language-majority households, in language-minority households both parent and child are undergoing parallel (but distinct) processes of language acquisition. Additionally, while immigrant parents – much like their language-majority counterparts – are socializing their children to and through their family language, and setting an explicit language policy for the household, in language-minority households children are also socializing their parents through implicit and explicit attempts to select the language of the environment, through cultural and linguistic brokering, and sometimes through explicit instruction, correction and evaluation of parental L2 speech. And because, when seen in a new light, sometimes the obvious is the most compelling, you and I, reader, will remember that here a luxury that language-minority parents do not share with their language-majority counterparts: for them, it is never a foregone conclusion that their children and grandchildren will speak their native language(s) (Fishman, 1989: 465).

We return now to Spolsky's definition of *family language management*: conscious attempts made by adult speakers 'to control the household sociolinguistic environment by selecting a language to speak with each other or with the children, or give explicit instruction' (Spolsky, 2009: 16). In first-generation Latino families in LEV communities in the Midwest, adults with the potential to influence the family's linguistic environment may or may not be the parents, and may or may not reside within the same household. These may include: other adult relatives living in the same household permanently or for extended periods of time; adult children living away from home or in the same household; other parents in the immediate neighborhood and in parents' closest circle of interaction; teachers, medical professionals and social workers; community and religious leaders; and extended family members who may be physically located in another region of the United States or in the parents' country of origin. This influence can take place through: increased exposure to either Spanish or English for the children; criticism or praise of parental strategies; shared caregiving; modeling of parenting behaviors; access to resources through the medium of the family language; offering of advice; providing expressed evaluations of language, language varieties and language users; and generally by providing (or failing to provide) a speech community where children can develop the linguistic and pragmatic skills that will potentially allow them to use their family language with someone other than their parents.

The reader will remember that for King *et al.* (2008: 910) the core of family language planning consists of decisions and actions taken by parents or other caretakers in three areas: *status planning, corpus planning* and *acquisition planning*. Table 1.2 summarizes how these areas differ in language-minority and language-majority households in LEV settings.

Social Capital and Social Networks

The third element of the theoretical framework described here relates to the concepts of *social network* and *social capital*. Outlining the necessary conditions for minority language vitality at community, regional and national levels, Lo Bianco (2008a, 2008b) argues that revitalization efforts

Table 1.2 Family language planning in language-minority and language-majority households

Areas of family language planning	Language-minority household	Language-majority household
Status planning Whether and when to use one or more of the family languages	Parents control children's exposure to language(s), with direct input from children and adults in the family, community (e.g. teachers, school counselors, religious and community leaders, caregivers, social workers, medical professionals) Family bilingualism/multilingualism framed by schools as a problem Bilingual skills are source of social capital Use of family language in public spaces risks exposure to ethnic stereotypes, xenophobic discourses	Parents control children's exposure to language(s), with indirect input from other adults in the family, community Family bilingualism/multilingualism framed by schools as an asset Bilingual skills are source of personal capital Use of family language in public spaces does not risk exposure to ethnic stereotypes, xenophobic discourses
Corpus planning What language or language variety is used for what types of literacy	With few exceptions, literacy is not supported by school system nor by linguistic landscape in community Limited and inconsistent exposure to standard varieties and formal domains Limited availability of print materials Development of literacy unlikely without parents' active, extensive, sustained management	Literacy supported by school system and the community's linguistic landscape Consistent and sustained exposure to standard varieties and formal domains Abundant availability of print materials Development of literacy possible even without parents' active, extensive, sustained management
Acquisition planning How, when and where to teach what language or language varieties to which members of the household	Children and parents undergoing parallel processes of language acquisition Intergenerational transmission of family language is not a given Parents are not primary source of native-like input in majority language Children have limited exposure to balanced bilingual/bicultural adults	Only children undergoing process of language acquisition Intergenerational transmission of family language is a given Parents are primary source of native-like input in majority language Children have limited exposure to balanced bilingual/bicultural adults

Source: Adapted from King et al. (2008).

must take into consideration: *capacity development* – the development of personal language proficiency and use, through formal and informal learning; *opportunity creation* – the development of domains in which use of the language is natural, welcome and expected; and *desire* – investment in learning the language, because proficiency in it brings certain rewards (Lo Bianco & Kreeft Peyton, 2013: 1). Attempting to account for differences in transmission outcomes among Midwestern Latino families, despite parents' overall positive attitudes toward Spanish, I have proposed elsewhere a three-factor model to understand intergenerational transmission of Spanish in the context of the United States (Velázquez, 2013). Success in this effort, I argue, depends on *quality and amount of exposure, children's opportunities for use* and *relevance*. In Velázquez *et al.* (2015) we operationalize at speaker level what Lo Bianco and Kreeft Peyton (2013) define as *opportunity*: the use of the family language with interlocutors and in domains where Spanish is natural, welcome and expected. They define this as *viability of the family language* (Lo Bianco & Kreeft Peyton, 2013: 2). Viability is subsumed under the broader concept of *language relevance*, which they define as 'language viability at the point in time of data collection. (…) not what speakers intend to do, or why they intend to do it, but what they report as actually taking place in common, every-day interactions' (Lo Bianco & Kreeft Peyton, 2013: 3). It seems appropriate to point out here that relevance is not a discrete feature of languages, but a dynamic property of social interactions. The main thrust of the present argument, then, is that speakers do not (or not only) choose a language or language variety because of emotional or aesthetic reasons but, above all, because they find it to be the most viable option to access and share social capital – i.e. material, informational or emotional support. In aggregate, these choices determine the structure of their personal network of interaction and the patterns of their everyday behavior (Hawe *et al.*, 2004). An unavoidable part of this everyday experience is the experience of class. For speakers of Spanish in the context of the United States, the dimension of socio-economic class makes possible the following distinction: for university-educated, middle-class, upwardly mobile L1 and L2 speakers, Spanish can primarily be a source of personal capital – i.e. a source of academic and economic advancement and individual recognition, whereas for working-class speakers it is primarily a source of social capital – i.e. a way to access networks of support.

In their study of social capital, self-esteem and online social network use among college students, Steinfield *et al.* (2008) argue that differences in the strength and type of social ties result in different types of capital: *bonding social capital* – found between individuals in tightly knit and emotionally close relationships, such as family and close friends; and *bridging social capital* – found in loose connections between individuals such as colleagues or acquaintances (Steinfield *et al.*, 2008: 436). Influenced by Granovetter's (1973) seminal work on social network theory, they posit that both types of social ties are useful, and accrue material and psychological benefits to the members of a network. In sociolinguistics, social network analysis (SNA) has been a frequently used research approach since it was introduced to the field by Jim and Leslie Milroy in the 1980s (Milroy, 1987; Milroy & Milroy, 1992). Researching language use in Belfast, L. Milroy (1987) devises a network strength scale using five indicators to establish the level of multiplexity and density of the interviewed speaker's social ties. She finds a statistically relevant connection between phonological variation and the speaker's personal networks. Since then, SNA has been adapted and incorporated into numerous variationist and linguistic contact studies because it allows for the study of small, mobile groups, traditionally invisible in other models (Milroy & Milroy, 1992), because it offers plausible explanations of the spread of a linguistic feature among speakers who are separated by ideological and/or physical barriers (Milroy, 1987, 2002), and because it explains the survival of minority languages in environments where there is a strong pressure to shift (Milroy & Li, 1995), and the construction of shift-resistant minority language networks as a support system in stigmatized, marginalized communities (Zentella, 1997). Velázquez (2012) is an analysis of mothers' social network in 15 Mexican American families residing in the city of El Paso, TX, the ethnolinguistic enclave of La Villita, in Chicago, IL, and the city of Lincoln, NE. Examining the network features of primary language of exchange, density, strength of ties, level of integration to local, regional and transnational networks and gender segregation, findings in that study suggest that in these families intergenerational transmission of Spanish was influenced not so much by network density and multiplexity as by mother's perception of benefit/cost, mother's participation in networks where Spanish is vested with social capital, and mother's own competence in English and Spanish. Why look at first-generation mothers' social networks in order to study family language maintenance and loss in their children?[3]: First, to understand the resources available to mothers as they engage in parenting in a new environment; and secondly, to understand the resources available to children as related to language socialization, quality and amount of exposure to Spanish, and opportunities for use (Velázquez, 2014a, 2014b).

Even when they do not incorporate an SNA component, several studies of heritage language (HL) maintenance conducted in other contexts and at different points in the bilingual lifespan support the idea of parents' social network as determinant in children's later maintenance in the family language. To name just two examples: Cho (2000) studies self-reports of proficiency in Korean in a group of second-generation adults, and finds an relationship between adult HL attainment and the variables of *negative external feedback, degree of ethnic connection, frequency of interaction with speakers of the HL* and *degree of acceptance of HL values.* Tannenbaum and Howie (2002) study maintenance patterns among nine- to 12-year-olds in a group of Chinese-speaking immigrant families in Australia. They find that children were more likely to use and prefer to use their parents' mother tongue when they perceived their family to be more cohesive and low in hierarchy, had fewer negatively loaded emotions associated with their parents, and showed indications of a secure attachment pattern. In both cases, the reasons for use or non-use of the family language went beyond demographic and social factors, and included individual, attitudinal, affective and identity/ethnic orientation factors which necessitated childhood participation in adult networks where the family language was vested with social capital.

Globalization, Midwestern Style

(1) This is Nebraska, a state with a population of 1.8 million, and 2.4 million heads of cattle (Bergin, 2014). It is 2010, early morning in the city of Lexington – overall population 10,204, of which 60.4% is Latino. A Mexican immigrant prepares to start her shift at one of the nation's largest meat-processing plants. She came to join the members of her extended family already working here, but left her parents and siblings behind. This year, Mexico is the second largest importer of US beef and pork, and the first worldwide consumer of US chicken (USDA). So it is at least theoretically possible that the members of the same family are processing the meat that their relatives will eat some 2000 miles away.[4]

(2) It is the first week of school for a student in the south side of Omaha – overall population 434,353, of which 13.1% is Latino. Because he has recently arrived from Guatemala he is placed in one of the few Spanish/English dual language programs in the state. The teacher, herself an immigrant from Latin America, addresses him in Spanish. It takes her a little while to realize that he doesn't understand what she is saying, because he is mostly monolingual in a Mayan language.

(3) The day is blustery and the coffee isn't great, but it's hot and keeps coming. The conversation is lively. The very blond and very blue-eyed manager of this restaurant chain in Lincoln – overall population 268,738, of which 6.3% is Latino, serves us a third cup and finally decides to chat with us in Spanish. He tells us that he is from California, his wife is Mexican, and his children are adopted Nebraskans. We talk for a while about the common reasons that brought us here: we found work; it's a good place to raise a family. He asks where we are from, and when I mention the name of my town, overlooking the Pacific Ocean on the border between Mexico and the United States, his face lights up. He laughs at the coincidence. He explains that he was born in California, but that his grandparents on his mother's side came from the same town as me. He then starts reciting family names and kinship ties and I find myself, in the middle of the prairie, playing a game that I have jokingly called my city's sport of choice: *How are your people related to my people?*

The personal reasons that brought us all here are not so different from those that brought European homesteaders in the 19th century, but the force, speed and ramification of these collective movements is unprecedented. Gouveia (1994) writes:

> At its most fundamental level, globalization entails a radical change in strategies of capital accumulation aimed at resolving the world capitalist crisis that began in the late 1960s. It is premised on the capacity of fractions of capital to move into an international market of money, commodities, and labor, unconstrained by geographical borders. But globalization means much more than economic change. Most significant for social scientists is the understanding of globalization as not only an economic but also a political process with significant social implications. (Gouveia, 1994: 125)

How do the economic, political and social forces that made possible these encounters impact Latino communities in the Midwest? It is to this question that we turn in Chapter 2. Chapters 3–8 are focused specifically on household language dynamics, and Chapter 9 presents a theoretical model of minority language maintenance in LEV settings.

A note on research positionality

It seems important to address here Fishman's admonition about the perils of ignoring the observer's paradox (Labov, 1972), and about researcher biases when conducting research in minority language communities:

> Involvement, whether more or less positive or more or less negative toward the minority perspective, is an inevitable byproduct of the interaction between the observer and the topic observed which characterizes the social sciences as a whole. [...] The posture of science, in the social sciences, surely requires that this involvement be admitted and that it be carefully watched in order to note (rather to deny) the biases that this interaction introduces. [...] These biases can be countered and eliminated, at least in part, and others can only be replaced or confronted by counter-biases. The confrontation of biases provides the patient student with opportunities to weigh and compare, and thereby, to arrive at a more considered (although still not impartial) point of view. (Fishman, 1989: 699)

I am a middle-class, university-educated speaker of Mexican Spanish and a first-generation immigrant to the United States. I am also an employee of the largest university in the state of Nebraska. Depending on the interaction and the purpose of the interaction, I approach the community and the social networks described herein as an in-group community member (e.g. as friend, neighbor, client, acquaintance), as an out-group observer (e.g. as a university researcher), and also as a member of a hybrid space (e.g. a professional, bilingual Latina who often gets recruited to serve as a resource both because I work for the university and because I'm a member of the local community). The line that separates those roles is, of course, rarely clear-cut.

As a trained sociolinguist and as newly arrived to the city, in the two years previous to data collection I participated in community celebrations, volunteer programs and other activities that allowed me to learn about the community. Although I had attended several functions in the school where the workshops for this project were offered, and although I was a second-order acquaintance of the mothers in this study, I did not personally know any of the families before they agreed to participate.

A few questions to continue the conversation ...

(1) One of the main points in this chapter was that language experi-ence takes place along five dimensions: the materiality of language and its use; speaker perceptions about those conditions; beliefs about self and others in the speech community; emotional responses about language; and about language users. In your opinion, what comes first? Language use or emotional responses about language (or language variety) and its users? Why do you think this may be the case?

(2) In communities with low ethnolinguistic vitality for Spanish in the United States, it is often the case that prestige functions of Spanish (e.g. teachers, school administrators, doctors, lawyers, police officers, judges, politicians) are not performed by speakers of local varieties. Does this matter? Why would this be relevant for children and teens growing up in bilingual households?

(3) Figure 1.1 in this chapter describes the intersecting nature of the different speech communities to which the members of a Midwestern, first-generation Latino household can lay claim. If you had to draw a figure based on your own language experience, what would it look like?

Notes

(1) Participant names and surnames used throughout this book are pseudonyms, and identifying details have been omitted for privacy reasons. These vignettes are a recon-struction based my field notes. All translations are mine. Italicized segments are quotes originally spoken in Spanish and jotted down in my notes after each session.

(2) Velázquez (2013) includes a discussion about the dangers of training university stu-dents to develop an expert voice about local Latino communities without helping them to develop the cultural competence that would allow the students to be part of them.

(3) Focus on maternal social networks does not negate the impact of fathers' social net-work on household language dynamics. Among the families in this study, however, mothers were the primary caregivers, were in charge of most child-rearing decisions

and spent more time with their children than their partners. A stronger case for the gendered nature of the intergenerational transmission process in LEV is presented in Chapters 2 and 9.

For ease of comparison, and as a way to ensure that children had stable sources of input in Spanish, the study presented in the following chapters (as well as Velázquez, 2008, 2012, 2013, 2014b) focuses on two-parent households where both parents were native speakers. This does not in any way negate the diverse nature of possible family arrangements among Latino families in LEV communities. These arrangements may include blended families, one-parent households, households where one parent is a native speaker of English, households where one parent is a native speaker of another language, households where children are being raised by grandparents or adult siblings, etc. The mechanics of maintenance and loss in families from LEV communities where only one parent is a native speaker of Spanish is in fact, an area ripe for research.

(4)   Population estimates are from the Census Bureau for the year 2013, and can be accessed at http://quickfacts.census.gov/qfd/states/31/3128000.html. Export data are from the US Department of Agriculture for the period of January–October 2014, and can be accessed at http://www.ers.usda.gov/data-products/livestock-meat-international-trade-data.aspx#26019. The actual distance between the cities of Lexington, Nebraska and Guadalajara, Jalisco, is 2750 km (1708 miles). Guadalajara is used here for illustrative purposes because several communities in the state of Jalisco have a 100-year history of emigration to the United States.

2 Latino Language Experience in the US Midwest

Magdalena: We speak Spanish so they won't forget

Why do I want my children to maintain Spanish? Because communication within the family is important and, because we speak Spanish at home, dialogue is important. Because someone who speaks two languages has more opportunities at work, and more opportunities to come into contact with more people. To communicate with a new culture and to express who we are and what we want. You have a greater chance of helping people who need interpretation at the doctor, at school, etc. Magdalena hates misspellings with a passion. Pen in hand, she marks them in the notes that her children's school address to her in Spanish. *It's disrespectful*, she tells me. *It's a school: they should be able to get this right.* Her Spanish orthography is a point of pride for her. She rewrites the notes she takes during our meetings with clear penmanship. She keeps a separate notebook for her English class. She considers her answers carefully. Eloquence, elegance and clarity are important. Pride in one's ability to use language is important. One of her regrets is not having had the chance to go to college when she was younger.

Magdalena is the type of person near to my linguist heart: the type of person who interrupts a conversation about childrearing to ask why a verb is conjugated one way and not the other; why some words in Spanish and English are similar and some are not. After enrolling me in her plan, she tries – and fails – to convince the other moms in the group to hold a Spanish class just for mothers. *If we don't write well in Spanish*, she tells me, *if we forget what we know, how are we going to help our children?* Lately, she has started correcting misspellings in the English signs she sees around town. She has been studying English for some time and feels more confident.

Today Magdalena calls late afternoon to ask me how one says 'my body feels numb' and 'it tingles'. She has taken her mother to the clinic and needs to interpret on the spot. Somewhere past 9:30 pm she calls again to let me know that her mom is all right. A little dehydrated and with high blood pressure, but all right. I thank her. She's calling me from work, from one of the office buildings she cleans at night. About to say goodbye, I ask her: Are you about done? *In a little while*, she says, *until 12:30*. I am absolutely certain that tomorrow morning Magdalena will drop off her two boys at school in time to get to her English class at 8:00 am and, two hours later, will be at our workshop for mothers.

These are the words that greet the visitor ascending the northern staircase of the Nebraska State Capitol: HONOUR TO PIONEERS WHO BROKE THE SODS THAT MEN TO COME MIGHT LIVE / HONOUR TO CITIZENS WHO BUILD AN HOUSE OF STATE WHERE MEN LIVE WELL. On entering the majestic limestone building, as the beauty of a space dedicated to democracy unfolds before one's eyes, one image will be largely absent from representations of the many generations of Nebraskans whose mettle and hard work helped to build the state.[1] Few in number during the first half of the 20th century, Mexican Americans in Nebraska were disproportionately represented in beet farming, railroad construction and meat packing, three industries that would prove to be fundamental for the economic expansion of the state.

Because the murals in the vestibule and foyer are static, another important element of Nebraska history will be missing: the chorus of languages other than English that have been spoken in this prairie even before the Homestead Act of 1862: Lakota and Dakota, Omaha, Ponca, Pawnee. Later came Russian, German, Czech, Japanese, Swedish, Spanish, and more recently Vietnamese, Arabic, Kurdish, Dinka, Karen and Q'anjob'al.[2] Nebraska, like the rest of the states in the Midwest, was formed through immigration. Networks of ethnic solidarity were as important for the survival of pioneers in the late 19th century as they are for 21st century immigrants and refugees (Cayton *et al.*, 2006; Sittig & González, 2016).

Over the course of the past century, most of the linguistic heritage that European homesteaders brought with them would be gone from Nebraska towns and cities as a result of assimilation, internal migration, xenophobia or outright linguistic suppression.[3]

One exception is Spanish, spoken in the state since the first *betabeleros* came to work in the fields at the westernmost edge of the state, lost many times over at the individual level, but maintained at the community level as the lifeblood of families, parishes and communities in rural and urban centers alike: in Minden, Harvard, Hershey and Minatare; in

Cozad, Omaha, Schuyler and South Sioux City; in Grand Island, Madison and Crete. As Saenz and Cready (1997: 5) point out, 'The formation of Mexican American communities in the region facilitated the entrance and settlement of newer cohorts of Mexicans and Mexican Americans, with newcomers tapping social networks in their social and economic adjustment to life in the Midwest'. Despite low overall ethnolinguistic vitality Spanish was, and continues to be, the key to accessing those networks.

Until the second half of the 20th century, to speak of the Latino experience in the Midwest was primarily to speak of the Mexican and Mexican American experience (Grajeda, 1998). The same is true of Nebraska, where a scant Hispanic presence was recorded from the time of the Spanish military expedition of Villasur in 1720, until the arrival of the first Mexican sugar beet farm workers in the 1900s (Davis, 2002; Garza, 2009; Rochín *et al.* 1996). During the second part of the century, Puerto Ricans, Cubans and Central and South Americans settled in the state in greater numbers as a result of interrelated historical developments and economic factors (Rochín, 2000).

Unlike any other immigrant group in the history of the Midwest, Mexicans and Mexican Americans were vigorously recruited twice to come to work in the region's fields and factories between the 1900s[4] and 1964, and were also subject to massive repatriation campaigns, deportation raids, discrimination and harassment after their labor was no longer needed (Gonzales, 2009; Santillán, 1989; Valdés, 1989). Social and spatial segregation was also part of this experience, as Garza (2009: 91) writes: 'Aside from detrimental health issues, the importation and widespread use of Mexican families in the beet fields of northeastern Colorado, as well as Nebraska, created an invisible class of rural workers who were fed and housed in company towns well outside the view of the general population.' Explaining the main reason for the small number of Mexican farm workers who chose to remain in Nebraska after the 1920–1921 Depression, Roger Davis (2002: 23) notes that 'The stereotypes and discrimination discouraged Mexicans from settling in rural areas'.

Cashman (2006) goes a step further, in describing how the lived experiences of its members impacted the linguistic landscape of Midwestern Mexican American communities over the course of the 20th century:

> The rich complexity of Mexican Spanish in the Midwest reflects a long history of immigration, migration, segregation, discrimination, deportation, neglect, struggle, cultural renaissance, and recontact. The sociohistorical realities of Mexican and Mexican American Chicano communities are embodied in the diverse language practices of their members. Due primarily to labor-recruiting practices and 'chain-migration,' the Spanish of central and southern Mexico predominates in the Midwest. (Cashman, 2006: 344)

Davis analyzes the push/pull factors that stimulated Mexican immigration to the Platte River Valley in Nebraska between 1890 and 1996.

As 'push' factors he cites the Mexican Revolution of 1910 and the Mexican economic crisis of 1980. As 'pull' factors he cites opportunities for field labor and railroad employment and, after 1980, the technological shift in the meatpacking industry and the Immigration Control & Reform Act of 1986 (Davis, 2002: 2).[5]

Midwestern sugar beet production began at the turn of the century in response to a national demand for sugar which quintupled thanks to the unprecedented period of population growth that followed the Civil War. Many Russian, Slovak, Bohemian and Russian German immigrants, who had made up most of the labor pool for that industry before WWI, joined the army, migrated to urban centers in search of higher wages or bought land and became farmers themselves. Smaller in number, Japanese workers suffered the backlash of anti-Asian measures (Garza, 2009).

In order to address this labor shortage, sugar companies began recruiting thousands of Mexican and Mexican American workers in Texas, New Mexico and Arizona, and later in Mexican colonies in cities like Detroit and Kansas City (Valdés, 1989). Indeed, Garza (2009: 90) reports that by 1920 some 13,000 Mexicans had been hired by the sugar beet companies in places such as western Nebraska. By the end of WWI, the expansion of industrial production and restrictions on European immigration led to greater labor shortages and increased recruitment efforts. As explained by Vargas (1991), the 15-year period between the start of WWI and the Great Depression would see large-scale immigration of Mexicans to the United States, and the formation of a Mexican immigrant working class in the Midwest. Vargas estimates that there were 63,700 Mexicans in the Midwest by 1927, with that number going up to 80,000 during the summer beet farming season (Vargas, 1991: 7).

The importance of Spanish as a source of social capital and a vehicle for economic survival can be better understood if one takes into account the role of kinship and ethnic solidarity networks in early Mexican American settlements in rural communities throughout the Midwest:

> Lured by the promise of jobs, workers first took in the characteristics of sojourners or single male migrants, and only later brought their families with them. In fact, for the sugar beet companies, recruiting laborers without families was expensive, as single men tended to move at the first notice of a higher paying job elsewhere. By recruiting entire families, the companies insured that male heads of family would stay in one place. Moreover, the entire family could participate in picking the crop. Since the sugar beet industry was extremely labor-intensive and required a high degree of stoop work, hiring families made sense from the company's point of view. It would also lead to charges of exploitation, which by some accounts were justified. (Garza, 2009: 91)

And just as Mexican labor was instrumental for the growth of the beet farming and railroad system, those two industries were key in the settlement of Mexican American communities throughout Nebraska – as were automobile factories and steel mills in other Midwestern states like Michigan, Illinois and Indiana. For example, García (1996: 10) writes that railroads were important in determining the location of Mexican enclaves in some Midwestern states and that the sugar beet industry 'created a permanent agricultural force in the Midwest and became a major pool of laborers for other businesses in the region. Many beet workers, or *betabeleros*, moved to cities in search of higher wages, steadier work, and education for their children. As a result, they were the core of many Mexican colonias'.

Describing the social environment where Midwestern Mexican Americans born between 1915 and 1926 grew up,[6] Santillán (1989) highlights the particular importance of Spanish – and language brokering in general – for the construction of the social bonds that allowed families and communities to prevail in the face of inclement weather and isolation, as well as racial and economic discrimination:

> The Mexican-born population in the Midwest, by 1920, had already reached about thirty thousand and nearly 150 satellite communities flourished in this ten-state region, principally in Kansas, Iowa, Nebraska, Illinois, Indiana, Michigan, and Wisconsin. These early Midwest Mexican settlements were, in the real sense, 'communities,' with both Catholic and Baptist churches, mutual-aid societies, fiestas, orchestras, dance, and theatre groups, Spanish language newspapers, small businesses, and organized sports. Mexican neighborhoods were oftentimes separated from the rest of the city by either railroad tracks or a river. [...] The G.I. Generation was raised in a bilingual and bicultural environment, with strict rules often requiring that only Spanish be spoken at home. The children usually translated for their parents whenever the occasion required social contact with Anglo society. [...] The majority of parents instilled the Mexican culture in their children because they feared that, without such reinforcement, the process of assimilation would eventually destroy altogether their traditional Mexican culture. (Santillán, 1989: 120)

Santillán points out the importance of the social and economic contribution of Mexican American women during WWII. Like their neighbors, Mexican American women in the Midwest and Southwest labored as riveters, crane operators, welders and assemblers, and engaged in industrial work, meatpacking and farm work. 'They were secretaries, shipbuilders, nurses and seamstresses. Some enlisted in the military and served overseas, and thousands assisted in the home front by planting victory gardens, collecting scrap metal for armament, organizing war bond drives, working for the Red Cross', and 'organizing social clubs for Mexican American servicemen who were often barred from public establishments because of racial discrimination' (Santillán, 1989: 116).

From the wives who followed their husbands to the Great Plains in the 1930s and started families and communities in railroad boxcars (Vargas, 1991), to the women who maintained solidarity networks during the

Great Depression and those who collaborated in the 1940s war effort, women were fundamental for the consolidation of working-class Mexican American communities in the region. Their contribution, as García (1996) explains, was often invisible:

> Both organized and informal community life depended on the interpersonal abilities, social networks, and organizational skills of women. The vital contributions to the economic well-being and social dynamics of the community, however, remained largely unrecognized and unrewarded by their contemporaries. Women encountered prejudice, discrimination, exploitation, poverty, and insecurity in the workplace and the home. Sex and gender established and circumscribed the world in which they lived and worked. (García, 1996: 83)

The Bracero program, signed in 1942 between Mexico and the United States, allowed US employers to contract seasonal labor. Davis (2002) estimates that between 1942 and 1947 some 62,000 Mexican workers entered the United States. This program, however, had little overall impact on Mexican immigration to Nebraska. The state's Latino population remained static between 1940 and 1950 because of the pull of the West Coast's demand for labor and, within the Midwest, discrimination and anti-Mexican sentiment (Davis, 2002: 38). The decades between 1950 and 1970 were prosperous for the state of Nebraska. This was thanks in large part to increased mechanization of agriculture, improved transportation and rising commodity prices. Mexican immigration to the United States during this period remained relatively low as a consequence of a period of sustained economic growth known as the Mexican Miracle (1946–1976). Still, even as Mexican immigration to Nebraska during this period was low compared to national levels, it increased to pre-Depression era levels (Davis, 2002).[7]

A second moment of demographic expansion for Latinos in Nebraska took place between 1975 and 1995. By 1980 Nebraska's Latino population saw an increase of 300%. Davis (2002) attributes this expansion to three factors: first, to the transformation of the meatpacking industry which moved away from large urban centers and relocated to rural communities throughout the Midwest and other regions of the country without a long history of Latino settlement; secondly, to the Mexican Economic crisis of 1980; and finally, to the passing of the US Immigration Control & Reform Act of 1986, which opened a path to legal status to previously unauthorized individuals who met requirements and were already in the country.

Two features of this period of growth bear directly on the landscape of Nebraska towns and cities. The first was the arrival and settlement in the state of Latinos of other national and regional origins, which fostered greater intra-community diversity. As Rochín (2000: 245) points out, 'As the meatpacking industry has restructured and established plants in Great Plains communities, it has attracted Latinos from immigrant and Latino family networks in California, Texas, Mexico, and Central America'. The second, and most important factor is that during the 1990s and onward, Latino population growth reversed net population loss in many Nebraska communities (Gouveia & Stull, 1996; Rochín, 2000). As Rochín and Siles (1996: 2) write: 'Latinos and Blacks sustained the general population base of Nebraska. Concomitantly, without the growth in both Latinos and Blacks, Nebraska would have lost congressional representation and federal grants for the 1990s.' These are not, of course, the only factors involved in the decision to migrate. Macrostructural factors are always in dynamic tension with the individual decisions of social actors.

Is the Past Present?

The second decade of the 21st century finds Nebraska Latinos in the middle of an anti-immigrant climate in which they are often made the target of xenophobic discourses which, on the one hand, preclude the implementation of public policies that facilitate the integration and social mobility of new arrivals and, on the other, obscure the contributions of several generations of Latinos born and raised in the Great Plains. Today, as was the case during the first two decades of the past century, community and family resiliency in working-class Latino neighborhoods throughout the state is possible because of social bonds that are in large part replenished and maintained by women. Thus, the fundamental role of women is as both economic and social agents.

Complex intergenerational language negotiations take place every day in Nebraska Latino households. Unlike their forbears, second-generation Nebraskans today have the opportunity to choose between assimilation and integration – or a selective combination of both. It is their choices that will determine in the coming decades whether Spanish will survive, and how, and for what purposes, even as the impact of their contribution for the economic and demographic wellbeing of the state becomes ever more evident.[8]

The Importance of the Second Generation

Latinos make up 10.7% of the total population of Nebraska. They are also the largest minority group in the state. Between the years of 2005 and 2014, the rate of Latino population growth was more than five times higher than the overall population (Aliaga Linares & Cogua-Lopez, 2016: 1). Importantly, although Latinos make up 55% of the total foreign-born population, most Nebraska Latinos (64%) were born in the United States (Pew Hispanic Research Center, 2014). In fact, since 2007, the share of US-born Latinos grew twice as fast as their foreign-born relatives and neighbors (Aliaga Linares & Cogua-Lopez, 2016: 1). Overall, Nebraska Latinos are young. In 2014 the median age for Latinos was 24.[9] Twenty-nine percent of Latinos in the state were 17 or younger and, as a group, Latino children represented 16% of the total K-12 student population in the state (Pew Hispanic Research Center, 2014). As Aliaga Linares and Cogua-Lopez (2016: 1) point out, 'this trend highlights the importance of the second generation as the primary source of demographic growth'.

In 2009, when data for the present study were collected, only 5% of Lincoln's total population of 247,882 was Latino. That same year, some 9955 people over the age of five spoke Spanish at home. According to Census estimates, by 2016 the city's population was 6.3% Latino and some 13,530 persons over the age of five spoke Spanish at home (ACS 1-year estimates; US Census Bureau 2015a). As of 2014, 15 Nebraska counties had a Latino population greater than 2000. Counties with highest percentage of Latino residents were Dawson (33%), Dakota (37%) and Colfax (43%). The largest Latino populations in the state live in Douglas and Lancaster, which correspond to the Omaha and Lincoln metropolitan areas (Aliaga Linares & Cogua-Lopez, 2016).

With a land area larger than Austria, Belgium and the Czech Republic combined, and a population count barely reaching 2 million, Nebraska is sparsely populated but increasingly diverse. In 2010, minorities represented 17.9% of the total population of the state. In many communities across the state, minorities are also the motor for demographic growth. Between 2000 and 2010, Nebraska's racial/ethnic minority population grew by 50.7%, while the non-Hispanic White population grew by only 0.4%. In 2000, 29 counties in Nebraska had minority populations of 5% or greater; by 2010 that number had increased to 45 counties (Zhang, 2015). In 2010, foreign-born residents comprised 6% of Nebraska's overall population; this represents a 298% increase from 1990 figures (Zhang, 2015). Forty-one percent of foreign-born Nebraskans were born in Mexico, followed by India, El Salvador, Vietnam and China. Nebraska is also a refugee resettlement destination. According to Nebraska Department of Health and Human Services figures, 818 refugees arrived in the state in fiscal year 2010 (Zhang, 2015).

Immigrants contribute in important ways to the economic base of the state. In 2014, Nebraska's foreign-born households contributed more than one in every 20 dollars paid in state and local tax revenues, and earned 4.9% of all income earned by Nebraskans that year. Latino immigrant households in particular earned $1.2 billion dollars in 2014, and paid $267.6 million in taxes (New American Economy, 2016).

As in other communities in the Midwest, working-class first-generation Latinos in Nebraska rank low on many key socio-economic indicators and in comparison to non-Latino White populations, and have less access to the resources that would grant them access to social mobility (Kayitsinga, 2015; Martinez et al., 2015). As Aliaga Linares and Cogua-Lopez write, this has lasting implications for second-generation

Nebraskans and, by extension, for the long-term wellbeing of the state as a whole:

> The importance of this second generation poses major challenges, as their fates are also impacted by the socio-economic conditions of their households and to some extent by the integration of their foreign-born parents [...] The young character of this population, composed largely of children and adolescents, represents one of Nebraska's greatest demographic assets. This demographic shift calls attention not only to the imperative to grant opportunities to this upcoming generation, but also to the need to create a dynamic environment in which immigrants and later generations can thrive. (Aliaga Linares & Cogua-Lopez, 2016: 9)

Although not all Latino Nebraskans speak Spanish, household language planning, language brokering and bilingualism continue to be central to the experience of an important segment of second-generation Latinos in the state. Aliaga Linares and Cogua-Lopez (2016) report that 'for the period of 2011–2013, around half (51%) of US-born Latinos routinely spoke Spanish at home, which represented a slight increase from 47% for the period of 2005–2007'; they write, 'In contrast to the adult US-born population, US-born Latino children are increasingly more likely to live in households where Spanish is spoken. The proportion of US-born Latino children who speak Spanish at home rose from 52% in the 2005–2007 period to 58% in the 2011–2013 period' (Aliaga Linares & Cogua-Lopez, 2016: 4).

Household Profiles

The 19 families in this study were first-generation two-parent households with at least one child under 18 living at home. Median household size was five. In 26% of these households there were more adults than children. All adults were native speakers of Spanish and included children older than 18 and living at home, grandparents or other members of the extended family. Two households included at least one child under 18 who was related to, but not the son or daughter of the respondent. At least two families had children under 18 living in Mexico. In nine of these families the father had lived in the United States between one and ten years longer than the mother. In two families the mother had lived in the United States between one and three years longer than the father. The shortest period of residence in the United States for either parent was one year. Eighty-nine percent of the parents in this study were born in Mexico. In one family the father was Mexican and the mother Guatemalan. One family had migrated to the United States from Peru after having lived in Argentina.

The parents

All parents in this study were native speakers of Spanish and were born outside of the United States. None of them was a native speaker of

English. The median age for the father was 37, and 35 for the mother. This was higher than the state's median age for native-born Latinos, which was 12, and slightly higher than the median age for foreign-born Latinos, which at the time was 34. Sixty-eight percent of the fathers worked in the construction or industrial sectors, 16% worked in the service sector, 11% were reported by their spouses as employed but unspecified, and one was unemployed. Seventy-nine percent of mothers were homemakers, and 21% worked in the service sector. The median years of schooling in Spanish for either parent was nine years.

The children

There were 52 children between the ages of 20 years and 11 months in these 19 households. Three were excluded from this study because they were older than 18. Fifty-six percent of the children in these families were born in Nebraska, 10% were born in another US location and 34% were born in their parents' country. Only 21% had received any formal instruction in Spanish – all outside of the United States. Median years of instruction in Spanish for these children were three years. All school-aged children in these households attended schools where English was the language of instruction. Eight percent were attending or had completed high school, 17% were in middle school, 38% attended elementary school, 6% were in preschool and 31% were not old enough to attend school. The youngest children interviewed for this study were five years old.

Mothers' Social Networks

One way to understand household language dynamics in these 19 families from the perspective of the mothers is to examine the basic structure of their social networks. Consideration of key characteristics of the actors in their closest networks of interaction beyond the home affords us information about potential sources of ideas about parenting, language development, bilingualism and, in more general terms, about life in the United States. Additionally, for the children in these families, the number and type of social actors in their mothers' networks were also potential sources of exposure to Spanish and English, of opportunities for use and for socialization to both languages.

The features of mothers' social networks were analyzed (as opposed to fathers' or children's, for example), because in these 19 households mothers spent more time with the children during daytime, participated in more Spanish-dominant networks and, for the most part, were in charge of planning, monitoring and facilitating their children's schedule outside school.

Thus, mothers were presented with two questions intended to understand the basic features of their social network. First, the respondents were asked to name *people whom you consider closest to you, that do not live in your household.* This question was meant to generate data on network connections potentially vested with bonding social capital, in other words, individuals perceived by the respondents as sources of emotional and material support. The second question presented to the respondents was: *Please name five people you see more than three times in a normal week that don't live in your house.* This was asked in order to gather data about interactions potentially vested with bridging social capital, i.e. social exchanges that presented opportunities to access ideas, resources and experiences not circulating in the speaker's most intimate circle of interaction.

Overall, the networks described by the 19 mothers in this study shared four features: gender segregation, locality, multiplexity and language dominance. In other words, the overwhelming majority of network actors recalled by the respondents as closest to them were female, interacted face to face with them, shared more than one social connection, and spoke Spanish.

Mothers' closest network of interaction

A total of 120 individuals were recalled by the respondents as members of their closest circle of interaction outside their household. The median number of actors was six. Most social actors identified by the respondents were female (72%). Of the total number of males named by the respondents as closest to them and not living in their household, only 12% were unrelated to them by kinship or marriage. In contrast, 59% of the females identified as closest to the respondent and not living in her home were not relatives – e.g. friends, neighbors.[10]

Most actors (75%) recalled by the respondents as members of their closest circle of interaction lived in Lincoln and interacted with them face to face on a regular basis. Another 11% of actors lived in Mexico, 3.5% lived elsewhere in the Midwest (Nebraska, Kansas or Illinois), 3.5% lived in other US locations (Responses included California, Colorado and other states outside the Midwest), 3.5% lived in South America (Argentina and Peru), and 2% lived in Texas.

Overwhelmingly, Spanish was the language of interaction in all the networks described by the adult participants in this study. The respondents reported most often interacting in Spanish with 93% of the actors identified by them as members of their closest network. The respondents reported interacting in English and Spanish with only ten of the 120 actors recalled. Of these social actors, seven were children or teenagers in their extended family or their neighborhood (whom the respondents reported addressing primarily in Spanish, while they responded in English). Three were adult women who were not speakers of Spanish (with whom the respondents reported interacting haltingly in English). Two were friends and one was the respondent's sister-in-law. Only one respondent reported interacting primarily in English with one of the actors in her closest circle of interaction. This actor was identified by the respondent as a female manager at work.

Five people you see more than three times in a normal week

When we examine the characteristics of individuals recalled by the respondents as interacting with them on a regular basis, three features come to light: gender segregation, network multiplexity and Spanish language dominance. In fact, 86% of the individuals recalled by the respondents as someone who did not live with them but whom they saw more than three times in a normal week were female. Concurrently, 44% were linked to them by more than one connection – e.g. were sisters and co-workers, friends and neighbors, or friends and classmates, and were also mentioned as members of their closest circle. Regarding network density, only 21% of respondents were able to recall five or more individuals who did not live with them and with whom they interacted more than three times in a normal week.

Spanish was also the dominant language within the acquaintance sector of these personal networks – i.e. people with whom the respondents interacted more than three times in a normal week but who were not necessarily listed as members of their closest circle. The participants reported interacting in English or both languages with only 17 of the 110 actors identified in this outer sector of their personal network. Other than the nieces, nephews and friends listed above, reported interactions in English were clustered in the spaces of the workplace (employers and co-workers), and the respondents' children's school (child's teacher and adult English as a second language instructors). Adult males not related to the respondent and named as actors in this network sector include one friend, two neighbors, landlord, employer and co-workers.

Spanish Beyond the Home

In a follow up item, the respondents were asked to recall the last person with whom they had spoken in Spanish and in English – not counting the interviewer or household members. Twenty-one interlocutors in Spanish and 19 interlocutors in English were named. Friends and extended family were most often cited as recent interlocutors in Spanish (13/21). These were followed by other mothers at school (4/21).

Other interlocutors in Spanish included co-workers, people at church, school interpreter and store patron (one token, respectively). The respondents recalled most recently interacting in English with: their child's teacher, their English as a second language (ESL) teacher and classmates or school staff (9/19); followed by social services agency staff and a medical professional (2/19); friends (2/19); and co-workers (2/19). Other responses included employer and store clerk (one token each). Two participants were unable to recall the last person with whom they had interacted in English in the recent past.

Asking the Meadowlark to Stand in for 'Bird'

The meadowlark is a small yellow bird with a black bib on the chest and a sweet song that it likes to sing over the summer grasslands. It also happens to be Nebraska's state bird. Because of this, whenever I ask myself what Latino communities in Nebraska have to teach us about other communities where Spanish and English are in contact, I often think of the meadowlark, sitting atop a fencepost along the I-80 highway. *How much does describing 'meadowlark' help us understand 'bird'?* And then again, *How much of 'meadowlark' can we understand if we limit ourselves to the taxonomy of 'bird'?* In other words, what can theories and models developed in other contact situations tell us about this experience? Such is our aim here – to locate 'bird' in the meadowlark, and to place the meadowlark in its rightful position within the universe of 'bird'.

The experience of Spanish speakers in Nebraska shares features with that of speakers in other communities within and beyond the Midwest. With a broader lens, it also shares much with the experience of speakers of other minority languages with limited public presence. Some of these features are: limited institutional support; limited opportunities to develop literacy; diglossia; language brokering by the second generation; language loss at the individual level and maintenance at the level of the ethnic community; and discursive construction of the minority language within the linguistic landscape (Hult, 2014) as a marked 'other' that does not contribute to a sense of place beyond ethnic neighborhoods.

The social experience of first-generation Latinos in Nebraska and other Midwestern, non-metropolitan communities can be subsumed as part of the New Latino Diaspora, which Johnson *et al.* (2016: 55) define as 'a demographic phenomenon that describes the immigration of Latinos from across Latin America to small cities and towns in the United States, which have historically not been popular destinations for Spanish speakers'.

At the same time, as illustrated in Table 2.1, Nebraska's low overall population density, coupled with high Latino growth in some areas of the

Table 2.1 Population density in several Midwest locations

	Chicago, IL	Minneapolis, MN	Omaha, NE	Lexington, NE	Schuyler, NE
Total population (2016)	2,704,958	413,651	446,970	10,004	6,106
% Latino (2010)	28.9	10.5	13.1	60.4	65.4
Population per square mile (2010)	3,217.9	7,088.3	3,217.9	2,273.3	2,405.5

Source: US Census Bureau, American Community Survey.

state and high concentration within specific sectors of the workforce, impact the conditions of linguistic contact and give unique characteristics to the social experience of Spanish speakers in the state.

First-generation Latino Nebraskans are more likely to hail originally from a non-metropolitan location and to have settled in the state after having lived previously in another US location. Roughly seven out of ten will speak a dialect of Mexican or Mexican American Spanish, but their everyday experience and social networks will likely include interactions with speakers of other varieties of Spanish, as well as interactions with speakers of other immigrant languages in their workplaces, neighborhoods and places of worship. Some first-generation Latino households will have experienced prolonged family separation, with one or both parents having migrated first. Some will include repatriation, circular migration and transnational schooling experiences (Hamann & Zúñiga, 2011; Zúñiga et al., 2016).

Overwhelmingly, with the exception of school districts in communities such as Omaha, Lexington and Fremont, Spanish language instruction at K-12 levels, as well as most university-level courses, is designed to address the needs of L2 learners, as the state offers few opportunities to develop Spanish literacy for HL learners. For many Latino Nebraskans, religious education is an important source of opportunities to develop Spanish literacy, as well as for community building.

At the level of the community, Spanish is often a source of social capital for working-class native speakers, and a source of personal capital for native and non-native middle-class speakers.

Finally, as opposed to other US localities where Spanish and English are in contact, in many Nebraska communities children have limited contact with middle-class, upwardly mobile bilinguals, and language norms are exocentric – i.e. advanced L2 speakers or middle-class native speakers who grew up in communities where Spanish is a majority language teach, plan and evaluate language.

Politically, Latino Nebraskans – foreign born or not – are often the target of anti-immigrant discourses and public policies. For example, in attempting to understand how the legislative environment shapes the context of reception for Latinos and Latino immigrants in the region, Martínez et al. (2012) analyze bills enacted in 12 Midwestern states between 2009 and 2010, and conclude that 'Legislation in Nebraska, Iowa and North Dakota are examples of laws that are exclusionary from the mainstream by way of immigration status or perhaps meant to dissuade immigrants from moving to the state on a permanent basis' (Martínez et al., 2012: 62).

In 2006, Vogt et al. reported the results of a poll of 2482 rural Nebraskans' perceptions of, among other topics, Latin American immigration. Over two-thirds (69%) of non-Latino respondents disagreed with the statement that rural Nebraska communities should communicate important information in Spanish as well as in English. In contrast, 76% of Latino respondents agreed that rural Nebraska communities should communicate important information in Spanish as well as English (Vogt *et al.*, 2006: 5).

Fifty percent of the respondents disagreed with the statement that immigrants from Latin America strengthened rural Nebraska (Vogt *et al.*, 2006: 5). The respondents with higher education levels, or who had friends, relatives, close acquaintances or co-workers who were recent Latin American immigrants, were more likely to agree that immigrants from Latin America strengthened rural Nebraska. In the same survey, Latino respondents (61%) were more likely than non-Latino respondents (39%) to say that Latin American immigrants faced discrimination and barriers to inclusion in the community (Vogt *et al.*, 2006: iii).

In economic terms, Latinos in the Midwest face challenges similar to Latinos in other regions of the country, as Vega *et al.* (2011: 79) point out: 'Low educational attainment in a deindustrialized region and an increasingly service-orientated and changing economy'. Employment concentration in specific sectors in the economy gives the state's Latino communities distinct features. For example, Gouveia and Powell (2007) outline some of the obstacles for the successful integration of immigrants: Nebraska has little recent experience with immigration; there is a lack of jobs at the top of the employment scale; the state is predominantly white; and immigrant communities lack the social and political capital of immigrant destinations with a larger history of settlement (Gouveia & Powell, 2007: 17). At the same time, they write, Nebraska presents several advantages that could serve as factors in the successful integration of Latino newcomers across the state:

> Labor competition among immigrants is not as intense as in California or New York; there are plenty of jobs at the bottom of the scale where immigrant labor is most wanted; [...] a growing immigrant presence is creating mid-tier jobs that, until now, were nonexistent in the state. Absent are what would technically qualify as 'inner-city' neighborhoods and 'inner-city' schools and the disadvantages associated with such contexts in places like Los Angeles or New York. Also, the state lacks some of the most egregious history of segregation and anti-minority sentiments found in southern and border states. [...] positive outcomes for the second generation will be measured by, or highly correlate with, the extent to which these new destinations provide them with sufficient educational opportunities to shrink the distance between the abundant unskilled jobs their parents occupy and the scarcer well-paid jobs the state's economy produces. (Gouveia & Powell, 2007: 2)

Like most of the children and adolescents interviewed for this study, 64% of Latino Nebraskans are US born. As stated elsewhere in this chapter, the successful integration of this second generation into the labor market and more generally into the wider social fabric of the state is of utmost importance not just to their families, but to the overall wellbeing of the state.

In terms of human capital, Nebraska's Latino population growth in rural and urban counties reversed a population decline which was reported in the 1990s (Carranza *et al.*, 2002). Latino children make up 16% of the K-12 student population in the state. The productivity of these children and adolescents once they enter the workforce will be crucial for the state's economic base. Vega *et al.* (2011: 79) write: 'As the baby boomers move out of the economy and become dependent on the productivity of others, their wellbeing becomes more directly tied to that of Latinos [...] how social and political institutions integrate them and their children foreshadows the capacity of the nation to meet tomorrow's challenges.'

In the following chapters we abandon the macro lens of the community and take up the micro lens of household dynamics and individual perceptions about language use. In Chapter 3 the reader will find a detailed description of the study from which the data presented here derive.

A few questions to continue the conversation …

(1) For an ethnic minority, two possible outcomes of prolonged social isolation and economic discrimination are language shift (the gradual abandonment of the group's language in favor of that of the majority) or language maintenance. After reading about the experiences of Mexican Americans in the first half of the 20th century, can you identify some of the factors that might foster one outcome over the other?

(2) As described in this chapter, Spanish speakers in several non-metropolitan communities throughout Nebraska and other parts of the Midwest live in localities with low population totals but high Latino concentration. How might their everyday language experience differ from that of a speaker who lives in a large metropolitan center with both high Latino concentration and high demographic density?

(3) Think about your own community. What is the oldest neighborhood in the city or town where you live? If you pay attention, can you see the presence of languages other than your own? In the names of the streets? The shops? The names of the foods? The street signs? How many languages can you identify?

Notes

(1) Stephen Roberts' murals, representing 'heroic enterprises associated with Nebraska history', were added to the central room of the 14th floor in 1996. These eight paintings are a truer depiction of the diversity of the state's population. See http://capitol. nebraska.gov/building/rooms/memorial-chamber.

(2) Indeed, a news item published in the *Lincoln Journal Star* newspaper in March 2005 proclaimed the city of Lincoln as one of the most linguistically diverse areas in the United States. In this piece, the city's linguistic diversity is framed by the reporter as a problem. Tellingly, the only two sources cited were the local chief of police and a Washington, DC non-profit dedicated to the promotion of English as the official language of the United States. See http://journalstar.com/news/local/lincoln-is-land-of-many-tongues/article_8f68e513-303c-5089-b8e8-47629ad10068.html.

(3) A consequence of anti-German sentiment following WWI, the Siman Act of 1919 was a Nebraska state statute that prohibited 'any private, denominational, parochial or public school, [to] teach any subject to any person in any language other than the English language'. It also forbade foreign-language education before the eighth grade. In 1920 Robert T. Meyer was tried, convicted and fined in Hamilton county, Nebraska, for teaching German to fourth-grader Raymond Parpart. The Nebraska Supreme Court affirmed his conviction and Meyer appealed to the Supreme Court of the United States. In 1923 *Mayer v. Nebraska* (262 U.S. 390) the justices found that the Siman Act violated the due process clause of the Fourteenth Amendment of the Constitution. See http://nebraskahistory.org/exhibits/we_the_people/wwi_council_of_defense.htm. Justice James C. McReynolds delivered the majority opinion on 4 June 1923. A portion of it reads: 'No emergency has arisen which renders knowledge by a child of some language other than English so clearly harmful as to justify inhibition with the consequent infringement of rights long freely enjoyed' (Crawford, 1992: 237).

(4) According to census data for that year, only 20 Mexicans lived in Nebraska in 1900. By 1927, a survey cited in Davis (2002: 7) estimated that there were 10,000 Mexican railroad workers in the Great Plains, of which 1500 were in Nebraska alone.

(5) Sugar, corn, cattle and railroads were the catalysts for overall population growth in Nebraska, which had surpassed one million by 1900 (Davis, 2002: 4).

(6) Santillán (1989: 119) refers to this as the G.I. Generation – Mexican American men and women born between 1915 and 1926 who would go on to fight, work and organize during WWII.

(7) According to Davis (2002), Nebraska's Latino population in 1950 was 1851, and had reached 7177 by 1970. According to Census Bureau estimates, in 2016 Latino Nebraskans made up 10.7% of the state's total population.

(8) A careful reader of this manuscript has rightly pointed out that the distance between assimilation and integration is rarely the result of a conscious decision; instead, it is the result of an accumulation of everyday, mostly unnoticed and mostly unremarkable choices about how one chooses to live one's life and interact with others.

(9) In 2014 the median age for non-Hispanic Whites in Nebraska was 40 (Pew Hispanic Research Center, 2014).

(10) A *comadre* (one's child's godmother) is understood here as a form of symbolic kinship, and was counted in our analysis as family.

3 Language in the Small Spaces: A Description of this Project

Teresa: I don't work

Teresa takes one of the 100-calorie cookie packs we set out as snacks for our first meeting, and observes it as one would observe an artifact from a foreign planet. When she opens it, she stares into the void, and for the first time in my life I notice what she is seeing: that it is mostly air, mostly negative space to set off a few thin cookies sliding at the bottom of the bag in all their sadness. Because she is very polite, she takes her coffee and her forlorn cookies and goes back to her seat. But I understand, or think I understand, the oddity: a cookie that is valuable not because it tastes good, or is nourishing, or beautiful to look at, but because there is less of it. An un-cookie.

Not that she hasn't seen them before, of course. Teresa has seen 100-calorie cookie packs. What is strange in this context is that THIS is what I've chosen to share with them, what I've brought of myself, the level of effort I've put forth to make them feel welcome in our workshop. I learn this at the next parents' group meeting. The tables are set up in the school cafeteria with food that the moms have prepared: tamales, flautas, three kinds of salsa, fruit, tostadas, atole, horchata. My eye wanders among that bounty and Teresa is adamant about fixing me a plate. This is what she teaches me that morning: that invisible work is the kind of work that builds social bonds; that there is community in food; that there is a sense of accomplishment, of valuing the other and valuing oneself. *This is what I prepared for you.*

So, let's call it what it is: a workshop for mothers who want their kids to be bilingual. The default gender marking of the plural obscures an important reality in these and many other communities. We advertised in Spanish: *Taller para padres de familia* – Workshop for parents. But it is exclusively the mothers' faces I see looking at me week after week. It's only the mothers who ask the questions and bring things and stories to share with the group; only the mothers who cook for school fundraisers and extend a network of solidarity and kindness. Not that the fathers don't want their children to be bilingual. Not that they don't love their children. Not that they don't work hard. Not that they may or may not come to parent teacher conferences. It's that this part of childrearing is gendered. I look at the group and ask myself if a father would know off the top of his head, without consulting anyone, who is having a baby next month, who has children in Mexico, whose husband is looking for a job, who can babysit at a pinch, who can make six dozen tamales with a day's notice, who knows how to see a doctor without health insurance or what are the requirements to enroll a child in catechism. In all the months of our work together, only one father comes to our sessions, and then only for one meeting.

The core of the experience described in this book is a sociolinguistic study conducted between January and June 2011 in the city of Lincoln, NE, a community with low ethnolinguistic vitality for Spanish (henceforth, LEV). Despite the fact that Latino children drive an important proportion of demographic growth in the region, and that many of these children are growing up in first-generation bilingual households where parents and children are undergoing different processes of language acquisition, little is known about language dynamics in Latino households in non-metropolitan Midwestern contexts that are geographically distant from other US locations with high vitality for Spanish.

Justification

This study was designed as a community-based, family-centered and culturally relevant project for the study of language maintenance/loss in Latino families newly arrived in the state, and it was predicated on two overarching notions. The first is that first-generation families bring with them diverse cultural practices, values and beliefs that can benefit both the families and their new communities (Maldonado & Licona, 2007). If understood, these practices can be used as strengths and resources, rather than as barriers to education, success or integration into the wider community (Villenas, 2001; Villenas & Moreno, 2001). The second of these notions is that one piece of social/cultural capital that immigrant families bring with them is language. Bilingual/bicultural skills provide family members with social, instrumental and psychosocial advantages that help them to be resilient and adapt to their new environment (Bankston, 2004). Yet, regardless of positive parental attitudes toward Spanish use and transmission, and despite the fact that very often one or both parents are Spanish dominant, many families report a decline in their children's use of Spanish as early as the first year after their arrival.

Sociolinguistic studies conducted in Latino communities have afforded us three important insights about minority language maintenance in the United States: (1) the crux of intergenerational transmission encompasses the quality and time of exposure to the home language, opportunities for its use and its relevance beyond the home domain (Velázquez, 2008); (2) if a minority language is to survive in a community, it must survive first in the home (Fishman, 2001; Worthy & Rodríguez-Galindo, 2006); and (3) mothers/primary caregivers are the key node in the process of intergenerational transmission or loss of a heritage language (Okita, 2002; Potowski, 2008). The mother's perception of the instrumental value of the language in her children's life as well as her self-perception as an agent in her children's language development are fundamental in determining the amount and quality of opportunities for use (Velázquez, 2009).

The primary drive for this research owes much to the work of Reyes & Moll (2008: 148), who conceptualize language development as a sociocultural process where 'those being socialized to language are agents, not mere initiates. Language and literacy are socially constructed, culturally mediated'. From this perspective, studies exploring the development of language and literacy must go beyond describing only the relationship between caregiver and child, to include the household, the extended family and the community.

'Caregivers', they write, 'model for the young child, in many different ways, the acceptable ways of interacting in accordance to their cultural practices' (Reys & Moll, 2008: 148). And beyond the home, it is spaces such as church, community events, neighborhood parties and catechism, where children have the opportunity to participate in minority language literacy events, that allow them to develop and maintain their bilingualism (Reys & Moll, 2008: 154). Concurrently, this project was designed to take González et al.'s (2006: 149) concept of community funds of knowledge – diverse bodies of knowledge existing in households and communities that develop from people's social histories and from their everyday practices – and investigate it as it relates to intergenerational (non-)transmission of Spanish first-generation households in an LEV community.

Project Goals

Based on the previous rationale, the original goals of this study were to:

(1) identify household and community factors that foster the use or non-use of Spanish within these families;
(2) describe the role of each language in the process of acculturation of each household member;

(3) investigate parental attitudes toward the use and transmission of Spanish;
(4) investigate children's attitudes toward the use and transmission of Spanish;
(5) identify household language dynamics;
(6) find out if mothers perceive themselves as agents in their children's linguistic and academic development;
(7) explore what skills mothers possess that can help them increase their children's development in either/both languages; and
(8) find out if mothers can be trained to function as agents for the main- tenance of Spanish in the household.

In its original design, this study was to be conducted over the span of one school year. To test Goal 8 above, potential participants were to be recruited into one of three groups. In *Group 1*, a parent and one child would participate in two sociolinguistic interviews at the beginning and end of the school year. In addition to participating in the interviews, *adult respondents in Group 2* would attend school-based informational meet- ings about child language development and successful strategies for rais- ing bilingual children. Finally, in addition to participating in the interviews and attending the informational meetings, *adult participants in Group 3* would participate in a series of hands-on workshops requiring parents to test different strategies to stimulate Spanish use at home. This distribution of the respondents was one of the few features that survived the transition from the first to the second iteration of the study.

The original version included the following prediction: that after one school year of differential treatment, greater evidence of Spanish language shift would be observed in Group 1 (no treatment, only interview); a mini- mal, temporary positive effect on children's use of Spanish would be observed in Group 2 (only information); and greater evidence of mainte- nance would be observed in Group 3 (interview + information + training). The null hypothesis was to be, of course, that parental training and infor- mation would have no effect on children's use of Spanish and on their self-perception as bilinguals, and that differences observed in patterns of language use between families and within each family after a school year would be due to normal stages of language development in a minority language setting, and not to the systematic training of the mothers.

Whose perspective? Try it again, keep going

The attentive reader will notice several flaws in the original design of this study. To name only a few: Can language maintenance be measured in the span of one school year? How is one to tease apart language loss from non-acquisition? How would one measure the potential relationship between the treatment and participant attitudes? How would one account for external factors that may impinge on household language use during the time of data collection?

But most importantly, the original design for this study was flawed because it was constructed from an outsider's perspective, and without taking into account the specific conditions of the community under study. In their research into language and literacy development in two Mexican American communities, Schecter and Bayley (2002) highlight the importance of distinguishing between etic and emic definitions of language maintenance. In other words, they remind us about the importance of studying bilingual communities and families from the perspective of their members. In specific terms this means, for example, considering each family's definitions of, and goals for, language maintenance. They write: 'We have found it worthwhile to identify the different meanings that participants ascribe to the idea of minority-language maintenance as well as the different roles that they envision for home and sometimes school, in achieving these goals' (Schecter & Bayley, 2002: 81).

In practice, an improvement of this design required that the principal investigator start over, drawing from the experience of the members of the research team as members of the local Latino community. It required reconsidering our assumptions, consulting with key community members and, finally, establishing a formal research collaboration with the public school district.

The second iteration of this study took into consideration, for example, that a research intervention of one school year would result in a considerable intrusion into school and family dynamics, that it was impracticable to recruit both parents because childrearing duties and interactions with the school were mostly performed by the mothers, and that any interviews conducted at home would have to be conducted by female native speakers. Additionally, we asked both parents to choose which of their children they would like to participate and, with their permission, we asked for the child's assent before conducting our interviews. On the one hand, this likely led to the selection of children with the highest oral competence – thus limiting our access to children with less fluency in Spanish. On the other hand, this aligned more closely with parental choice, household-internal dynamics and parental understandings of fluency and sociopragmatic competence – i.e. which of their children would be able to politely interact in Spanish with a stranger for an hour.

But perhaps the most problematic of the original goals of this project was Goal 8: *Find out if mothers can be trained to function as agents for maintenance of Spanish in the household.* This goal is problematic because it is predicated on an asymmetrical relationship between respondent and researcher, a relationship that privileged my ideas of the value, impact and challenges of family language transmission over a speaker's own understandings of her own experience. Further, it presupposes that mothers are empty vessels that can/should be trained to perform tasks that may or may not be aligned in the same way or for the same reasons with her own purposes. It presupposes as well that mothers have nothing to teach the researchers and nothing to teach other mothers about raising bilingual children in the context of the United States – a thoroughly disproven idea, as can be attested throughout the chapters of this book.

With these considerations in mind, our research goals for the second iteration of this study were as follows:

(1) record and analyze reported patterns of household language use;
(2) investigate maternal attitudes toward the use and transmission of Spanish;
(3) investigate children's attitudes toward the use and transmission of Spanish;
(4) compare mothers' and children's attitudes and perceptions of the viability of Spanish;
(5) investigate maternal participation in networks where Spanish is vested with social capital;
(6) investigate maternal perceptions of agency in children's linguistic development; and
(7) determine if, at the point of data collection, intergenerational transmission of Spanish had occurred with at least one child under 18 in each household.

Children's literacy in Spanish was not studied because none of the children in these 19 households was receiving formal instruction in their family language at the time of our interviews. Working definitions of linguistic maintenance and loss as understood in this study are summarized in Table 3.1.

Table 3.1 Components of language maintenance and loss

Two concurrent but different processes ...

Acquisition		Maintenance
Results can be...		
null	partial	complete
Linguistic maintenance means ...		
Knowing how	Knowing where/with whom	Wanting to
Language competence	Language socialization	Attitudes, motivations
Two related, but not necessarily concurrent processes ...		
Bilingualism		Biliteracy
Driven by home and minority-language institutions and practices		Driven by school and majority-language institutions and practices

Intergenerational transmission was determined by answering the following questions about each child and teenager interviewed for the study:

(1) Can they understand oral Spanish?
(2) Can they speak enough Spanish to sustain a conversation with an adult who is not a member of the household?
(3) Is their oral production age appropriate?
(4) Can they narrate a story in Spanish?
(5) Is the quality of this narrative comparable to a similar narrative in English produced by the same child?
(6) Are they socialized to use the language (i.e. do they know where/when/how to use Spanish with what interlocutor, in which context, for what purpose)?
(7) What are their attitudes toward Spanish, English and bilingualism?

Sample

Twenty-five families were recruited. In order to participate, families had to live in two-parent households with at least one child under the age of 18 living at home. All parents were native speakers of Spanish and L2 speakers of English. Six families were excluded from analysis either because they relocated mid-study or because they failed to meet one or more participation requirements (Velázquez, 2014b). For purposes of comparison, only two-parent households were included. It bears saying, of course, that one-parent households, households where one parent did not speak Spanish, and households where children were being raised by a relative or guardian other than the parents were excluded for our benefit, not because they were not a part of the community we were studying.

Recruitment

In order to access different social networks, the participants were recruited in three different groups. All families were recruited using snowball sampling. The geographical distribution of working-class first-generation Latino families within the city, the sensitivity of the topics to be discussed, participant privacy considerations and the pragmatic challenges of being allowed into the space of the home to conduct project interviews made the use of a random sample not only unviable, but wholly inadequate to address the questions in this study. The use of the recruitment strategies described here likely lead to an overselection of parents with a desire to transmit Spanish to their children. This is not at all a drawback, but precisely the point: to understand how/why positive attitudes to the family language are not enough to guarantee its intergenerational transmission.

Families in Group 1 were not members of the school community to which the families in Groups 2 and 3 belonged. They were invited to participate by word of mouth through the principal investigator's personal and professional networks, and through Spanish language flyers posted by members of the research team in restaurants, stores, community organizations and social agencies that served a high proportion of Spanish-speaking clientele. **Families in Group 2** had at least one child attending the school where the workshops and informational meetings were to be held. They were invited to participate in the study by word of mouth, and by the school's bilingual liaison and the principal investigator. Informational sessions about bilingual language development were advertised by the school, were free, and were open to any parents interested in raising their children bilingually. The sessions were held in Spanish. Simultaneous interpretation was offered by the school for parents who did not speak Spanish. **Families in Group 3** also had at least one child attending the school, and were selected to participate in a four-month long, hands-on workshop for parents interested in helping their children develop their bilingual skills and maintain Spanish. Aside from fulfilling other project requirements, the participants in Group 3 had to submit a written application in which they explained why it was important for them that their children acquire and maintain their family language. The invitation to apply was open to any parent in the school who was raising children in a Spanish/English bilingual household. At the time of data collection, several of the mothers in Group 3 were participating in an externally funded, school-wide family literacy project. As part of that program they were attending ESL classes provided by the school.

Compensation and participant time commitment

Participation in this study required a significant time commitment over the span of six months. It also required that the families disrupt their

Table 3.2 Participant time commitment and compensation

Group 1	Group 2	Group 3
Time commitment: 4 hours over the span of 6 months	Time commitment: 10 hours over the span of 6 months	Time commitment: 20 hours over the span of 6 months
• Two sociolinguistic interviews with mother and one child	• Two sociolinguistic interviews with mother and one child • Attendance at 4/6 school information sessions	• Two sociolinguistic interviews with mother and one child • Attendance at 4/6 school information sessions • Attendance at 8/10 workshops • Language journals/ assignments
Child respondent received: One book in Spanish	Child respondent received: One book in Spanish	Child respondent received: One book in Spanish
Adult respondent received: One $50 gift certificate for local supermarket	Adult respondent received: One $50 gift certificate for local supermarket Printed materials	Adult respondent received: $240 in supermarket gift certificates Printed materials

schedules and open their homes to the members of the research team. It required as well that parents speak with us about what are often sensitive topics involving private household matters. Because of this, all participants received compensation as detailed in Table 3.2.

Instruments and Data Collection

Two sociolinguistic interviews were conducted with the mother and one child in each household. The first interview took place at the beginning of the study, and the second six months later. Mothers were interviewed using an instrument designed to collect data on: perceived language competence; perceived role in their children's linguistic development; attitudes to Spanish transmission; maternal understandings of bilingualism; reported patterns of household language use; and family strategies related to maintenance. The full instrument can be consulted in Appendices 2 and 3.

Children's responses were organized in two age groups: the first, identified as *children*, includes 11 respondents between the ages of five and ten; the second, identified as *teens or adolescents*, includes eight respondents between the ages of 12 and 17. The median age for all respondents younger than 18 was nine years. Children and adolescents were interviewed using an instrument designed to gather data on their level of aural and oral competence in Spanish, their perceptions about the viability of Spanish in their everyday life, and their attitudes toward Spanish, English and bilingualism. Both instruments can be consulted in Appendices 4 and 5.

All instruments, recruitment materials and assent/consent documents were prepared in Spanish and English, and approved by the internal review boards of the University of Nebraska and the local school district. The instruments used in this study were adapted from Velázquez (2008), and have been used previously to study patterns of intergenerational Spanish (non-)transmission in the city of El Paso, TX, the neighborhood of La Villita, in Chicago, and in Lincoln, Nebraska. Sessions were audio-recorded and transcribed by the members of the research team. The corpus for this study comes from 33 hours of recorded interviews, plus field notes produced by the principal investigator, final research reports prepared by members of the research team, and written materials produced by the mothers in Group 3.

Research sites

Research was conducted at two sites. All interviews were conducted in the respondents' homes. All parental information sessions and all workshops took place in a multi-purpose classroom provided by the school, an elementary school with a high percentage of immigrant and refugee student population. At the time of data collection, 93% of the children in the school participated in the federal free or reduced lunch program and 47% of the students were Latino. In that same time period, 43% of K-12 students district-wide participated in the free or reduced lunch program and 11.4% were Latino (Lincoln Public Schools, 2011).

Research team qualifications

Interviews were conducted in Spanish by female bilingual interviewers who were native speakers of Latin American Spanish and who lived in the same community as the interviewees. Interviewer gender, language variety and locality were crucial components for establishing rapport with potential participants, gaining access to the respondents' social networks, and participation in local female communities of practice where Spanish is vested with social capital. School information sessions and workshop activities were designed and led by the principal investigator, who is a sociolinguist and a specialist in language acquisition, with support from one of the members of the research team. At the time of data collection, one of the two research assistants was a graduate student completing an MA in Spanish. The second research assistant was a lecturer in Spanish with a BA in social work. A female undergraduate project assistant majoring in education provided childcare and bilingual enrichment activities for small children who attended project activities with their mothers. The two research assistants in this study helped to recruit participants, conducted and transcribed most of the home interviews in this study and provided their insights into the local Latino community. The design, instruments, analysis, human research protocols, translations, research supervision, workshop design, materials and execution, family and community outreach and interinstitutional coordination were the responsibility of the principal investigator. All members of the research team were asked to keep field notes for the duration of the project. Project assistants prepared an end-of-project research report. The principal investigator field notes became the basis of the vignettes that open each chapter in this book.

A few questions to continue the conversation ...

(1) The number of families that participated in this study is relatively small: 19 families. What are the drawbacks of working with a sample of this size? Are there any benefits? In other words, what type of questions can be asked of a larger pool of respondents (e.g. 1000 versus 19 households), and what type of questions can be asked of a smaller group (e.g. 19 versus 1000).

(2) The interviews for this study were conducted by female bilingual interviewers who were native speakers of Latin American Spanish and who lived in the same community as the interviewees. Taking

into account the topic and space of these interviews, do you think the participants' responses would have changed if the interviewers were male, second-language speakers of Spanish or speakers of non-local varieties of Spanish?

(3) Think about your own experience. If you had to participate in an interview and you had to talk about sensitive topics, what interviewer characteristics would make you feel most comfortable? If you are bilingual, do you think that your level of anxiety, your way of speaking and/or the tone or structure of your answers would change depending on the language used by the interviewer?

4 In What Language Do You Pray? Household Language Use and Parental Strategies for Management

Josefina: You do what you can

In appreciation for their participation in our project, the mothers in this group receive a $40 supermarket gift certificate each month. Today is the first day of the month, so everyone receives theirs before the start of our session. As we are setting up, everyone is getting coffee and talking about what they bought with last month's certificate. After her turn, we tease Ana because she used hers 'to spread the wealth': she bought the ingredients she needed for the food she prepared for a fundraiser at her church and another at the school.

Josefina bought lunch ingredients for a month, and surprised her husband at the cash register when she took out only $1 in cash from her wallet. He asked her, wanted to know: Are they paying you or paying you because of our son? She proudly recreates the dialogue for us: 'No, I told him, no, they're paying me for me, for my effort, for what I know.' And, because Josefina, like the rest of the women here, also takes English classes several times a week in this same room, her youngest son has told his friends that her mom and him go to the same school. It's Rosario's turn and she says that she thought long and hard about what to get: 'You have to make it last.' Someone else asks if you have to spend the whole amount in one go; I realize that she is trying to save it. I tell them that I want to nominate them for Secretary of the Treasury because they can do so much with $40. We laugh. As I listen to the conversation, I note that none of them bought anything for themselves. I know it's a supermarket, but still. No shampoo, no pretty soap, no cosmetics, no deodorant, no fancy cookies. Different expectations.

In this chapter we will examine the point of intersection of two household language dynamics: overt parental policies and the everyday language choices of all family members. It is in some sense a ground-level perspective of what language management looks like in the intimate spaces of the home. Understanding patterns of language choice in everyday interactions is fundamental to discerning the mechanisms of family language maintenance and loss because, by their nature, these interactions differ from public uses of the family language (be they fully functional, merely formulaic or purely symbolic), which require a display of identity, are planned, adult driven, ritualized and most often follow a social script. We refer here to the type of interactions where language is a salient feature of ethnic affiliation, such as participation in religious services, weddings, soccer clubs, social and civic events within the local Latino community, paying and receiving visits from Spanish-dominant friends and relatives and visits to another country, for example.

As Spolsky (2009: 24) points out, parental efforts to manage children's language exposure most often fall in line with one of three broad strategies: (a) attempts to control the home language environment; (b) planned interaction with speakers of the target language; and (c) requests for outside support (e.g. playgroups, language schools, community activism). These strategies, he adds, can be enacted through overt language policy and/or by linking language choice to specific interlocutors or interactions:

> Those trying to control the sociolinguistic environment may attempt to be absolute ('don't you ever let me hear you speaking that other language!'), or be determined by presence of certain individuals ('you must speak that language when your grandmother is here!') or restricted to specific times, such as reading a story in the language to the children before they go to bed, or setting a language to be used at certain times. (Spolsky, 2009: 25)

Patterns of language use in the 19 households in this study were determined by collecting four types of data: overall language environment; reported language choice; parental language policies; and language management efforts carried out by various members of the family. The mother in each family reported the patterns described in this chapter. The drawbacks of using reported data are several and have been discussed elsewhere in detail, as well as their long history in in studies of Spanish in the United States (Potowski, 2004). To cite only three: Are the respondent's recollections reliable? Is the interviewee reporting actual use or her idea of how things should be? Are these responses stable over time? While acknowledging these drawbacks, we invite the reader to consider those presented by alternative approaches. Experiments conducted outside the home, and survey methodologies used in isolation require that both researcher and participant have a common understanding of the task and the topics at hand, and may be biased toward what the researcher wants to hear, rather than actual use. Even the gold standard of prolonged, in-home ethnographic observation would in this case be prohibitive in terms of cost and time commitment on the part of the researcher and, most importantly, would require a serious intrusion into family life and would alter the observed interactions by the presence of the observer and by the lens of her interpretation of the intimate events observed.

In this study, in order to test the stability of responses, the same questions were asked at the beginning and, several months later, at the end of the study. For a richer understanding of language use in these families, the reader is invited to compare the results presented here with those of Chapters 7 and 8 which describe children's language use as observed and recorded in actual interaction with the members of the research team.

Parental Language Management Efforts

The mothers in this study were presented with nine language-planning statements and were asked if any of them applied to their household. Five of these were strategies commonly cited in how-to guides targeted at middle-class parents interested in raising bilingual children (e.g. Baker, 2014; Bourgogne, 2013; King & Mackey, 2007; Pearson, 2008). Another four were related to the use of English in the home, and were included based on the findings of preliminary research conducted in the same community. These statements are presented in Figure 4.1. The contrast between the parents' language management efforts and the reports of language choice, described in the following pages, is illustrative of one of Spolsky's main points: parental policies and efforts do not always align with actual use. It also resonates with Barron-Hauwaert (2010), who argues that, despite their original intentions, parents in multilingual households need to re-evaluate their approach as life situations and family needs change over time. This is, of course, a point well understood by any parent attempting to raise young children, regardless of linguistic environment.

Figure 4.1 summarizes several findings regarding parental language policy and planning in these households. The first is the percentage of

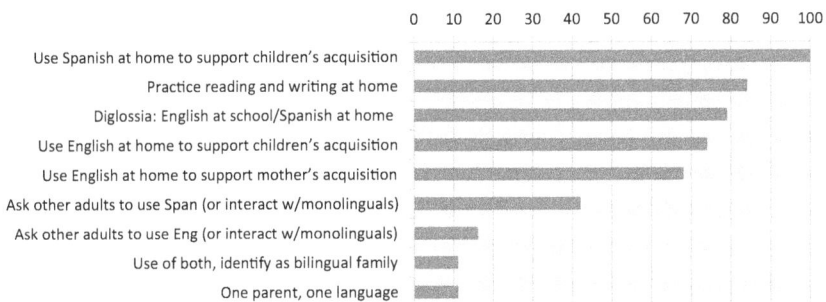

Figure 4.1 Parental language management efforts (percentage of report; N = 19)

mothers that reported their children as their main source of opportunities to practice speaking in English. This contrasts with several mothers' belief that they used the same amount of Spanish with each of their children. This is relevant for the purposes of Spanish maintenance efforts because it suggests an overestimation of exposure to the family language. It also highlights the need to take into account that in immigrant households children and parents are undergoing different – but intersecting – processes of language acquisition (Velázquez, 2014b).

The second finding we will highlight here is that most mothers who reported that they did not explicitly ask adults to speak to their children in Spanish or English explained they did not do so because the adults in question were monolingual in either language. Taken together with the low percentage of families who self-identified as bilingual, this underscores the limited contact that the children in these families had with adult bilinguals.

Finally, despite its popularity in guides targeted at middle-class parents, the one-parent-one-language (OPOL) approach was either irrelevant or not viable for most parents in these families. This result should be of interest for those concerned with bridging the disconnect between theoretical approaches to bilingual language development and socially embedded language experience (for a thorough critique and discussion of the origins and limitations of the OPOL approach, see Barron-Hauwaert, 2011).

The respondents' evaluation of their own planning efforts provided a clearer picture of the different beliefs and processes of accommodation that converge in everyday household interactions. Several mothers explained that their original choice of allowing greater use of English at home when their first child was small stemmed from the fear that speaking Spanish would hinder the child's success in school. An equal number reported regretting the choice several years later, once their children were fully integrated in school (and/or had siblings with whom to interact in English), and the evidence of Spanish attrition was ever more present in family communication.

Extract 4.1 Molina family, Session 1

Mother: Pero porque aquí, esta pregunta que el inglés lo va a aprender en la escuela este, yo esa, esa la hubiera yo pensado antes y a lo mejor yo hice mal a mi niño lo dejé que se juntara con personas que, que hablaban más este, inglés, porque yo no sé, pensé que era, se le iba a hacer difícil en la escuela, pero ahora lo veo y ahora es más difícil para mí [...] Porque sí, ahora yo veo a mis niñas y yo les trato de hablar más español y de ponerles la tele en español y eso, este, porque yo veo que ellas lo van a aprender además, Uhhuh.
Researcher: Cuando entren a la escuela
Mother: Entonces yo, a lo mejor aquí fue mi error de que...

Mother: *But because here, this question about [eldest child] learning English at school, I mean, that one, I should have thought about that one before, and maybe I hurt my child because I let him interact with people that, that spoke more, English, because I don't know, I thought it was going to be harder at school for him, but now I see that it's harder for me [to communicate with him]. Because yes, now I see the girls [youngest children] and I try to speak to them in Spanish, and to have them watch TV in Spanish and such, because I see that they are also going to learn [English], Uhhuh.*

Researcher: *When they go to school*

Mother: *So I, maybe it was my mistake that…*

For María Luisa Martínez, the mother in Extract 4.2, this moment of anagnorisis came precisely at school, while watching her older daughter interact with other children:

Extract 4.2 Martínez family, Session 2

Researcher: Muy bien. ¿Y él? [Referring to respondent's two-year-old child]

Mother: Apenas empieza a decir unas palabras. Yo yo yo le empezaba como por ejemplo a a a decir palabras en español como los zapatos y él empezaba a decir 'shoes, shoes', pero un día en la escuela me cayó el *veinte1 y dije* 'estoy haciendo mal' porque no tengo por qué hablarle en inglés si él al rato agarra su inglés yo le tengo que enseñar desde ahorita el español y ya se me quitó esa maña y ya ahora ya le digo 'los zapatos, los zapatos', y ando al jugo también, siempre le decía juice y ahora ya yo le digo jugo […] Porque sí siento que estaba, que estaba cometiendo, yo pienso, más no lo sé, pienso que estaba cometiendo un error en estarle enseñando palabras ya en inglés y digo ¿pero por qué? si ése lo van a ver en la tele, o con [eldest daughter] o con los niños que juega afuera, yo le tengo que empezar a enseñar, pero el español.

Researcher: *Very well. And him? [Referring to her two-year-old child]*

Mother: *He's just starting to say some words. And I was starting to, for example, to tell him words in Spanish, like 'zapatos', and he was starting to say 'shoes, shoes', but one time in [eldest daughter's] school, I realized it and told myself 'I'm making a mistake' because I shouldn't be speaking to him in English because in a while he will pick up English, so I have to start teaching him Spanish now, and I lost the bad habit, and now I tell him 'zapatos, zapatos', and I'm like 'jugo', because I always used to call it juice, and now I call it jugo […] Because yes, I do feel that I was making a, I think so, but I can't be certain, but I think that I was making a mistake in teaching him the words in English, and I ask myself why? They're going to see it [English] on TV, or [speak it] with [eldest daughter], or with the children in the neighborhood, I have to start teaching him, but teaching him Spanish.*

The segment in Extract 4.3 illustrates the ideological tension between the respondent and her older brother, who insists in speaking English to her son, despite her requests:

Extract 4.3 Lara family, Session 1

Researcher: Le pedimos a los familiares y amigos adultos que les hablen en español
Mother: Sí, pero a veces no nos hacen caso [Giggles]
R: ¿A veces les hablan en inglés?
Mother: S- uh, por ejemplo, uhh mi hermano es de un pensamiento diferente [...] Él dice que para qué (1) van a hablar en español si están aquí [...] él es de pensamiento muy distinto [...] Sí, aquí viene y luego se pone a estarle hablando al- al inglés a mi XXX [Child]
R: En inglés, y hhmm, y usted no le dice háblele en español, háblele en español, sino que lo deja
Mother: Sí, le digo que le hable en español pero él- mi hermano dice que está bien que me hablen inglés porque así yo también voy a practicar el inglés.

Researcher: *We ask adult relatives and friends to speak to them in Spanish*
Mother: *Yes, but sometimes they don't listen [Giggles]*
R: *Do they sometimes speak to them in English?*
Mother: *Y- uh, for example my brother is of a different mind [...] he says that what's the use of them speaking Spanish if they are here [...] he has a very different opinion [...] Yes, and he comes here and starts talking in English to my [child's name]*
R: *In English, and hhmm, you don't tell him to speak to him, speak to him in Spanish, but you just let* him
Mother: *Yes, I tell him to speak to him in Spanish, but my brother says that it's good that [the children] speak English, because that way I can practice [speaking in] English too.*

The segment in Extract 4.4 illustrates two conflicting parental management efforts. On the one hand, Susana Sánchez, the mother, accommodates to English in order to be understood by her older children in everyday interactions, but attempts to teach them to read and write in Spanish. On the other hand, her husband Carlos insists in speaking only in Spanish with his children, but believes that teaching them basic literacy skills will confuse them.

Extract 4.4 Sánchez family, Session 1

Researcher: Hablamos los dos idiomas porque somos una familia bilingüe
Mother: ((pause)) No somos una familia bilingüe todavía ¿verdad? ((laughs)) pero, pero sí tratamos de hablar un poquito los dos [...] porque por ejemplo mi hijo menor no me entiende muchas veces, entonces le tengo que hablar lo poquito que yo sé, o mi hijo mayor le tiene que traducir a mi hijo menor, para enseñarle,

o sea que sí manejamos, no es que seamos una familia bilingüe pero sí tratamos de entendernos
[...]
Tanto en español como inglés, si él no me entiende todavía, o no me entiende mucho el español porque él empezó a hablar aquí en Estados Unidos, cuando él empezó a hablar, el empezó a hablar en inglés. Él estaba muy baby cuando llegamos, entonces su, su, su, su, sus primeras palabras fueron en inglés. O sea, cuando él empezó a hablar, sí entendía muchas palabras en español, pero cuando él empezó a hablar [...] Más fluido en inglés ¿Sí? Entonces, insisto, no es que seamos una familia bilingüe, pero tratamos [...] de comunicarnos

R: Ok. Otra estrategia si, si la usan o no. Hablamos inglés con mis hijos porque estoy aprendiendo y necesito practicar

Mother: Yeah, definitivo

R: Los pongo a leer o escribir en español para que practiquen

Mother: Te soy sincera, no lo hemos hecho mucho y las veces que lo hemos intentado lo he dejado de hacer porque mi esposo se pone así de nervioso y él dice que, él no quiere confundir más, más al, al niño menor porque él dice que, que él se confunde, yo insisto que no, pero él dice 'es que si tú le hablas y tú le dices en español que se ponga a leer o que se ponga a escribir, se va a confundir y entonces no va a saber ni cuál es cuál, y no estoy de acuerdo'

R: Uhhuh

Mother: Pero cuando hemos intentado que ellos, que él principalmente [youngest son] escriba en español, lo hemos parado por eso, porque él [husband] dice que se puede confundir

R: [...] otra estrategia, tu esposo le habla en un idioma y tú le hablas en otro idioma. ¿Usan esa estrategia?

Mother: ((pausa)) No me quiero jactar pero, pero mi esposo le habla en puro español

R: Uhhuh

Mother: Pero muchas de las veces, insisto, el menor no entiende mucho y entonces yo le hablo de la otra manera

Researcher: *We speak both languages because we are a bilingual family*
Mother: *((pause)) No, we aren't a bilingual family yet, right? ((laughs)) but, but we do try to speak a little of both [...] because for example, my youngest son often doesn't understand me, so I have to speak to him with the little English that I know, or my oldest son has to translate for the youngest, to teach him, so we do use, it's not that we're a bilingual family, but we do try to make ourselves understood*
[...]
both in Spanish and English, if he [youngest son] doesn't understand me yet, or doesn't understand much Spanish it's because he started to talk here in the United States, when he first talked, talked in English. He was a baby when we got here,

so his, his, his, his first words were in English. I mean, when he started to speak, he did understand a lot of words in Spanish, but then he started to speak [...] more fluidly in English right? So I insist, it's not that we are a bilingual family, but we try [...] to communicate with each other

R: *Ok. Another strategy. Do you use it or not. We speak English with our children because I'm learning and I need to practice.*

Mother: *Yeah, absolutely*

R: *I make them read and write in Spanish so they can practice*

Mother: *To tell you the truth, we haven't done it a lot, and when we have, I've stopped doing it because my husband gets very nervous, and he says that he doesn't want to confuse [our youngest son] more. He [husband] says he can get [child] confused, and I insist that he won't, but he says 'if you tell him to read or write in Spanish, he's going to get confused, and he's not going to know which [language] is which, and I don't agree [with you teaching him to read and write]'*

R: *Uhhuh*

Mother: *But when we have tried to teach them to write in Spanish, him mainly [youngest son], we've stopped because of that , because he [husband] says that he can become confused*

R: *[...] another strategy, your husband speaks to him [youngest son] in one language and you speak to him in another. Do you use this strategy?*

Mother: *((pause)) I don't want to boast, but my husband only speaks to him in Spanish*

R: *Uhhuh*

Mother: *But a lot of times, I insist, the youngest doesn't understand a lot, so I speak to him in another way*

Another form of assessment of language management efforts is self-evaluation. Velázquez (2014b) explores the perceptions of agency that the mothers in that study held regarding their children's linguistic and academic development, and about the household practices they perceived as potentially conducive to the maintenance of Spanish. A central argument of this paper is that focusing on maternal perceptions of agency is pertinent because in immigrant households, parents – in particular, mothers – must negotiate transnational and local pressures either to foster bilingualism in their family or to encourage subtractive assimilation to English. Additionally, because they bore the primary responsibility for daily childrearing tasks, and because they regulated much of their children's schedules, activities and opportunities for interaction outside the home, the mothers in these families played a fundamental role in family language planning and language management (Velázquez, 2014b: 138).

Overall, the 19 mothers in these families did not perceive that their children's bilingual development depended exclusively on them. Fifty-eight percent of respondents perceived that fostering their children's use of Spanish depended either on her husband and her, or on the whole family (understood as both nuclear and extended). Not surprisingly, perceived agency for children learning English was primarily located in the school and the community (Velázquez, 2014b: 143). All the mothers in this study could name concrete activities in which they commonly engaged that, from their perspective, helped their children to maintain Spanish. All but one listed activities performed by their husband that served the same purpose. However, the respondents' own recollection of each parent's contribution to the maintenance of the family language differed in number and quality. Overall, activities listed as commonly performed by the mother required a greater expenditure of time and effort, as well as planning and arrange-ment of family schedules.

A major axis of family language dynamics was the distribution of household duties and the amount of interaction between each child and each parent. In the overwhelming majority of these households, the mother was responsible for the day-in-day-out tasks of childrearing, because the father worked outside the home most of the day and inter-acted with the children primarily in the evenings and on weekends (this included those households in which the mother held part-time employ-ment in the service sector). This distribution made the mother the de facto main source of transmission of Spanish. The fathers' role in their children's language development should not be overlooked, however, as they played a key function in determining patterns of household lan-guage exposure. Some fathers (Carlos Sánchez and Juan Gallegos, for example) spoke primarily in Spanish to their children, refusing to accommodate to English. This choice increased the children's opportu-nities to use the family language. Compared to their spouses, other fathers (José Antonio Ortiz and Raúl Quiñónez, for example) used more English or both languages when interacting with their children, which increased the children's opportunities to use English when inter-acting with adults at home. In Chapter 9 the reader will find a thorough discussion of the gendered distribution of childrearing tasks in these households, as well as its relevance for the intergenerational transmis-sion of Spanish.

Household Language Environment

As described in the coming pages, the children and adolescents in these families lived in home environments that favored direct and indirect expo-sure to the family language. Spanish-language media was, for most of them, part of their everyday soundscape; the overwhelming majority of adult interactions around them took place in Spanish. According to their mothers' report (summarized in Figure 4.2), all of them spoke Spanish in a normal week, and they most commonly did so with their parents (84%

Mothers who reported children spoke Spanish

Mothers who reported children spoke English

Mothers who reported children consumed TV and music in Span

Mothers who reported Spanish literacy only for eldest child or children

Mothers who reported all of her children knew or were learning to read/write in Span

0   25   50   75   100

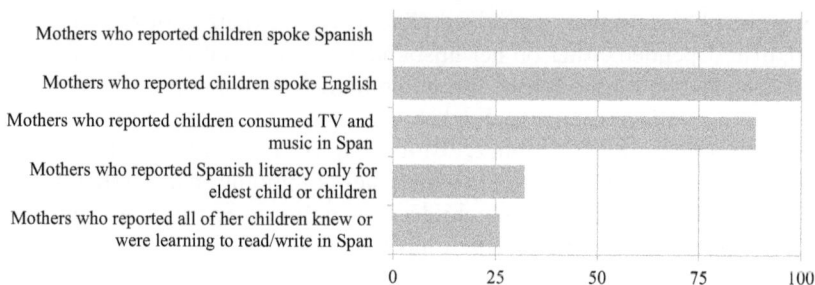

Figure 4.2 Household language environment in a normal week (percentage of report; *N* = 19)

of responses), with siblings, friends, and other relatives in the same age cohort (63%), with unspecified relatives in the same household (26%) and, to a lesser extent, with adults at church (10%), in their neighborhood (5%) or daycare (5%).

At first glance, then, these would appear to be favorable conditions for maintenance. This perspective changes, however, when we compare these patterns to those for exposure to English. According to their mothers' report, all school-aged children in this study spoke English in a normal week, and they most commonly did so with friends, siblings, and other relatives in the same age cohort (63%), with teachers and classmates (63%) and, to a significantly lesser extent, with adults and children in church, daycare or at work[2] (5%, respectively). In only two of these families (10% of responses) were children reported as consistently speaking in English with their father (for patterns of sporadic use of English with either or both parents, see next section). These results mean, then, that for the children and teenagers in these families language choice was strongly compartmentalized along the axes of diglossia and generational cohort, as illustrated in Table 4.1.

Looking at Table 4.1, the reader will note what is missing at the core of this diagram: adults who can function fully in both languages in both spheres of interaction, that is to say, a critical mass of adults that can socialize these children to bilingualism, and increase their opportunities for the development of language in different contexts and registers. Of equal importance to the likelihood of Spanish maintenance in these families is the fact that, despite the 84% of mothers who reported they had made (or had attempted to make) their children practice reading and writing in Spanish, only 26% reported that their children knew how to do so. A slightly higher percentage (36%) reported that only their eldest child knew how to read and write in Spanish. Of those who knew how to read and write in Spanish according to their mothers' report, 39% had been taught by her, 17% by both parents, and 17% had attended school in another country. Two mothers reported that their

Table 4.1 Compartmentalization of language choice for school-aged children

Private spaces/functions		Public spaces/functions	
Adults		*Adults*	
+ Spanish		+ English	
– English		– Spanish	
Peers		*Peers*	
Not in school	*School-aged*		
+ Spanish	+ English	+ English	
– English	– Spanish	– Spanish	

children had learned basic reading skills in Spanish by decoding labels and signs in everyday interactions (with help from the parents and other adults). Another two mothers responded that their children had learned their ABCs in Spanish at their local preschool. Only one mother (5%) reported that her husband had taught their child to read in Spanish. At the time of data collection all school-aged children and adolescents in these families were attending schools where English was the medium of instruction.

Two additional patterns will be mentioned here: at least four of the mothers who reported that they had attempted to teach their firstborn how to read and write in Spanish also reported abandoning this goal when their second child was born. The data are insufficient to ascertain what motivated this choice. Possible reasons could include: that she had more work with two children at home; that she felt the pressure to shift to English once the eldest child was in school; that the eldest child was using English with the younger siblings; or because (as happened in some of these cases) the mother began a part-time job in the service sector, and thus had less time to dedicate to this effort. Although not the focus of this chapter, it should also be mentioned here that Spanish-language youth church groups and religious education classes were, for several of the families in this study, major spaces for the development of literacy, and a source of opportunities of interaction beyond the home.

Household Language Dominance

In an attempt to establish patterns of household language dominance, the respondents were asked to report on the language most commonly used by family members when engaging in 15 common household interactions (Appendix 3). Reported data were collected both by interaction and by communicative dyad (i.e. mother to child, child to mother, father to child, child to father, etc.).[3] Interactions reported as most commonly taking place in Spanish were given a score of 2; those reported as most commonly taking place in either or both languages were given a score of 1, and those reported as most commonly taking place in English were given a score of 0.

Under this criterion, hypothetical scores of 30 or 0 would describe monolingual households in Spanish and English, respectively. Households with a score greater than 15 were classified as Spanish dominant, and households with a score lower than 15 were classified as English dominant. As summarized in Table 4.2, all households in this study were classified as Spanish dominant, with important differences by interlocutor and type of interaction. Excluding babies and toddlers, all children and parents in this study spoke Spanish, but parents spoke more Spanish than children, and slightly more mothers spoke more Spanish than fathers. Greater use of Spanish was reported in the youngest children, with increased use of English in direct proportion to the number of years a child had attended school.

While the majority of mothers reported that their older children preferred to speak in English among themselves, this was not by itself understood as evidence of Spanish attrition, as most of these children and teenagers interacted in Spanish with Spanish-dominant adults and peers, and could function in domains and spaces that were socially marked for Spanish (e.g. church groups and family gatherings). In contrast, Spanish attrition or, to be more precise, the reduction of Spanish viability in the domain of the home was presumed when the mother reported instances in which miscommunication obstructed ordinary household interactions, and instances in which the mother reported feeling that her children did not understand her when she spoke (Josefina Gallegos, for example). In Extract 4.5, Marina Ortiz describes how her eldest children's preference for English when interacting among themselves and with their father (as well as her inability to speak the language), leaves her unable to

Table 4.2 Reported language dominance by household

Spanish-dominant households	100%
Households where parents spoke more Spanish than children	79%
Households where mother spoke more Spanish than father	37%
Households with more than one child where eldest spoke more Spanish	0%
Households with more than one child where youngest spoke more Spanish	48%
Median age of youngest in households where youngest spoke more Spanish	3.5 years
Median age of eldest in households where youngest spoke more Spanish[a]	9 years

Notes: Percentage of report; N = 19.
[a] Four families had children over the age of 18 (three of them living at home at the time of the study). Adult children living at home or elsewhere, as well as minor children living in another country and children living in the same household temporarily or permanently but not the respondent's offspring were not included in this calculation.

comprehend segments of household conversations, particularly those related to homework.

Extract 4.5 Ortiz family, Session 1

Researcher: ¿Qué idioma usan ellos entre hermanos? [Referring to respondent's two eldest children]

Mother: Inglés [...] y batallo bastante de que hablen español porque no les entiendo, hay cosas que sí les entiendo, hay cosas que no...

R: [Hay cosas que no... ¿generalmente ellos siempre hablan en inglés?

Mother: Sí.

R: Eh, cuando ellos le hablan al papá, ¿lo hacen en inglés o en español?

Mother: Algunas veces en español y algunas en inglés, pero más en inglés

R: En inglés. ¿Qué cosas, de éstas que tengo aquí, ¿cuáles son algunas cosas que más utilizan el inglés?

Mother: Cuando hacen las tareas

R: ¿Para hacer las tareas?

Mother: Ajá.

R: ¿Sobre todo los dos mayores?

Mother: Uhuh.

Researcher: *What language do they use amongst siblings? [Referring to respondent's eldest children]*

Mother: *English [...] and I struggle a lot to make them speak in Spanish, because I don't understand them. There are things that I do understand, and things I don't...*

R: *[There are things you don't... Do they generally speak in English?*

Mother: *Yes.*

R: *Eh, when they speak to their father, do they do it in English or Spanish?*

Mother: *Sometimes in Spanish and sometimes in English, but more in English*

R: *In English. What things [interactions], from the things I have listed here, what are some in which they use more English?*

Mother: *When they do their homework*

R: *To do homework?*

Mother: *Uhuh.*

R: *Mostly the eldest [children]?*

Mother: *Uhuh.*

In Extract 4.6, María Luisa Martínez articulates her understanding that her inability to communicate fluently in English combined with her daughter's inability to understand what she had said in Spanish resulted in occasional breakdowns in communication, which she tried to resolve by accommodating to English, despite her favorable attitudes toward

Spanish maintenance (for more on maternal attitudes toward transmission and use of Spanish, see Chapter 5).

Extract 4.6 Martínez family, Session 1

Researcher: ¿En su hogar, ustedes usan las siguientes? [Strategies] 'el inglés lo van aprender en la escuela, así que en la casa les hablamos español a nuestros hijos' ((Pause 0.5)) ¿Usan esa estrategia? ¿Están de acuerdo?

Mother: No, porque como le digo, hay veces que la niña necesita que yo le hable, que le explique a veces en inglés, y yo trato de decirle como puedo, yo trato de decirle en inglés qué es, porque a veces ella no entiende.

Researcher: *In your home, do you use the following? [Strategies] 'They're going to learn English at school, so at home we speak Spanish to our children? ((Pause 0.5)) Do you follow this strategy? Do you (both) agree?*

Mother: *No, because, like I told you, there are times when the girl [my daughter] needs me to speak to her, to explain sometimes in English, and I try to tell her as best as I can, I try to tell her in English what it is [I'm talking about] because she sometimes doesn't understand.*

Language Choice in Everyday Interactions

Once we establish that a household is Spanish dominant, can we then assume that Spanish will be equally viable[4] for all activities in which parents and children interact? Based on the experience of these 19 families, the answer appears to be no. In this section we examine language use by type of interaction in order to better understand household language dynamics. Additionally, we identify which kinds of interactions, if any, were most resistant to the use of English. Reported data on parent–child interactions can be further classified by communicative function: *storytelling* (tell a story, tell a joke); *solidarity* (tell a secret, console, ask for money/favor); *convey emotion* (express affection, express anger); *exert authority* (scold, warn); *religion* (pray together); *recreation* (play, sing together); *Spanish literacy* (read for fun[5]); and *convey information from outside home* (do homework/teach something, give information).

The respondents were asked which language was most commonly used by each parent and each child when engaging in these interactions. Spanish was given a score of 2, English was given a score of 0, and interactions that were reported as taking place in either or both languages were given a score of 1. Activities that did not normally occur in a specific household were coded as N/A. Viability of Spanish for a specific interaction was established when the score of reported use was more than half of the possible score for parents and children. To clarify, the results related to language viability do not mean that Spanish was used 100% of the time, but that it was the unmarked choice for carrying out that specific interaction.

In 74% of these households viability of Spanish was established for all parent–child dyads in all interactions. In 16% of households Spanish was not reported as a viable language for completing homework or teaching something. In one of these households (5% of responses), Spanish was not viable for asking a favor or asking for money (most commonly done in English) and, in another, when playing or reading for fun. Another five interactions received slightly lower scores, but still above the midway point. These were singing, expressing affection, asking for money, doing homework and reading for fun. Expressing affection was classified by the respondents as taking place in both languages when the set phrase 'I love you' was inserted in an exchange in Spanish. Overall, praying was the interaction most resistant to English, as no adult was reported as using anything but Spanish when praying with his/her children, and only seven out of 52 children were reported as using both languages in family prayer (no child was reported by their mother as using English when praying with the family). Interactions least resistant to English were singing, doing homework and reading for fun. The use of both languages when asking for a favor or (in the case of children) asking for money is explained in the next section.

In order to test the stability of responses, the same instrument was used at the beginning and end of the study. The results were stable for 14 of these households (74% of responses). In four households (the López, Aparecido, Gómez and Ortiz families) an increase in the mother's use of Spanish with the youngest child was reported. An increase in the father's use of English with the eldest child or children was also reported for the same households. In the Arroyo household, a considerable increase in the use of Spanish by the children was reported in asking for favors/money, telling a joke, telling a story and reading for fun.

Parents' and Children's Strategies for Household Language Management

In the last part of this chapter we examine the everyday creativity and accommodation that takes place in multilingual households. To some extent, all household members who could speak managed or attempted to manage the language choice of other members of the family. As will be seen below, some strategies favored use of Spanish, some favored use of English, while some emphasized solidarity and some emphasized exclusion. Regardless of language or family member, all of the strategies reported here share one communicative goal, which was the successful completion of the interaction at hand.

Parental strategies

Parental strategies can be situated within one of five broad categories. The first strategy was *pragmatic*, and was the most commonly reported for both parents and children: adults used more English when they needed to ask a favor from their children, and children used more Spanish when they needed to ask a favor from their parents. This is illustrated in Extract 4.7, where Elena Navarro, the mother, describes the accommodation that takes place between both parents and their two eldest sons.

Extract 4.7 Navarro family, Session 1

Researcher: Usted tiene un favor que pedirle a sus niños, ¿en qué idioma se lo pide?
Mother: Hmm, en los dos [giggles]
R: En los dos, okay. En- a: ¿quiénes?
Mother: A [Two eldest sons]- a los niños más grandes y la niña sí en español
R: [...] Sus hijos quieren pedirle dinero, ¿en qué idioma le- se lo piden?
Mother: En español
R: ¿Los tres?
Mother: Sí, en español los tres
R: [...] Su esposo tiene un favor que pedirle a sus niños, ¿en qué idioma le habla?
Mother: En los dos [giggles]
R: En los dos su esposo a sus niños
Mother: Sí
R: Okay, eeh a los dos mayores y ¿a la niña sí en español?
Mother: Sí. Sí, en español
R: Bueno ahora sus niños tienen- quieren pedirle dinero a su esposo, ¿en qué idioma le hablan?
Mother: En español

Researcher: *You have a favor to ask your children, in what language do you ask it?*
Mother: *Hmm, in both [giggles]*
R: *In both, okay, In- to: whom?*
Mother: *To [Two eldest sons]- the oldest kids, and to the youngest in Spanish*
R: *[...] Your children want to ask you for money, in what language do they ask for it?*
Mother: *In Spanish*
R: *The three of them?*
Mother: *Yes, the three of them in Spanish*
R: *[...] Your husband has a favor to ask your children, in what language does he speak to them?*

Mother: *In both [giggles]*
R: *Your husband to your children in both*
Mother: *Yes*
R: *Okay, eeh to the two eldest, and to your [youngest] child in Spanish?*
Mother: *Yes. Yes, in Spanish.*
R: *Well, now your children have to ask your husband for money, in what language do they speak to him?*
Mother: *In Spanish*

The second most commonly reported parental strategy was *refusal to switch* when addressed in English by their children. This included instances in which the mother exaggerated her inability to comprehend English in order to force her children to use Spanish (in the Pérez and Quiñónez households, for example), and households in which the father allowed the child to speak in English, but pretended not to pay attention until addressed in Spanish (the Martínez family, for example). The third strategy was *mother's use of English with her children*. As explained at the beginning of this chapter, this was reported in households where the respondent was learning English and her children were one of her few sources of input.

Perhaps the most creative parental strategies were those intended to *circumvent obstacles related to completing homework and reading* with their children. The reader will remember here that all school-aged children were attending classrooms where English was the medium of instruction, and that families had reduced access to age-appropriate books in Spanish.[6]

Bedtime reading strategies included cases where parents read an English-language book and then translated and paraphrased in Spanish, and instances where a Spanish-dominant parent read passages of a book in English with heavy exegesis in Spanish. In an interesting example, Mateo Pérez had a *special* book (i.e. a book written in Spanish) which he would only take out to read to his children at bedtime. Importantly, in all of these cases, the intimate family ritual of bedtime reading with the youngest children in these families was marked for Spanish, because children and parents were expected to address each other in the family language and according to the mothers' report they did, for the most part.

Strategies related to homework included cases where the child read the assignment in English and the parents supervised or answered questions as best they could using Spanish, and cases where the completion of homework by the youngest children was undertaken as a joint family effort with participation (and pooling of linguistic resources) of parents and teenage children (in the López household, for example).

Linguistic re-contact

Although several of the children in these families had travelled to their parents' country of origin, only Dora Alicia García related that her husband had taken their boy for a three-month stay in Mexico as a deliberate (and successful) attempt to help him reacquire the family language after they had noticed that her eldest son was not comprehending or using Spanish.

Children's strategies

Compared to their parents, the language management strategies employed by the children in these families involved greater sensitivity to context and communicative goals. Most code-switching strategies were used by older children and teenagers, and would most often be deployed to include or exclude someone in a conversation (e.g. households in which the eldest children spoke English among themselves and in Spanish with youngest siblings; and households such as the García family, where the eldest child told his secrets to his mother in English so his youngest siblings didn't understand). Other examples of the use of switching strategies include cases where the eldest child switched to Spanish with the expressed purpose of making sure his parents understood him (Gallegos household), and cases where the child was angry and switched to English when addressing his mother to express distance (or, in the words of Rebeca López, 'para hacer una malcriadez': *to misbehave*).

Most of the strategies employed by the children and teenagers in these families were related to language brokering. These included several forms of paraphrasing, interpretation, exegesis, and other strategies aimed at ensuring comprehension. In some households (in the García family, for example), the eldest son would translate his siblings' homework for his parents. The children in the López and Quiñónez families, for instance, would relate a story from school in English and proceed to rephrase it in Spanish to make sure that their mothers understood them. In the Sánchez family, the two eldest sons were English dominant, and were in the habit of interpreting for each other in order to be understand/be understood by their mother.

Compared to the other types of interaction surveyed, storytelling is by definition an activity that requires greater control of linguistic structure. Not surprisingly, then, children in these households were most comfortable relating a story in their stronger language (for results of the children's storytelling task, see Chapter 8). What is noteworthy, however, is that even very young children in these families commonly chose the language according to the type of story, interlocutor and space in which the narrated events took place. For example, according to their mother's report, the children in the Navarro family most often used English when telling her a story about something that happened at school, and Spanish if the story was invented. Similarly, Luisito Quiñónez, a five-year-old boy, pre-ferred to use Spanish when talking with his mother about things that happened at home, and English when talking about things that happened at daycare.

The final group of language management strategies to be discussed here includes management practices that are common in language minor-ity households but are for the most part absent in the dynamics of mono-lingual households. These relate to children's evaluation and monitoring of their parents' speech. In the case of these 19 families this included cases in which the children corrected their parents' pronunciation (in the López and García households, for example), cases in which the youngest child in the household equated her/his mother's inability to speak English with lack of education. Of equal interest are maternal strategies to overcome or reframe the effects of these negative evaluations. Whenever her youngest daughter criticized her pronunciation of a word in English, for example, Rebeca López would verify the word's correct pronunciation by consult-ing with her older children. In another example, Carina Quiñónez reframed her inability to speak English with her five-year-old by explain-ing to him that she had a lot of things in her mind.

In this chapter we examined the intersection between overt parental policies and everyday language choices. Based on mothers' reports of household language practices, I have argued that the children in these families lived in home environments that favored direct and indirect exposure to Spanish, but that it was not equally viable for all activities in which the parents and children interacted. The results suggest that for the children and teenagers in these families language choice was strongly compartmentalized along the axes of diglossia and genera-tional cohort.

While the mother was the de facto source of Spanish input and opportunities for literacy development, the father played a key function in children's language development both in families in which he refused to switch to Spanish and in families in which he addressed them in English (increasing the children's opportunities to use either language at home). We will return to this point in Chapter 9. An important finding discussed in the preceding pages is that both the parents and the chil-dren engaged in efforts to manage household language dynamics. Compared to their parents, however, the language management strate-gies employed by the children and adolescents in these families involved greater sensitivity to context and communicative goal, and most com-monly related to language brokering and evaluation/monitoring of their parents' use of English.

At the beginning of this book I made the case that the language dynamics in these 19 families are both illustrative of those present in many language-minority households around the world, and that they arise from the unique social and economic conditions present in New

Latino Diaspora communities. In Chapter 2 we have situated their experiences within the larger context of Latino households in the United States. In the following chapters we will examine three additional forces that impinge on these dynamics: mothers' and children's attitudes toward and motivations to use Spanish (Chapter 5), mothers' and children's self-perception of proficiency in both languages (Chapter 6) and children's observed skills in Spanish (Chapters 7 and 8). We will end by describing a theoretical model which attempts to account for language maintenance in low vitality settings.

A few questions to continue the conversation ...

(1) Many children growing up in first-generation bilingual households are the main source of input in the majority language for one or more adults in their lives. What impact might this state of affairs have on their own process of acquisition of the family language? What impact might this have on their acquisition of the majority language?

(2) As described in Chapter 2, some first-generation Latino households in the Midwest experience prolonged family separation due to differential migration, repatriation or circular migration. What might the impact of this separation be for the overall development of the children and teenagers in these families? What emotional, physical and economic impact might it have on the parents? What role do bilingual skills play in these dynamics?

(3) Think back over your own experiences. What are three things you did with your family when you were growing up that made you feel like a member of your family? What role did language (or languages) play in learning those family practices or acquiring family traditions?

Notes

(1) *Caer el veinte* (literally: for the coin to drop): 'To realize something that was evident or that should have been noticed before.' *Diccionario de Mexicanismos.* See https://www.academia.org.mx/obras/obras-de-consulta-en-linea/diccionario-de-mexicanismos.

(2) The response 'At work' refers to one teenager who had a part-time job at a fast-food restaurant after school. Two mothers (10% of responses) did not respond to this item. Data are insufficient to ascertain if they meant to convey that they believed their children did not speak English, that they didn't know with whom their children spoke English outside the home, or if this lack of response is related to the wording of the item or to an unidentified condition at the moment of interview.

(3) Adult–adult interactions, which overwhelmingly took place in Spanish, were not included in this instrument.

(4) Language viability is understood here following Velázquez *et al.* (2015): On the week of the study speakers were using their family language with certain interlocutors and in certain contexts because they deemed it apt, appropriate, and suitable to carry out these interactions.

(5) A difference was made between reading for fun and homework, because homework reading was in English by default.

(6) Some children's books in Spanish were available through the public library system.

5 Mothers and Children: Attitudes and Motivations to Use Spanish

Juana: She reads in English but we talk to her in Spanish

This the writing prompt: *What I would do for my children or with my children if the day had three more hours, or if I earned a hundred dollars more each month.* I unfold the piece of ruled paper and read Juana's answer: *Talk, communicate more. Play, read stories, eat dinner together, fun times. Go to the library, to the park, museums, to the movies, to the theater. Disneyland. Take them to Chuck E. Cheese's. Pool, ballet, soccer practice.* I read the rest of the answers and I notice that in these dream scenarios, no-one answers 'I would buy something'. All have to do with having more time, sharing experiences. So, we talk about time, and about how, for several of the moms in the group, the need to be at work is the main cause of not having more time to spend with their kids. Need to pay bills first. Elena, who doesn't work outside the home, asks if it's possible to work fewer hours in order to spend more time with the children. Juana speaks about the low salaries: *If I earned $100 a day, I wouldn't have to work all week, I would work only three and spend more time with them, but I don't earn that.* Magdalena says that she has talked with her husband about the possibility of not working in the afternoons, so she can be at home with her kids. But they're older now, she says, they want to go out to play with their friends. They're more independent now. Stages. She says that maybe, if she were at home in the afternoon, she would be watching TV or on the computer, and the kids would be playing outside, so instead she goes to her job. But in the evenings and on weekends, she explains, the children expect to spend time with their parents. This is non-negotiable. Ana has elementary-aged children, one teenager, and an adult daughter who is married and lives in another state. She agrees: *Children need you differently* *at different stages.* Juana is none too convinced: *My sister works all the time, and her boy, my little nephew, is always with me. Even on the weekends, when she is off work, the boy still wants to be over at my house.*

In Chapter 4 the reader was presented with a ground-level perspective of what language management looked like in the households included in this study. We examined family language dynamics and parental strategies for maintenance as reported by the mother in each family. This chapter centers on what they thought about their own use of Spanish and about their children's acquisition and use of the language. Understanding speaker perceptions about language is important to understand language use because what we think about ourselves, about others and about the relationships and practices that shape our shared experience has a direct impact on the material conditions of life.

A positivist paradigm of the study of language attitudes is predicated on an understanding of the speaker's articulation of their own experience as subjective, and thus unreliable in any attempt to understand linguistic choice. In reality, both the speaker's perceptions and the observer's interpretation of those perceptions are subjective; the meaning of that experience is socially constructed, the question itself modifying the experience. The space where language choice and language transmission take place is a social space mediated by perceptions that condition our experience. These perceptions help us to interpret it, to give it meaning, to seek or avoid an interaction, thus changing the nature of the experience itself. Writing about the relationship between the individual and society, Raymond Williams reminds us about 'The essential relation, the true interaction, between patterns learned and created in the mind and patterns communicated and made active in relationships, conventions, and institutions'. 'Culture', he writes, 'is the name for this process and its results' (Williams, 1961: 72).

At the scale of the household, attitudes and motivations are the motor for the use and transmission of a family language. They are not articulated in a vacuum, but rather they are the site where individual language choice meets larger, community-wide language ideologies (Alarcón & Parella, 2013; Edwards, 2009; Lapresta-Rey *et al.*, 2017; Woolard & Schieffelin, 1994).

For the purposes of the present discussion we will understand language attitudes as beliefs about language and its users (Baker, 1992). Following Karan (1996, 2000, 2011), we will operationalize these as *general, self* and *goal* beliefs; that is: what the speaker perceives as the 'normal' state of affairs about a language and its users; perceptions about self-efficacy in use and transmission; and perceptions about what should be done about this state of affairs. We will also distinguish between *language attitudes* and *language motivations*. We understand motivations – communicative, religious, instrumental, solidarity and social identity – as intrinsically linked to the cost/benefit calculation that underlies language choice (Karan, 1996, 2000, 2011).[1]

At the scale of the community, motivations have been understood as a major force in language shift and maintenance. For Karan (2011: 145), motivations are predictors of ethnolinguistic vitality because 'actions are the results of decisions, and decisions are shaped by values and motivations'. Speaker choices regarding transmission or non-transmission of Spanish are motivated by beliefs about language, and that these are a reflection of underlying tensions present in a multilingual community (Martínez, 2006; Velázquez, 2009).

At the scale of the family, the importance of positive parental attitudes for the transmission of a minority language is borne out by two decades of studies of bilingual child language development (De Houwer, 1999; Lanza, 2007; Okita, 2002). Also documented is the fact that positive parental attitudes are not by themselves strong predictors of language transmission (Schecter & Bayley, 2002). This leads to the conclusion presented in Velázquez (2013) that positive attitudes to the family language are a necessary but insufficient condition for transmission. An analysis of maternal attitudes toward the intergenerational transmission of Spanish in these 19 families is discussed in Velázquez (2013). What is presented here for the first time is a comparison of these results with children's perceptions of viability of the family language, as well as the sociolinguistic context in which these attitudes were articulated.

Data Collection

Data on maternal attitudes and motivations were obtained during the two interviews conducted for this study.[2] Maternal perceptions about the benefits and costs of speaking Spanish and English were surveyed using four open-ended items: *What are some good things about speaking Spanish? What are some bad things about speaking Spanish? What are some good things about speaking English?* and *What are some bad things about speaking English?* Maternal attitudes toward the use and intergenerational transmission of Spanish in the context of the United States, about bilingualism in their children, and about the potential link between language and cultural identity were surveyed using a 12-item Likert scale.

Maternal motivations to use and transmit the family language were surveyed using 24 open-ended questions. These were based on Karan's perceived benefit model, and were intended to explore communicative, instrumental, religious and economic motivations. An additional item was added to explore the fear of linguistic discrimination as a potential motivator not to transmit the family language. The inclusion of this item diverges from Karan's original model,[3] and was included to take into account the long and well-documented history of linguistic discrimination suffered by many speakers of Spanish and other minority languages in the context of the United States. The respondents were also presented with two open-ended questions: *In your opinion, what are some advantages and disadvantages of speaking Spanish to your children?* and *Why do you speak Spanish to your children?* These were intended to test the stability of the responses collected earlier during the same interview, and again a few months later. Unless otherwise noted, participant responses remained stable when asked during the second iteration of the sociolinguistic inter-view. This chapter ends with a comparison of mothers' and children's perceptions about Spanish and bilingualism, as well as a brief discussion of why understanding the differences between them is a key component of understanding patterns of intergenerational transmission and loss.

Is Spanish Good, Desirable, Useful? Maternal Attitudes toward Spanish

The functional separation of Spanish and English in the respondents' everyday experience – i.e. diglossia – was evidenced indirectly by their responses to the questions: *What are some good things about speaking Spanish?* and *What are some bad things about speaking English?* When asked about the potential advantages of speaking Spanish, most responses (39%) were related to communicating with family members and other speakers of Spanish locally and abroad. In contrast, 48% of responses regarding the potential advantages of speaking English were related to economic opportunities or job performance. Responses related to com-munication with others in English represent 33% of responses and refer, in all instances, to communicating with strangers in the wider community. Other perceived benefits to speaking Spanish – four or less tokens listed by the respondents – were: *being bilingual, it's my language, economic opportunities, it's my culture, it's easier* and *I can express myself better.* Additional responses listed as advantages of speaking English include: *being bilingual* and *not feeling ignored.*

Interestingly, this functional separation was accompanied by a percep-tion of the desirability of bilingualism which runs counter to monoglossic language ideologies.[4] When asked about the importance of knowing and using both languages, for example, all but one of the mothers in this study responded that it was very important that their children be bilingual. When asked about potential disadvantages of speaking Spanish, 79% of the respondents answered that there were none; three respondents answered that the use of profanities was a potential bad thing about speaking Spanish, and one reported fear of discrimination. Asked about the potential disadvantages of speaking English, the same three speakers alluded to the use of profanities. The rest of the women in the group responded that there were no disadvantages of speaking English. Indeed, contrary to xenophobic discourses that posit the immigrant as unwilling to learn the majority language, all the women in this group were motivated to learn, and saw it as an inescapable precondition for being successful in the United States, not only for economic success, but as a counter-measure to social isolation. Or, as Fernanda Gómez eloquently puts it in Extract 5.1, to avoid *feeling like a shadow*:

Extract 5.1 Gómez family, mother, Session 1

Researcher: ¿Cuáles son las cosas buenas de hablar inglés?
Mother: Pues la comunicación, el no sentirse, el no sentirse como una sombra en todo lugar.

Researcher: *What are the good things about speaking English?*
Mother: *Well, communication, not feeling, not feeling like a shadow everywhere.*

In Extract 5.2 Carina Quiñónez equates the ability to speak English with *being someone* in her new community:

Extract 5.2 Quiñónez family, mother, Session 2

Researcher: ¿Cuáles son algunas cosas buenas de hablar inglés?
Mother: Pues lo bueno de hablar inglés es para comunicarse con las demás personas de aquí [...] O para entenderles también [...] Para entenderles, eso es lo bueno porque [...] Si no hablamos no somos nada.

Researcher: *What are some good things about speaking English?*
Mother: *Well, the good thing about speaking English is to communicate with other people [who are from] here [...] to understand what they say too [...] to understand them, that's the good thing because [...] if we don't speak [it] we're nobody.*

Another way to explore speaker attitudes about their family language and about bilingualism is to examine the perceptions of desirability of aural, oral and literacy skills in both languages. Research conducted in a group of Mexican American middle-class households in the border city of El Paso, TX (Velázquez, 2008, 2009) suggests that mothers assigned differential value to their children's development of literacy skills in Spanish and English. For example, while they reported that their children's ability to comprehend and speak Spanish was very important for instrumental, emotional and identity reasons, they tended to underestimate local varieties of Spanish, and placed a lower value on the development of Spanish literacy.

Based on those findings, potential differentials in the perceived desirability of Spanish and English were surveyed in the present study by asking the respondents to assign a ranking of *very important, somewhat important, not very important* and *don't know* to each of the four basic skills in either language. The responses were later assigned a numerical value of 3, 2, 1 and 0, respectively. Thus, any result above 35 represents a skill that was understood by all the respondents in the group as 'important to very important'. A ranking of 54 describes a skill that was unanimously ranked as very important. Both results are taken here as indexes of desirability. On a follow-up item, the respondents were asked to rank how important it was for them that their children develop each of these skills in either language. This second measure was understood as an index of desirability of transmission in the case of Spanish, and as an index of desirability of acquisition of the majority language in the case of English.

As a group, a high perception of desirability was found for both languages. Seventy-nine percent of the mothers ranked all skills in Spanish and in English as 'very important'. No respondent assigned a ranking lower than 'important' in either iteration of the survey for either themselves or their children. Examined in greater detail, slight differences in perceived desirability were observed. For example, Consuelo Luna and Graciela Fernández ranked reading and writing in English – which was for them still in its nascent stages – as 'important', while they ranked reading and writing in Spanish, their dominant language, as 'very important'; i.e. the former was a goal, whereas the latter was a precondition to carry out the activities of everyday life. In contrast, Fernanda Gómez, also an L2 learner of English, ranked Spanish literacy as 'important' because she took it as a given, while she ranked reading and speaking in English as 'very important' because she was highly motivated to learn English; i.e. carrying out the activities of everyday life in her native language was taken as a given, whereas acquisition of the majority language was a priority.

The perceived importance of English for economic and social mobility is again evidenced by the fact that all but one of the mothers in this study assigned the highest possible ranking to every skill in English in both iterations of the sociolinguistic interview. The perceived importance of bilingualism/biliteracy is suggested by the fact that 69% of the respondents assigned a ranking of 'very important' to all skills in both languages. A slight difference was reported regarding literacy in Spanish. While all respondents ranked the ability to read, write, speak and understand Spanish as 'very important', three of the mothers in the group – Fernanda Gómez, Consuelo Luna and Marina Ortiz – assigned a ranking of 'important' to their children's acquisition of reading skills in the family language.

Beyond communicative, solidarity or social identity motivations, most respondents also reported an instrumental view of Spanish literacy, as illustrated in Extracts 5.3 and 5.4:

Extract 5.3 Molina family, mother, Session 2

Researcher: ¿Qué tan importante es para usted que sus hijos... [sepan] Para leer y escribir en español...

Mother: Oh, es importante para, porque los puede ayudar para más adelante en su futuro y en el trabajo y para hablar pues para comunicarse con la personas para poder desenvolverse con la comunidad.

Researcher: *How important was it for you that your children [...] To read and write in Spanish...*

Mother: *Oh, it's important to, because it can help them later on in their future and at work, and to speak, well, to communicate with people, to be able to function in the community.*

Extract 5.4 Quiñónez family, mother, Session 1

Researcher: ¿Para qué le sirve a sus hijos saber español aquí en Estados Unidos?

Mother: Para que puedan ayudar, ayudarme en primera [...] Y pues más adelante ¿verdad? si él llega a crecer aquí, y tiene un trabajo, si logra acabar los estudios y agarra un trabajo, él puede agarrar un mejor trabajo como bilingüe.

Researcher: *What use is it for your children to know Spanish here in the United States?*

Mother: *So they can help out, help me, first of all [...] And later on, right? If he grows up here, and he has a job, if he completes his studies and gets a job, he can get a better job being bilingual.*

Intra-community variations in Spanish literacy are highlighted in Extract 5.5, in which Juana Molina recalls the situation of one of her acquaintances, who was illiterate in her native language and was trying to learn to read and write in English. Her point is relevant because it reminds us about community-internal variation, which is often erased in socio-linguistic models that presuppose an ability to read and write in all speakers who migrated as adults.

Extract 5.5 Molina family, mother, Session 1

Mother: Es muy importante, porque ahí es donde dice usted qué tan importante poder este, escribir el español, yo, es importante porque yo conocí a una señora que iba a clases de inglés y no sabía ni español y entonces ella quería, no sabía escribir el español, y entonces ella, porque la maestra era bilingüe, entonces hablaba español e inglés, entonces dijo que dio, les estaba, estaba dictando algo, pero lo estaba diciendo en español, entonces ella no sabía ni escribir su nombre, ni su nombre en español, pero entonces yo le decía que a lo mejor ella va a aprender pronto el inglés [...] Pero ella decía que no porque no, pues ella en español ni inglés, estaba más perdida ((laughs))

Researcher: Sí, porque a veces cuando usted tiene una, por lo menos una de las lenguas, uno de los idiomas bien formado.
Mother: Ella sí tenía la lengua, pero lo que no sabía era escribir.

Mother: *It's very important, because there, where you ask how important is it to be able to, write in Spanish, I, it's important, because I met a lady that was going to English classes and didn't even know Spanish, so she wanted, she didn't know how to write in Spanish, so she, because the teacher was bilingual, so she spoke Spanish and English, so she said that she gave them, she [the teacher] was dictating something, but she was saying it in Spanish, so she [the woman] didn't even know how to write her name in Spanish, so I told her that maybe she was going to learn English very soon [...] but she said that she wasn't, because no, well, she couldn't, not in English and not in Spanish, she was quite lost ((laughs))*
Researcher: *Right, because sometimes when you have one, at least one of both languages well formed.*
Mother: *She did have the language, what she didn't know was how to write.*

Although the respondents ranked aural, oral and literacy skills as 'important' to 'very important' for both languages, which suggests a positive view of bilingualism, a slightly higher index of desirability of Spanish for self than for children was observed. The reader is reminded here that the small size of the sample does not allow us to claim statistical significance for this finding. This is indeed one of the major compromises of sociolinguistic studies of this nature: a sample large enough for statistic inference allows for broad generalizations, but does not afford us rich detail; on the other hand, in-depth examination of a smaller sample does not allow us to conduct inferential analysis.

A valid question at this point in our discussion is why the results for the desirability of children's acquisition of Spanish literacy were so high in households where none of the children was receiving formal instruction in the language. One way to interpret these results is that the respondents were answering what they thought the interviewer wanted to hear, i.e. they were saving face. Another potential explanation is that they self-selected, i.e. they agreed to participate in a study about Spanish use in their family.

If, however, we conceptualize the transmission of Spanish as one of the many tasks in the constellation of childrearing duties, a simpler explanation appears: the road that separates best intentions from actual outcomes is an upward slope which requires endurance and patience from all those involved. That is, the gulf between parenting intentions and actual practice widens and narrows with changes in the family's life cycle. It is precisely these ebbs and flows that are described in the chapters of this book.

A second type of responses related to general, self and goal beliefs about language were gathered using a 12-item Likert scale. These were designed to examine the respondents' attitudes, first toward Spanish use, and secondly toward transmission. This scale included four numerical measures: strong positive attitude toward Spanish (+2); somewhat positive attitude (+1); somewhat negative attitude (−1); strong negative attitude (−2); and don't know, N/A (0). The respondents were read each item and asked if they agreed with it or not. Two items were included to survey **general beliefs related to monolingual language ideologies**: *People who come to live in the United States should learn English and forget their Spanish* and *I don't need to teach Spanish to my child(ren) because I live in the United States*. The results for these two items show no evidence of the reproduction of monolingual language ideologies in this group of speakers; 100% of the respondents disagreed with these items. In contrast, all the respondents reported strong agreement to the items *It's important that my child(ren) value(s) and feel(s) comfortable in her/his/their two cultures* and *My children know that being bilingual is important*, which suggests the respondents' positive attitudes about bilingualism and multi-culturalism. The results for these items were stable in both iterations of the sociolinguistic interview.

A second group of items was included to survey beliefs about perceived links between cultural transmission and transmission of the family language. The results suggest that, as a group, the respondents conceptual-ized a link between transmitting their culture and teaching Spanish to their children; 95% of the respondents agreed with the item: *Not teaching Spanish (to my children) is to deny them a part of their culture*. Equally high were responses to the item *When they help their children to maintain their Spanish, parents are giving them a very valuable gift*, with which 95% of mothers agreed (17/19) or somewhat agreed (1/19). Eighty-four percent of mothers agreed (15/19) or somewhat agreed (1/19) with the item *Mexican/Mexican American/Latino parents have the obligation to teach Spanish to their children*, which suggests a perception of Spanish trans-mission as part of successful childrearing.

Is Spanish harmful?

Delving deeper into general and normative beliefs related to linguistic transmission, three items were included to survey three examples of folk linguistics linked to monolingual language ideologies. These folk beliefs are unsupported by research on bilingual child language acquisition (as well as by the existence of billions of multilingual humans around the world), but are very common in US public discourse about the benefits and drawbacks of bilingual child language acquisition. In general terms, these beliefs can be summarized as follows: that working-class immigrants harm their children cognitively, academically and/or emotionally when they speak a language other than English to them, because they slow down their children's acquisition of the majority language and their integration into the wider community. The reader is invited to notice the absence of its opposite: public discourses about the harm that non-immigrant, upper-middle class parents may cause their children by speaking to them in a second language. The former is framed as an example of bad parenting, while the latter is framed as parental investment in their children's future.

In the present study it was hypothesized that a high percentage of maternal agreement to any of the following three items would suggest some degree of speaker internalization of community-wide language ideologies that position monolingualism in English as the norm, and as an aspirational goal for first-generation immigrant households wishing to integrate successfully into the national fabric (Baron, 1992; Cummins, 2000; Wimmer, 2009). Interestingly, the results for these three items suggest two opposing forces within this constellation of beliefs. One hundred percent of the respondents disagreed with the item *When they speak to them in Spanish, Mexican/Mexican American/Latino parents harm their children*, a result that provides no evidence of internalization of the belief that acquisition of the family language is detrimental to children's emotional or cognitive development. On the other hand, the lowest overall scores were found for the items *Speaking two languages to children can be confusing for them* and *If children don't want to learn Spanish you shouldn't force them*. Forty-seven percent of the mothers in this study agreed with the proposition that speaking more than one language to a child is confusing to them (one mother declined to answer this item). Sixteen percent agreed with the belief that children should not be expected to speak Spanish if they didn't want to. The results for these two items are, as will be argued in greater detail at the end of this chapter, of utmost importance to mapping the tensions between positive parental attitudes to Spanish as a language, and actual household language practices.

Is Spanish transmissible?

The last two items to be discussed here relate to speaker self-beliefs about their own ability to impact their children's language development. As argued by Lanza (2007) and De Houwer (1999), strong parental perceptions of agency are prerequisite for the successful childhood acquisition of a minority language. The results suggest strong maternal perceptions of agency as related to the transmission of Spanish to their children. Ninety-five percent of the respondents disagreed with the item *No matter what their parents do, Latino children living in the United States will forget Spanish*. The item *I don't speak good Spanish, so I can't teach it to my child(ren)* was included to survey potential linguistic insecurity. This item was used in Velázquez (2009) with a group of mothers in El Paso, TX. While it was useful in that study because some of the mothers in that group were heritage speakers of Spanish, in the present study the item was not very useful because all the mothers were Spanish dominant. Fifty-eight percent of the mothers surveyed in this study clarified or commented that the item did not apply to them. The rest of the respondents interpreted the item as a hypothetical (that is, as referring to a normative, rather than a self-belief).

Is it worth it?

The next question we will address here is why adult speakers of a language with low demographic density and limited public presence continue to use this language even though they are under constant pressure to shift. In other words, what part of their social experience makes this language viable, makes it still a positive result in the cost/benefit equation of language choice (to use Karan's terms). A preliminary and very simplistic answer is that the choice is obvious: first-generation immigrants who come into contact with the language of their receiving community as adults will rely on their dominant language regardless of indicators of ethnolinguistic vitality. A second plausible answer is that, in their process of adaptation to their new environment and even as their time of residence in their new community lengthens, speakers will rely on social networks where their native language is the most viable language for solving everyday problems and carrying out everyday interactions. I argue here, however, that these explanations are insufficient to understand language use in the small spaces.

I do this, first, because I believe that there is value in the critical examination of assumptions that underlie any state of affairs labeled as 'obvious', and secondly because I believe that analysis of a speaker's social network addresses the question of language choice as related to interlocutor, but largely leaves unexplored the question of *why*. In other words, that the tide will come in is obvious. What is not at all obvious is how the swells will hit the boat, or whether it will surge with the waves or be split in two.

Motivations to Use Spanish

Eleven items were included in this study to survey respondent motivations to use Spanish. These items were grouped into five motivational clusters: *instrumental, communicative, emotional/solidarity, religious* and *fear of discrimination*. It is important to note here that the results discussed in the following pages are not reports of actual use, but rather speaker articulations of the value of Spanish when engaging in different types of discourses, in different contexts and with different audiences. Also surveyed were speaker motivations to transmit Spanish to their children. The ways in which the respondents' understandings of the cost/benefit of speaking Spanish themselves differed from perceptions of the cost/benefit of Spanish use by their children hinged on perceived differences in the generational and social positioning of both, and were heavily influenced by immigration narratives that predicated children's educational attainment and future economic mobility on parental self-sacrifice. The hope that their children would access greater opportunities and would eventually outpace their parents economically was a recurring theme in the interviews conducted for this study. Indeed, this was presented by several respondents as one of the main reasons for their family's decision to emigrate.

Religious motivation

The respondents' strongest motivation to use Spanish was religious.[5] One hundred percent of the respondents reported praying in Spanish, and identified Spanish as the language they used when communicating with God. Eighty-four percent of the respondents reported a preference for attending religious services in Spanish. Only three respondents reported attending bilingual religious services. No participant in this study reported praying in English or attending religious services offered exclusively in English. Examined in greater detail, religious motivations to use Spanish impinge on more than one context and more than one type of discourse: from the intimate discourse of solitary prayer, to the ritualized, public discourses of liturgy.

Communicative motivation

The percentage of the respondents who reported relying on Spanish as their primary language of communication in everyday interactions was also very high. When asked *On a normal day, how necessary is it for you to use Spanish to communicate with other people?*, 53% of the respondents reported using Spanish *all day, all the time* or *a lot*. Together with mothers who reported needing to use Spanish *about 80% of the time*, 60 to 70% of the time or *most of the day*, 84% of the respondents reported a strong communicative motivation to use Spanish.

Another 16% of the respondents reported needing to use Spanish *about half of the time, only a little* or *somewhat*. One respondent reported needing to use Spanish only when speaking with her children and other members of her family; one reported needing Spanish when speaking with friends and needing English when speaking with members of the wider community; and one more reported that her choice of language depended on her interlocutor. Although several of the participants in this study were learning English and all ascribed high instrumental and communicative value to this language, none of the adult participants in this study reported relying exclusively or primarily in English in any of the contexts included in our survey.

Again, that first-generation immigrants rely heavily on their native language to carry out everyday interactions is not surprising. It is, however, crucial to the understanding of household language dynamics. The fact that the school-aged children in these families were exposed to English most of the day, and that they were almost universally more fluent in English than their mothers meant, first, that they were often engaging in language and cultural brokering for them,[6] and secondly that for most of these mothers, with limited participation in English-dominant social networks, their children were often their main source of English input and opportunities to practice speaking it.

Emotional/solidarity motivations

As expected, the results for motivations to use Spanish with children, family and friends were also high: 100% of the respondents reported that speaking Spanish with their children and their family was either *very important* or *important*. A difference between the motivations to use Spanish with both types of interlocutors is that, on the one hand, the respondents positioned speaking Spanish with the adult members of their family as an ineludible condition – i.e. their interlocutors were either Spanish dominant or Spanish monolingual. On the other hand, they positioned speaking Spanish with their children as a way to help them maintain the family language and learn about their parents' country of origin. Although still very high, the reported motivation to use Spanish with friends showed a slight difference: 90% of the respondents reported that speaking Spanish with their friends was either *very important* or *important*. Two speakers (10% of responses) explained that speaking Spanish with their friends was not very important to them because they were accustomed to mixing both languages in conversation; that is, that they were engaging in code-switching, not that they were interacting with English monolinguals. Only one respondent expressed a desire to use more English when interacting with her friends. No respondent reported interacting exclusively in English with either family or friends.[7]

Instrumental motivations

The respondents' lived experience of diglossia was evidenced in their responses regarding instrumental motivations to use their family language. While reports of motivation to use Spanish in the intimate spaces of home, prayer and friendship were very high, the results for motivation to use Spanish in public spaces relating to work and economic mobility were mixed. Once again, that speakers of a language with LEV should experience diglossia does not fall into the realm of the unexpected. What are relevant here are the differences in speaker perceptions of the instrumental value of Spanish when linked to a generalized, imagined other – i.e. 'successful people' – and when presented as linked to their concrete experience. In order to explore the perceived value of Spanish as connected to social and economic success, the respondents were asked *Here in Lincoln, what language or languages do successful people use?* Only two respondents imagined a successful, hypothetical other as an English monolingual. Most respondents (89%) imagined this successful 'other' as a speaker of more than one language. Three respondents imagined this generalized other as speaking both Spanish and English, but also felt compelled to clarify that if she/he spoke only one language, this language would be English. We understood the need to make this clarification as an articulation of the higher instrumental value ascribed by these speakers to the majority language.

When asked *How important is it to know Spanish to get a good job?*, 58% of the mothers in this study responded that Spanish was important to get a good job, 21% believed that it was important only if the person applying for the job also spoke English, and another 21% believed Spanish was not important to secure employment. Asked *Do you think there's an advantage at work if you know Spanish?*, 84% of the respondents answered yes, 11% responded no, and 5% responded that speaking Spanish at work was only an advantage if the employee in question also spoke English.

For the speakers in Extracts 5.6 and 5.7, differential ascriptions of the instrumental value of Spanish were closely grounded in their lived experience, more so than to their representation of success in an imagined other. Patricia Pérez worked outside the home in a mostly monolingual English environment. Based on her immediate experience, she perceived that viability *and* instrumental motivation to use of Spanish at work were negligible:

Extract 5.6 Pérez family, mother, Session 1

Researcher: ¿Le parece que saber español es una ventaja en el trabajo?
Mother: ((pause)) ahh en mi, mi trabajo no, porque ahí únicamente es inglés, las señoras hablan inglés, entonces para mí tiene que ser inglés, entonces yo no uso el español en mi trabajo, español únicamente en mi casa.

Researcher: *Do you think that knowing Spanish is an advantage at work?*
Mother: *((pause)) ahh at my, at my job no, because there it's only English. The ladies only speak English, so for me it has to be English, so I don't use Spanish at work, [I speak] Spanish only at home.*

Extract 5.7 Pérez family, mother, Session 2

Mother: Aquí yo creo que el español para conseguir un buen trabajo no se necesita porque pues aquí quieren que uno hable inglés [...] que entienda las cosas y pues nadie se las va a decir a uno en español, por aquí nadie está... no hay una empresa que diga 'hablamos español vengan, aquí hay trabajo' [...] todo es en inglés.

Mother: *I think that you don't need Spanish to get a good job because here they want you to speak English [...] that you understand things, and, I mean, nobody's going to explain things to you in Spanish, nobody is... there isn't a company that will tell you 'we speak Spanish, come on over, we have jobs' [...] everything is in English.*

In contrast, respondent Adriana Gallegos used her nieces' experience as evidence that, in some types of employment, knowing Spanish afforded economic advantages both for the (bilingual) employee and the (monolingual) employer:

Extract 5.8 Gallegos family, mother, Session 2

Researcher: ¿Qué tan importante es hablar español para conseguir un buen trabajo?
Mother: Es muy importante. [...] Sí, sí, muy importante, porque también, bueno aquí en Estados Unidos a lo mejor no importa tanto el español, en cualquier trabajo, pero hay muchos trabajos, [es] necesario, que es bien importante hablar español y le digo, tengo experiencias, por ejemplo las sobrinas de mi esposo [...] Ella [first niece] trabajaba en un banco, al compañero le pagan nueve dólares y a ella le pagan catorce [...] porque ella hablaba español. Igual la muchacha, la otra, [second niece], ella se salió de ahí [...] Y se metió a trabajar con un dentista y ahí la conoció otro dentista y le ofreció más dinero para que se fuera a trabajar con él, porque ella hablaba español, porque ya tenía la experiencia de ayudarle al dentista. [...] Y lógico, a esos dentistas les conviene más, porque cuando uno [Spanish-speaking patient] sabe, uno que no habla bien el inglés, uno sabe que allá hay una persona que habla en español [...], Y uno va a esos, va a esos lugares. [...] Entonces pienso que, que sí [...] que es muy importante.

Researcher: *How important is it to speak Spanish to get a good job?*
Mother: *It's very important. [...] Yes, yes, very important, because also, well, here in the United States maybe Spanish is not so important, but there are many jobs, [where it's] necessary, where it's very important to speak Spanish. And I tell you, I have experiences, for example, my husband's nieces [...] She, [first niece], worked*

at a bank, and her [male] co-worker was paid nine dollars and she was paid fourteen [...] because she spoke Spanish. The same with the girl, the other one, [second niece], she left that job [...] and she started working with a dentist, and she met another dentist there and he offered her more money so she would go work for him, because she spoke Spanish and she already had experience [...] And obviously, it's better for those dentists because when you [Spanish-speaking patient] know, when you don't speak English well and you know that they have a person who speaks Spanish there, you go to those places. [...] So yes, I think that, that yes [...] it's very important.

For Juana Molina, the potential benefits of speaking Spanish were not an exclusive parcel of Latino professionals:

Extract 5.9 Molina family, mother, Session 1

Researcher: ¿Qué tan importante es hablar español para conseguir un buen trabajo?

Mother: Pues por ejemplo un, un doctor, aquí hay mucha gente, latina que habla este, español y entonces si él por ejemplo, si el doctor supiera español e inglés, porque tendría que ser así porque aquí, entonces sí, el doctor ya no, ya no tendría que ocupar un intérprete [...] Y así como varias cosas, es que es una comunidad, y en esta comunidad hay mucha, mucha gente latina y en todos los trabajos yo pienso que hay gente que habla español, y que [...] tendría más trabajo porque es como que tiene dos trabajos porque habla dos idiomas.

Researcher: *How important is it to speak Spanish to get a good job?*

Mother: *Well, for example a, a doctor, there's a lot of people here, Latinos that speak, I mean, Spanish, and so, if he, for example, spoke Spanish and English, because it would have to be like that, because here, then yes, the doctor would not need an interpreter any more. [...] he would have more work because it's like having two jobs because you speak both languages.*

A quasi obvious but nonetheless relevant point to be made here is that in all participant responses, the instrumental value of Spanish was always predicated on the ability to speak English. Thus, in objective terms, the perceived instrumental value for these speakers lay not in Spanish per se, but in bilingualism. A second and equally important point is that for these speakers English monolingualism was not a mark of a successful person. Success, understood in terms of the responses recorded for this study, was not disconnected from family or community. This is to say that, for the adult participants in this study, an individual is able to achieve economic success *because* he/she has a family and a place within a Spanish-speaking network, and not *in spite* of this. Seeking to explore personal experiences of discrimination at work as potential motivations not to use Spanish (Hill, 1998; Urciuoli, 1996), the participants were asked *Have you ever been afraid of not getting a job because you speak English with an accent?* Sixty-nine percent of the mothers in this study reported they had not. Another 26% reported they had, in fact, been afraid of not gaining employment because of their accent,[8] and one mother explained that she had never been afraid of this happening to her because she did not speak English.

The results for this last item were not very enlightening. The wording of this item proved to be a flaw in the design of the instrument. The mothers in this group did not work outside the home or were employed in jobs that did not require intensive interaction in English with the public or with co-workers – e.g. one mom cleaned buildings at night and another took care of children in her home. Thus, it was unclear at the moment of analysis if the participants who reported not feeling afraid of not getting a job due to their accent did so because they had never looked for a job outside the home, if they had applied only to jobs in which fluency in English was not a precondition for employment, or if they believed that their level of fluency in English was such that it did not present a hindrance to accessing the local labor market.[9]

Two things are worth noting here, however. The first is that all the mothers who reported that they had, in fact, felt afraid of not being hired because of their accent had worked, were working or had applied for work outside the home. The second is related again to the flaws in the design of this item: the participant responses did not necessarily yield data on general beliefs about local conditions of employment, but about self-perceptions of language proficiency.

Motivations to Transmit Spanish

For the mothers in this study, the strongest motivations to use Spanish in their everyday lives were *religious, communicative* and *emotional/solidarity*. From this vantage point, a new set of questions presents itself for consideration: How do speaker motivations to use a minority language map onto motivations to transmit that language to their children? Does a speaker's motivation to use their dominant language necessarily mean that they will find value in their children's acquisition of it? For the same reasons? In the same contexts? With similar purposes? It is worth pointing out here that maternal motivations to transmit their family language to their children are not primarily about the children, but about the mothers themselves; that is, maternal motivations to transmit a minority language are an articulation of beliefs about child-rearing and agency. In other words, they are a type of self-belief.

Eleven items and two open-ended questions were included in this study in order to explore these potential motivations. Strong motivation to transmit Spanish was reported by all participants. Highest scores were recorded around *religious, cultural/linguistic transmission* and *emotional/solidarity* motivations.

Let us begin this section, then, with a discussion of the results for the two open-ended items included in the survey: *Why do you speak Spanish to your children?* and *In your opinion, what are some advantages and disadvantages of speaking Spanish to your children?* It was hypothesized that the first of these questions would yield responses related to self-beliefs, while answers to the second would yield articulations of general beliefs – i.e. speaker understandings about a perceived overall state of affairs. Table 5.1 summarizes the responses to the first of these.

Table 5.1 Why do you speak Spanish to your children? (tokens)

Why do you speak Spanish to your children?	
△ Because it's my language and they need to learn it	3
△ So they can learn my language/culture	2
△ Because I don't speak a lot of English	2
△ Because that's how I communicate	1
△ Because it's the language I speak better	1
○ Because it's our language/our culture	5
○ Because it's our custom	1
○ Because it's the language we bring	1
□ So they won't forget their language/culture	2
□ So that they can communicate with my family	1
NA	5

Contrary to our original expectation, while most responses to this first item were indeed articulations of maternal self-perceptions, the responses were of three kinds: *responses related to self-perceived cultural identity or language ability* (identified with a triangle in Table 5.1); *responses related to perceived cultural or linguistic heritage of the family* (identified with a circle); and *responses related to perceived children's cultural identity or linguistic competence* (identified with a square). Most respondents in this study cited no disadvantages of speaking Spanish to their children. As seen in Table 5.2, most perceived advantages of speaking Spanish with their children centered on their children, rather than on themselves.

Table 5.2 Dis/advantages of speaking Spanish to children (tokens)

Disadvantages of speaking Spanish to your children	
None	12
☐ None, as long as they also know English	1
☐ They mix it with English	1
NA	5
Advantages of speaking Spanish to your children	
☐ They can learn Spanish	5
☐ They can access future opportunities	3
☐ They can communicate with other speakers	2
☐ They won't forget Spanish	1
☐ They can travel	1
☐ They can practice	1
☐ They can learn about their culture/roots	1
△ We can communicate better	2
△ They can communicate with me	2
○ They can know our language/our culture	2
Many	1

Religious motivation to transmit

One hundred percent of all the mothers who reported praying with their children reported doing so in Spanish. According to their mothers' report, 94% of all the children in these families who had received or were receiving religious education at the time of the interview had done so in Spanish.

Linguistic transmission

In order to explore self-perceptions about agency as related to linguistic transmission, the respondents were asked *What language will your grandchildren speak?* Sixty-eight percent of the mothers in this group believed that their future grandchildren would speak Spanish and English, while another 16% responded that their grandchildren would speak Spanish. Taken as a group, 95% of the respondents imagined their future grandchildren as speakers of Spanish, both English and Spanish, or more than two languages. Only one mother in the group responded that the language or languages that her future grandchildren would speak depended on her children. These results are suggestive of a strong perception of individual agency in their children's language development – i.e. a self-belief – and also a perception of the existence of family and community conditions for their children's acquisition of Spanish – i.e. a general belief.

The reader will note here that when they were speaking about their (hypothetical) grandchildren, the mothers in this study were really speaking about their children. They were articulating an expectation of what they themselves needed to do for their children, and extending that expectation into the future. Also of note is that in this expectation, monolingualism was not the default.

Cultural transmission

The potential link between language and culture was explored by asking the respondents *Can you teach children about your culture without using Spanish?* Forty-seven percent of the mothers in this study believed that it was not possible to transmit their culture to their children without using Spanish. Four mothers (21% of responses), believed that it was possible, but that transmission would be incomplete. One mother responded that it was possible, but very hard. Two mothers believed that it was possible to teach their children about their culture without using Spanish, and another two responded *maybe.* Intriguingly, one mother believed that it was possible to transmit her culture to her children without speaking Spanish, but did not speak English herself. This may (although not necessarily) be related to a perception that English-dominant adults in the wider local Latino community could help her to transmit cultural practices to her children; that is, she was perceiving cultural transmission as a shared task.

Analysis of the results for the last four types of motivations to transmit requires greater nuance. Such is the case, for example, of emotional/ solidarity motivations. When asked *How important is it for you that your children speak Spanish with your family?*, 84% of the respondents reported that it was important or very important that their children communicate in Spanish with their extended family in order to maintain bonds of affection. The remaining three respondents (16% of responses) also reported that it was important that their children be able to speak Spanish with their family, but understood this not as a way to nurture ties of kinship and affection, but rather as a matter of communicative necessity, because it was the only way in which they could understand what their children said.

A second and very relevant difference was observed when speakers were asked *How important is it that your children have friends who speak Spanish?* While 95% of the mothers responded that it was important to them that their children interact with Spanish-speaking friends, most took it as a foregone conclusion that their children would switch to English when interacting with their peers. This is important because it points to a tension between the speakers' general perception of agency and their everyday lived experience. Extracts 5.10 and 5.11 illustrate the ways in which María Luisa Martínez and Juana Molina articulated this dissonance:

Extract 5.10 Martínez family, mother, Session 1

Researcher: ¿Qué tan importante es para usted que sus hijos tengan amigos que hablen español?

Mother: ¿Qué tan importante? [...] pues es importante porque conviven, es bonito convivir y platicar el mismo idioma a veces, aunque los niños de hoy en día aquí en este país ya cuando empiezan a hablar el inglés ya es bien difícil que entre los niños hablen el español, aunque sean puros hispanos, pero se agarran a hablar inglés ((laughs)) si es la verdad, yo he ido a fiestas y las niñas están hable y hable inglés aunque todos son hispanos, pero puro inglés.

Researcher: *How important is it for you that your children have friends who speak Spanish?*

Mother: *How important? [...] well, it's important because they interact, it's nice to interact and speak the same language sometimes, but kids nowadays in this country, when they start speaking English it's very unlikely that they will speak Spanish, even if it's just Hispanics, they start speaking in English ((laughs)) yes, it's the truth, I've been to parties and the girls are talking away in English, even if it's only Hispanics, but [they speak] only in English.*

Extract 5.11 Molina family, mother, Session 1

Researcher: Muy bien. ¿Qué tan importante es para usted, doña XXX, que sus hijos hablen español con otros amigos, con sus amigos o con otras personas de la comunidad?

Mother: Pues es importante porque, pero es difícil aquí porque más que no cuando llegan a la escuela ya nada más los niños aunque sean latinos, van a hablar inglés. Y este, pues es importante, pero ellos después, porque como agarran amistad y amiguitos y eso [...] Y es que como van a la escuela y eso, necesitaría que se juntaran con otra mamá que pensara igual que yo ((laughs)) y le dijera a sus hijos que, cómo que es importante y que ellos también aprendan a querer su idioma pero...

Researcher: *Very well, How important is it for you, Mrs. XXX, that your children speak in Spanish with other friends, with their friends, or with other people in the community?*

Mother: *Well, it's important because, but it's difficult here, because even if, when they get to school, the children only want to, even if they're Latino, they're going to speak in English. And, I mean, it's important, but later they, they make make friends and that [...] And because they go to school, I would need them [I would need?] to join another mom who thinks like me ((laughs)) [a mom] that would tell [teach] her children how important it is that they learn to love their language, but...*

Instrumental motivations to transmit

Two items were presented to the respondents in an attempt to survey instrumental motivations to transmit Spanish to their children. The first was based on a general belief about the usefulness of Spanish as related to economic and social opportunity: *How true is this phrase for you: Spanish opens doors?* Ninety percent of the respondents (17/19) agreed with this statement. Two mothers in the group agreed with the statement, but qualified their answer. For Consuelo Luna, the statement was true elsewhere but not in Lincoln. For Elena Navarro the statement was true in general terms, but the usefulness of Spanish depended on the specific community. Qualification of their answers suggests a perceived low value of Spanish as related to the local labor market.

Answers to the second item in this cluster point once more to a high perception of desirability for multilingual skills. Asked *What language(s) will your children need to have a good future?*, 90% of the mothers in this study responded that their children would need to speak more than one language in order to be successful – 48% responded that their children would need to speak both Spanish and English, and another 42% believed that they would need to speak more than two languages. Only one mother in the group responded that her children would need to speak Spanish to have a good future. None of the mothers in the group perceived that their children would need to be monolingual in English in order to be successful adults. Again, the overall results suggest that for this group of speakers the perceived source of individual capital that would allow their children access to social and economic opportunities was bilingualism, not monolingualism in either language.

The usefulness of the present type of microanalysis is highlighted in the response to this item given by Carina Quiñónez, who believed that her youngest child, who was growing up in the United States, would need to be bilingual in order to be successful as an adult, whereas her eldest child, who was growing up in a rural community in Mexico, would only need Spanish to get ahead in life. Carina Quiñónez's answer reminds us of the need to construct sociolinguistic models that account for the differences in socialization, educational attainment, patterns of language contact and access to economic opportunities for all siblings in transnational families.

Communicative motivation to transmit

While the adult participants in this study reported strong communicative motivation to use Spanish themselves, communicative motivations to transmit the language to their children were minimally reported. In fact, only three mothers reported communicative motivation to transmit Spanish. In these three cases (identified in Table 5.3 with a triangle) the onus was on the child to serve as a language broker and/or to

Table 5.3 Purpose of children speaking Spanish in the United States (tokens)

What is the purpose of your children speaking Spanish here in the United States?	
Economic opportunity	6
▲ Help me, speak with me	3
▪ Speak with my family	3
▪ Help others	3
▪ For everything	2
▪ They can speak in two languages	2
• We are Latinos, it's our language	2
▪ Speak w/people in my country	2
▪ Speak w/monolinguals	2
▪ Travel to another country	1
Not so much	1
NA	1

accommodate to a monolingual adult. These results are not surprising, considering that school-aged children in these families spent a large part of their day in English-dominant environments and could, for the most part, interact exclusively in English outside the home. What is important here is that, for most mothers in the study, responses to the question *What is the purpose of your children speaking Spanish here in the United States?* revolved around instrumental rather than communicative or social/solidarity motivations. That is, while mothers believed overall that Spanish was important for themselves and for their children, they conceptualized speaking Spanish as a source of social capital for them – i.e. it allowed them to carry out everyday interactions – while in the case of their children they conceptualized speaking in Spanish as a source of individual capital – i.e. it would help them access future economic opportunities.[10]

Fear of discrimination

Two items were included in our survey in order to explore the fear of discrimination as a potential motivation not to transmit Spanish. Both of these items were related to the use of Spanish in public: one was presented as a hypothetical situation while the other was presented as a statement with which the respondents could agree or disagree. The hypothetical situation was this: *Imagine that you are with your children at the super-market, and while you're paying, they're speaking in Spanish. The person standing behind you in line makes a rude comment. What do you do?* Apparently simple, this item was the most complex of those included in the survey in that it was intended to elicit three kinds of subjacent beliefs: general beliefs (e.g. *Is this scenario possible/likely where I live? Is it appropriate for a stranger to address my family in this way? Is it appropriate for me to respond?*); self-beliefs (e.g. *Am I able to answer in English? Am I able to protect my children from a stranger's aggression in a public space? Am I able to model appropriate behavior for them?*); and goal beliefs (e.g. *What should I do in this situation?*). The responses to this item are presented in Table 5.4.

The first thing worth noting here is that none of the respondents perceived this situation as impossible or far-fetched. The second thing to note is that, presented with this scenario, more than half of the respondents (58%) believed they would do nothing. However, their rationale for this answer ranged from unqualified responses (7/19), responses related to the speaker's perceived inability to understand or make herself fully understood in English (3/19), and one respondent who understood doing nothing as an indirect way to assert her pride in speaking Spanish in public. Three respondents (16%) believed that faced with this situation they would do something. These answers ranged from the symbolic (e.g. 'giving the eye') to the concrete (e.g. 'I would defend my children'). Two respondents believed that they would ask their children to do something – i.e. ask them to convey her message in English, or continue speaking in Spanish as a way to assert the family's right to use the language in public.

For three of the mothers in this study, this situation was not hypothetical, as they reported that they had indeed felt discriminated against for speaking Spanish in a place of business at least once. In Extract 5.12 Dora

Table 5.4 Fear of discrimination in public spaces (*N* = 19)

Imagine that you're with your children at the supermarket, you're paying, they're speaking Spanish. The person standing behind you makes a rude comment. What do you do?

Do nothing (58%)	
Ignore them or do nothing	7
Feel bad, feel discriminated against, but wouldn't say anything	1
Nothing, because I wouldn't understand what they said	1
Ignore them because I couldn't answer as I would like to	1
Nothing, because we should be proud of what we speak	1
Do something (16%)	
Give them the eye ('La miraría feo')	1
Defend my kids	1
Would say they're ignorant	1
Tell my children to do something (10%)	
I tell my children to tell them something (in English)	1
I tell my children (in Spanish) they can speak whatever they like	1
Not hypothetical, this has happened to me (16%)	
Has happened to me	3

Alicia García describes her understanding of her right to speak Spanish and protect her children, and also her frustration at her inability to respond in English.

Extract 5.12 García family, mother, Session 2

Researcher: Bueno, imagínese que un día usted está en el súper con sus hijos y mientras usted está pagando ellos están hablando español [...] La persona que está atrás de ustedes hace un comentario desagradable en inglés [...] ¿Usted qué hace?

Mother: Pues nada más porque no le podría decir en inglés ((giggles)) lo que pienso pero [...] pero yo creo que de todas maneras de alguna forma- voltearía y: esto es un país libre nadie (prohíbe) el español

R: (O sea) trataría de decirle algo, pues...

Mother: Sí, trataría de decirle algo (2) o sea que, le digo, si no sé, no sabría, porque sí me molesta eso mucho, ya me- ya me ha pasado y me molesta bastante, me quedo XXX y volteo y la miro y la... y ella me... o sea yo... yo siento o sea

R: [Claro, y sin poder decir algo peor.

Mother: Sí, sin poder decir algo, pero defendiendo siempre- lo- lo mío [...] Es lo único que tengo- yo creo que lo único que nos dejaron bueno nuestros padres.

Researcher: *Well, imagine that one day you're at the supermarket with your children, and as you're paying they're speaking in Spanish. [...] The person behind you makes a rude comment in English [...] What do you do?*

Mother: *Well, only because I couldn't tell them in English ((giggles)) what I think but [...] but I think that I would turn anyway, somehow, and I: this is a free country and no one (forbids) speaking Spanish.*

R: *(I mean) you would try to say something...*

Mother: *Yes, I would try to tell them something (2) I mean, I tell you, if I don't know, I wouldn't know, because it does bother me, it bothers me a lot. It has- it has happened to me and it bothers me a lot, and I'm like XXX and I turn around and I look at her and... and she... I mean I... I feel, I mean...*

R: *[Of course, unable to say anything worse.*

Mother: *Yes, unable to say anything, but always defending what's, what's mine [...] It's the only thing I have- I think it's the only good thing that our parents left us.*

In Extract 5.13 Susana Sánchez relates a situation in which she felt compelled to defend her mother, who was criticized by a store employee for shopping while unable to speak English. An interesting feature of this story is that she finds the intra-ethnic language policing of other Latinos – who either join in the mocking or silently acquiesce – even more painful and surprising.

Extract 5.13 Susana Sánchez, mother, Session 2

Researcher: [...] Y escucha, usted escucha un comentario desagradable de unas personas que están hablando en inglés. ¿Qué hace?

Mother: No sé, una vez, una vez me pasó que vino mi mamá, las primeras veces que mi mamá vino aquí, estábamos en, en, en la tienda y mi mamá se estaba midiendo un una ropa y entonces la muchacha que atiende le estaba, le hizo una pregunta, y le dice este, no recuerdo si le dijo '¿la vas a querer?' o 'te queda bien' o algo así, entonces mi mamá obviamente no habla español, I mean, inglés, no, no entiende inglés, digo, yo tampoco [laughs] mucho, pero, pero ya sé lo que la otra persona está diciendo, y entonces se acerca ella a otras la [...] que estaba atendiendo y, y le dice, le dice 'ay', dice, 'yo no sé entonces a qué viene' dice, 'Sí, sí, sí estos mexicanos' dice 'que no entienden' dice, '¿A qué viene si, si no, si no saben hablar' y entonces me acerco yo y le digo '¿Tienes algún problema?' le digo, 'Ella no habla español' I mean, otra vez, 'Ella no habla inglés' le digo '¿Tú tienes algún problema con ella?' le digo 'Ella no te va a entender' le digo, 'Dime a mí si, si tú quieres saber algo, porque ella no...' [...] 'Oh no, es que yo no sabía que ella no hablaba inglés' y que no se qué. Le digo 'Pues es que si tú tienes algún problema, dime' 'No, no, no, no pasa nada, no pasa nada, está bien todo', y así, y entonces de momento yo no supe qué hacer, solamente le dije 'Pues si tienes algún problema, pues dime, porque ella no sabe, ella no sabe inglés, ella no sabe lo que tú le preguntaste'.

R: Uhhuh

Mother: Dice 'Es que yo solamente le pregunté que si se iba a quedar con él, la ropa' o algo así, no me recuerdo muy bien qué es lo que dijo. Y entonces le digo 'Sí, pero es que ella no te, no te va a entender, aparte le digo, ella no es que vive aquí en Estados Unidos, le digo, ella viene de México. 'Oh, oh, lo siento', y que no sé que, se quiso disculpar de muchas maneras, pero lo, lo más triste de esto fue que a las personas que se arrimó eran hispanas, y empezaron a criticar a mi mamá en inglés junto con la persona anglosajona [...] Entonces a mí me dio entre coraje y tristeza que, que nosotros mismos como latinos nos empezáramos a, ahora sí que como decimos [...] a echar tierra, porque luego, como ellos sí hablaban inglés, las otras personas, pues le empezaron a dar la razón a, a la persona que hablaba totalmente inglés, y digo, qué pena, qué pena... [...] a mí entre que me dio mucho coraje y me dio pena por eso, porque digo ¿Cómo es posible que las otras personas son latinas también? Ellos tampoco en algún momento, yo no pienso que hayan sabido inglés, y entonces ellos seguían este, criticando a la, a la otra persona que no sabía, que no sabía nada de inglés.

Researcher: *And you hear, you hear a rude comment from people who are speaking in English. What do you do?*

Mother: *I don't know, it happened to me once, when my mom came, one of the first times that my mom came here, and we were in, in, in a store, and my mom was trying on some clothes, and, and the young woman, the employee asked her a question, and she told her, I can't remember if she asked her 'Are you keeping it?' or 'Does it fit?', or something like that, so my mom obviously doesn't speak Spanish, I mean, doesn't understand English, she doesn't understand English, I mean, neither do I, [laughs] not a lot, but, but I know what the other person is saying, so she goes to other clients and tells them 'Oh', she says, 'Then I don't know what she's here for', she says, 'These Mexicans', she says, 'They don't understand', she says, 'Why does she come if, if they can't, if they can't speak'. So, I go up to her and I tell her 'Do you have a problem?', I tell her, 'She doesn't speak Spanish', I mean, again, 'She doesn't speak English', I tell her, Do you have a problem with her? I tell her, 'She's not going to understand what you say', I tell her. 'Tell me, if you want to know anything because she can't...' [...] 'Oh no, I didn't know she didn't speak English', and so on and so forth. I tell her 'Well, if you have a problem, tell me'. 'No, no, no, no, there's nothing wrong, there's nothing wrong, everything is alright', and so on, and in that moment I didn't know what to do, I just told her 'Well, if you have a problem just tell me, because she doesn't know, she doesn't know English, she doesn't understand what you asked her'.*

R: *Uhhuh*

Mother: *She says 'I just asked her if she was keeping the clothing', or something like that, I can't remember exactly what she said. And then I tell her 'Yes, but she's not going to understand you, besides', I tell her, 'she doesn't live here in the United States', I tell her, 'she's from Mexico'. 'Oh, oh, I'm sorry', she wanted to apologize several times. But the saddest part was that the people she approached were Hispanic, and they started to criticize my mom in English together with the Anglo person. [...] So, I felt between anger and sadness that, we, ourselves, as Latinos, would start, as they say, to tear each other down, because they did speak English, and they started to agree with, with the person who spoke totally [entirely] in English, and I say, what a shame, what a shame... [...] I felt a lot of anger, and sadness, because of that, because I think, how is it possible that those other people are Latinos too? They didn't, at some point in time, I think that at some point in time they didn't speak English [either], and they kept criticizing another person who didn't know any English.*

The second item used to survey potential fear of linguistic discrimination was related to the children's use of Spanish at school. The mothers in this study were asked *How true is this phrase for you: 'I don't like my*

Table 5.5 Fear of discrimination at school (N = 19)

'I don't like my children speaking Spanish in school because I feel they might be discriminated against'

Not true	8
Not true, because they speak mostly English at school	2
It's ridiculous	1
Not true, because we have school interpreters	1
Not true, because they should feel proud	1
Not true, because this is a free country	1
Not true, because I want him to speak Spanish	1
Sometimes	1
Maybe	2
Yes	1

children speaking Spanish in school because I feel they might be discriminated against'? The responses to this item are presented in Table 5.5 and are of two kinds: perceptions related to what things were like (i.e. general beliefs); and perceptions related to what things should be like (i.e. goal beliefs). Because this was an item intended to survey perceptions about the suitability of children's use of Spanish in the school environment and not about school environments themselves, these responses do not address a central socializing force in their children's language development: all of the school-aged children in these 19 families were attending schools where English was the medium of instruction.

Youth Perceptions of Bilingualism

So far, we have explored maternal attitudes toward Spanish and potential motivations to use and transmit their family language. In the last section of this chapter we will compare these perceptions with those of their children. Youths between the ages of 12 and 17 were presented with ten items intended to survey perceptions about bilingualism and the viability of Spanish in their everyday lives.

When family and community language dynamics are observed from the perspective of the teenagers in this study, two main themes emerge: (A) their role as interpreters and cultural brokers; and (B) their socialization to diglossia. The first thing to note is that regardless of linguistic ability (which is described in Chapters 7 and 8), the eight teens who participated in this study self-identified as bilingual. Two qualified responses were recorded for this item. The first was from a 15-year-old boy who had arrived in the United States after the age of 12; he responded during the first interview that he was on his way to being bilingual, and with 'yes, almost' during the second interview. The second was from two US-raised girls aged 12 and 13, who responded that they were bilingual during our first interview, and four months later responded 'a little' or 'no' after struggling to understand some of the questions presented in Spanish during the second interview.

The perceived role of this generational cohort as interpreters and cultural brokers in their family, their school and the wider community is evidenced in their responses to the questions *How do people benefit from speaking Spanish* and *What does a bilingual person do?* Many of their responses revolve around accommodation to Spanish-dominant or Spanish-monolingual adults. This is important to the understanding of community language dynamics, because monolingual English speakers were not perceived by any of the teens in this study as being in need of accommodation – e.g. when a youth described an occasion in which he/she had to interpret between school personnel and a newly arrived student, the interpretation was framed as benefiting the student, not the adults who needed the help of a minor to perform their duties. The underlying belief here is that English speakers need no accommodation, not because they are bilingual but because English is perceived as the default language. Concurrently, the role of extended family, adult family friends and church members for the maintenance of Spanish is suggested in responses to the question *Aside from your parents, who are some adults that know how to speak Spanish?*

Teen responses to the question *How many people in your school speak both languages?* provide further evidence of socialization to diglossia. Optimistic answers to this question ranged between 20 and 27 speakers of Spanish at school. Most responses ranged between five and 15 speakers. Again, these responses are not data on the actual number of speakers but on the perceived viability of Spanish in the space of the school.[11] In all instances, the number of teachers or other school personnel who were reported by these youths as able to speak Spanish was extremely small. In several cases, the only adult reported by the teens as a speaker of Spanish at their school was the Spanish teacher. Most classmates and friends reported as speakers of Spanish were also reported as preferring to speak in English while at school. Additional comments to this question were *somos poquitos* 'we're very few' and *casi todos son güeros los que van a mi escuela* 'almost everyone who goes to my school is Anglo'.[12]

Despite the fact that these teens shared with their mothers a perception of the instrumental value of bilingualism, in their everyday lives they had limited contact with adult bilinguals in professional and institutional settings. In the space of the family and the immediate (Latino) community they interacted mostly with Spanish-dominant adults, and in the space of the school and the wider (non-Latino) community they interacted mostly with English-dominant adults. This state of affairs limited their opportunities to use the language, and their exposure to formal registers of

Spanish and to adults who could model what multilingual competence looks like beyond the space of the home.

Finally, while 100% of the teens in this study reported liking to speak both Spanish and English, most of these youths preferred to speak in English in all contexts except when speaking with younger siblings and with their mothers. In Extract 5.14 Lily Aparecido, a 17-year-old girl, touches on two dimensions of a three-way pressure faced by this generational cohort, a pressure that was mostly absent from their mothers' experience: first, social or family sanction for not speaking monolingual-like Spanish; secondly, school and peer pressure to speak monolingual-like English; and thirdly, adult expectations that they should be able to interpret and translate accurately between both languages in home, school and other community contexts:

Extract 5.14 Aparecido family, daughter, 17-year-old, Session 1

Researcher: ¿Te gusta hablar español?
Daughter: (2) Hmmm, a veces sí y a veces no, porque me hacen burla (1) porque
R: [¿Por qué?
Daughter: No puedo hmm decir cosas bien a veces, y por eso (1) me gusta hablar más en- en inglés que…
R: [¿Y quién se te- o que- quién se burla de ti?
Daughter: Mi familia ((giggles))
R: ((giggles))
Daughter: Mis tías, y mi mamá
R: Okay
Daughter: Cuando digo cosas
R: Okay. ¿Te gusta hablar inglés?
Daughter: Sí
R: Okay. ¿Para qué les sirve a las personas hablar español?
Daughter: (1) Hmm, (2) para comunicarse con otras personas de aquí también […] Y eh (2) ayudarlas (1) como- como algunas personas tienen más tiempo de estar aquí, conocen más y pueden ayudar a l- a las personas que (1) están menos tiempo aquí.

Researcher: *Do you like speaking in Spanish?*
Daughter: *(2) Hmmm, sometimes yes, and sometimes no, because they make fun of me (1) because*
R: *[Why?*
Daughter: *I can't hmm say some things correctly, and that's why (1) I like to speak more in- in English than*
R: *[And who, who makes fun of you?*
Daughter: *My family ((giggles))*
R: *((giggles))*
Daughter: *My aunts and my mom*
R: *Okay*
Daughter: *When I say things*

R:	Okay. Do you like speaking in English?
Daughter:	Yes
R:	Okay. How do people benefit from speaking Spanish?
Daughter:	(1) Hmm, (2) to communicate with other people who are from here too [...] And eh (2) help them (1) like- like some people who have been here longer, they know more and they can help those people who have been here less time.

Children's Perceptions of Bilingualism and the Viability of Spanish

Eleven children between the ages of five and ten were presented with nine items intended to survey perceptions about bilingualism and the viability of Spanish. Two patterns emerge for this cohort: strong communicative motivation, and socialization to diglossia. Seventy-three percent (8/11) of the respondents in the youngest age group either reported accommodating to the language of their interlocutor with the express goal of understanding or making themselves understood and/or identified this ability as one of the benefits of knowing how to speak both languages. Unlike the respondents in the teen group, children between five and ten reported accommodating to Spanish and English-speaking peers, as well as to adults who were dominant in either language. Articulations about the instrumental value of Spanish or about cultural or linguistic brokering were absent in this cohort.

Like teens in the 12–17 age group, the youngest children perceived themselves as bilingual and all reported having friends who spoke Spanish. Similar to youth responses, responses in the younger age group are also highly suggestive of socialization to diglossia. These responses include: one child's report of being told by teachers not to speak Spanish at school (Martínez household); one who described speaking English with his peers while doing classwork and switching to Spanish after it was done (Fernández household); those who expressed a preference for speaking Spanish at home and English at school (Lara, Martínez, García and Villareal households); children's reports that a teacher who purportedly spoke Spanish did not know how to communicate clearly in this language (Fernández and Quiñónez households); and identification of English as the language of their school (García, Gallegos, Navarro, Pacheco and Molina households). Extracts 5.15 and 5.16 are illustrative of the children's perception of English as the unmarked language within the space of the school:

Extract 5.15 García family, son, seven-year-old, Session 1

Researcher:	Bueno y ¿qué- qué es alguna cosa buena [de hablar español]?
Child:	[Y también lo- me gusta el español, hablarlo porque (1) porque lo hablo casi todo el día, pero en la mañana cuando estoy en la escuela no.

R: Hablas el inglés ¿no?
Child: Sí.
R: Aaahh, y hmm, ¿hay cosas buenas de hablar inglés?
          [...]
Child: (1) Hmmm (1) en la escuela a veces lo hablo porque- (1) porque
          este (1) porque allí es este- XXX (vienen) los niños que saben
          inglés [...] Y hay (bien) poquitos que saben español
R: Uh huh
Child: Y hay una clase arriba que es inglés y en- español, que aprenden
          a los niños españoles a hablar inglés.

Researcher: *Well, and what is something good about speaking Spanish?*
Child: *[And I, I like Spanish, I like speaking Spanish, because I*
          speak it almost all day, but not in the morning, when I'm in
          school.
R: *You speak English [in school], right?*
Child: *Yeah.*
R: *Aaahh, and hmm, are there good things about speaking in*
          English?
          [...]
Child: *(1) Hmmm (1) In school I sometimes speak it because (1) because*
          (1) because that's where the kids who know English go [...] And
          there are very few who know Spanish.
R: *Uh huh*
Child: *And there's a class upstairs that's in English and in- Spanish,*
          where the Spanish kids learn to speak English.

Extract 5.16 Navarro family, son, nine-year-old, Session 1

Researcher: Te- ¿a ti te gusta? ¿Hablar español?
Child: Hmm.
R: ¿Te gusta o no te gusta?
Child: [XXX] me gusta, y también inglés
R: Y también inglés, ¿te gusta hablar inglés?
Child: Uh huh [...] le puedo ayudar a mi mami con unas palabras
R: ¿En español o en inglés?
Child: Hmmm (2) ella va a la escuela para aprender las [...] En- las-
          en- mi lenguaje de escuela
R: Ah en inglés, ah, okay, (1) veo
Child: [Child's friend's name] (también) (ella necesita ayuda con unas
          palabras)
          [...]
R: [En inglés, sí, ¿y tú le ayudas?
Child: Sí.

Researcher: *Do you- Do you like speaking in Spanish?*
Child: *Hmm.*
R: *Do you, or don't you?*

Child: *[XXX I like it, and I also like speaking in English*
R: *And also in English, do you like speaking in English?*
Child: *Uh huh [...] I can help my mom with a few words*
R: *In Spanish or in English?*
Child: *Hmmm (2) she's going to school to learn the [...] in- the- in my*
            school language
R: *Ah, in English, ah, okay, (1) I see*
Child: *[Child's friend's name] (also) (she also needs*
                          help with some words)
                   [...]
R: *[In English, yes, and do you help her?*
Child: *Yes.*

Ending this chapter by saying that mothers and children shared positive attitudes toward Spanish and a strong perception of the instrumental and social value of bilingualism is insufficient to provide any insight into patterns of intergenerational transmission and loss. Concluding by saying that it is 'obvious' or 'common sense' that first-generation immigrants should want to transmit their language to their children erases the fact that 'common sense' arguments about speaker motivations to use and transmit a minority language are very often exocentric: common sense to whom? The same social categories – e.g. gender, class, educational attainment, housing segregation – are understood differently by speakers in different contexts. The perceived experience of a Spanish speaker in the (non-metropolitan) Midwest is thus different, but not less valid, than that of a speaker in Miami, Los Angeles, Hoboken or San Antonio.

The context for the articulation of these perceptions matters. For the three generational cohorts in this study, a very relevant feature of this context was their shared experience of diglossia. Moreover, for the mothers and children in these families, the speaker motivations to use Spanish differed according to generational and social positioning. For the mothers, the perceived instrumental value of bilingualism was influenced by an immigrant narrative of parental self-sacrifice for their children's economic future. Religious motivation, as well as a perceived connection between linguistic and cultural transmission, and maintenance of kinship and affection ties were also articulated as motivations for the transmission of Spanish. Although no reproduction of monoglossic ideologies was reported in the mothers' responses, linguistic anxiety is suggested in the belief expressed by some respondents, that speaking more than one language is confusing to children.

That the children and youths in these families were being socialized to diglossia is suggested by the fact that, while the teens in this study perceived themselves as bilingual, and as language brokers for the adults in their lives, they perceived English as the default language in their school and had limited contact with bilinguals in institutional spaces. Interestingly, it was the youngest children in these families who reported accommodating to both peers and adults according to the interlocutor's language. In the following chapter, we will examine the mothers' and children's reported proficiency in Spanish and English.

A few questions to continue the conversation ...

(1) As you have read in this chapter, all the adult participants in this study reported positive attitudes toward Spanish, as well as a strong motivation to transmit the language to their children. Despite this, many also described their children's preference for speaking English with their peers. What are some features of the context and everyday interaction in this community and these households which fostered the functional and generational separation of English and Spanish?

(2) Many of the children in these families translated between both languages for the adults in their lives. How might this practice help them develop metalinguistic awareness?

(3) Write a list of five good things and five bad things about speaking more than one language. What might be the source of these ideas? Who/what made you come to these understandings?

Notes

(1)   Instrumental motivation (pragmatic desire to obtain economic or social gains by learning, speaking or transmitting a language).

(2)   The reader will find the whole instrument in Appendix 2.

(3)   In his later work, Karan offers a more nuanced account of the potential motivations that influence language shift at the level of the community. Karan further allows for the possibility of combined motivations, that is, that motivations to use or abandon a language are not present in isolation from one another. For a full taxonomy of language motivations, see Karan (2011).

(4)   For more on this discussion, see Del Valle (2006), García and Torres Guevara (2009) and Mar-Molinero and Paffey (2011).

(5)   Strength of motivation is understood here as both the number of respondents who reported that using Spanish was important to them in this specific context and the degree of importance assigned by each speaker.

(6)   Aside from their mothers, children in these families performed language and cultural brokering activities for other adults in their family, school and the wider community. This included monolinguals or near monolinguals in Spanish and English. For a detailed discussion of language brokering performed by children in first-generation Latino families, see Faulstich Orellana (2009).

(7)   This, of course, does not mean that the respondents did not interact with anyone in English on a regular basis, but that their closest social networks were Spanish dominant.

(8)   It is unclear whether the respondent meant 'Because I have the accent of someone who speaks Spanish' or 'Because I speak Spanish'.

(9) Because of an error in data collection, five participants were not presented with this item during one or both interviews. The response total is higher than 19 because several respondents provided more than one answer.

(10) An early reader of this manuscript has correctly pointed out that the responses *helping others* and *speaking with monolinguals* are also suggestive of maternal perception of potential social capital for their children.

(11) As a point of reference, ethnic distribution totals for Lincoln Public Schools (LPS) show that there were 5031 Latino students enrolled in K-12 classrooms as of September 2015. This constituted 13.1% of the LPS student population. This state of affairs was not radically different at the time of our interviews. Even taking into consideration the fact that not all Latino students are speakers of Spanish, as well as the different socio-economic profiles of the schools, it stands to reason that the teens in this study shared their school days with a considerably higher number of speakers of Spanish. The point to be made here is that beyond demographic counts this is also, fundamentally, a question of visibility. See https://docushare.lps.org/docushare/dsweb/Get/Document-2076015/2015%202016%20Student%20Section.pdf.

(12) In informal Mexican Spanish, the word *güero* is used to describe either a blond person or an individual from the United States. It is used by the respondent as a metonym for Anglo. See https://www.academia.org.mx/obras/obras-de-consulta-en-linea/diccionario-de-mexicanismos.

6 Mothers and Children: Reported Language Competence

Carmen: Víctor, please, te dije que te estuvieras quieto

I was ill-prepared for the question that Carmen asks in the middle of our session today. Someone has just mentioned that there are two pregnant 13-year-olds attending a local middle school. The other moms join in, our conversation on child language development now officially derailed. This is the question: *If a mom got pregnant at 15, does this mean that her daughter will necessarily get pregnant at 15?* Juana follows up: So, does it work if I tell my daughter *'Don't have sexual relations or you'll get pregnant at 15 like I did?'* She hedges, *For example, let's say.* I answer frankly – and frankly by the seat of my pants. As honestly and as clearly as I am able, all eyes on me, expecting ... *¿y usted qué piensa?*

I say that the first thing I believe is that the human spirit is resilient, and that it has the ability to learn and to grow and to change in any circumstance and at every moment. I say that the mom could use her experience to provide alternatives to her daughter, or she could not learn and not allow her daughter to learn from it, and reproduce the conditions that led to the mom getting pregnant in the first place. Carmen asks: *but what happens when the mom AND the grandma both got pregnant at 15?* My lungs deflate a little. My heart hurts.

We talk a while more about reproducing the same conditions, about how guilt does not accomplish the same as thinking, about how the same experience can have different outcomes depending on the perspective of the participants. We talk about the importance of finding good role models for our daughters, about the importance of creating positive expectations for them. BUT this is the connection I could not articulate properly, this is the thing I wish I

> had said and didn't: self-esteem. Teaching our daughters that they don't need to throw themselves at the first dude that comes by in order to be loved. Telling our daughters – ourselves? – that we are enough. Quite enough.

In the present chapter, we will narrow down our focus onto speaker self-perceptions of linguistic competence. We do this because adult perceptions about the ease or difficulty with which they understand, speak, read and write in Spanish and in English are an indirect way to access household language dynamics. They have a lot to tell us about household opportunities for use, print environment, socialization to reading and other literacy events, availability of print materials, access to technology, and overall quality and amount of available input in either language. Additionally, comparing teen self-perceptions of proficiency with those of their mothers provides us with information about linguistic (non-)transmission, potential intergenerational shift and potential resiliency of one or more of these skills.

In order to examine self-perceptions of linguistic proficiency, mothers and adolescents (aged 12–17) were asked to rate how easy or hard it was for them to understand, speak, read and write in Spanish and English. The mothers were also asked to recall the last three things they had read and written in each language. This was done as an attempt to understand the role of literacy in their everyday lives and, by extension, to gather information on the type of Spanish literacy events taking place in these homes. The results for each generational cohort are presented in Figures 6.1 and 6.2.

As expected for a group of native speakers of Spanish who arrived in the United States after adolescence, the mothers in this study rated

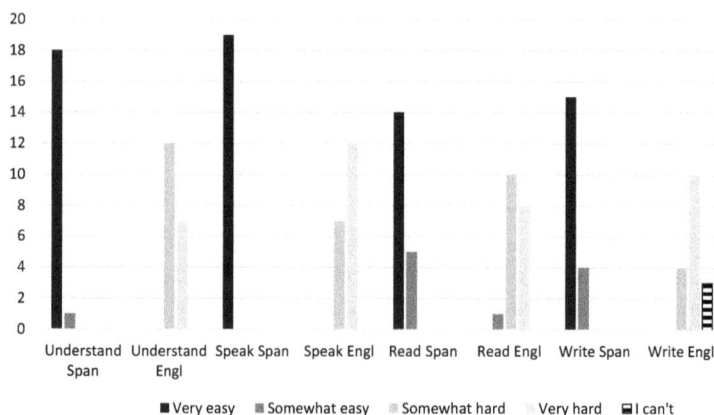

Figure 6.1 Mothers' perceived language competence (*N* = 19)

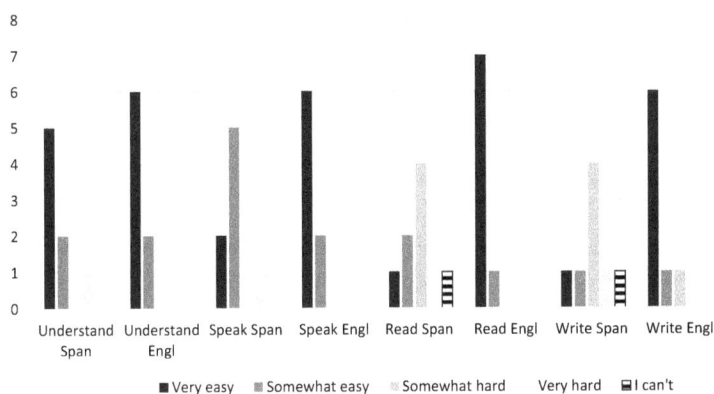

Figure 6.2 Youth perceived language competence (*N* = 8)

understanding, speaking, reading and writing in Spanish as very easy to somewhat easy. Linguistic insecurity and dialectal contact were evidenced in the responses given by Lala Rodríguez and María Luisa Martínez. For Lala Rodríguez, for example, speaking in Spanish was very easy, but she believed that her lack of education led her to mispronounce some words on occasion. Like her, Martínez believed that understanding Spanish was very easy, but she reported not understanding some words as used by speakers of a different variety of Spanish, and sometimes consulting their mother about their meaning. For Juana Molina, reading and writing in Spanish was very easy, but she reported writing very seldom in her strongest language because, as she explained, *Aquí casi no se escribe en español* 'One almost doesn't write in Spanish here'. An interesting case was that of Carina Quiñónez, who reported as one of her main Spanish writing activities the exercises and vocabulary lists she prepared for her five-year-old son. Quiñónez wrote vocabulary lists in Spanish and asked her son to identify and write the same words in English. Regardless of language, she perceived the development of literacy as one process, a process in which she could help her son with the household resources she had at hand.

Adult responses about perceived ease or difficulty in understanding, speaking, reading and writing in English also provide us with indirect evidence of late exposure to the majority language, limited input and limited opportunities to practice. Most mothers in this study ranked receptive skills in English as somewhat hard, followed by productive skills in English which they rated as very hard. Three mothers reported being unable to write in English. No adult respondent rated any skill in English as easy. These results do not mean that the mothers in this study did not interact with speakers of English in their everyday lives. They do not mean that they were not studying or had not studied English. They did not mean that they were not motivated to learn it, either. What they do mean is that they found communicating in English hard or very hard. This, in turn, impacted the amount, type and quality of their interactions in both languages.

A compelling household pattern emerges when we compare the maternal responses with those of their 12- to 17-year-old children. In a sense, the youth responses provide us with a mirror image of adult self-perceptions. While their mothers rated all skills in Spanish as very easy and all skills in English as somewhat hard or very hard, most teens rated all skills in English as very easy, and for 50% of them reading and writing in Spanish as somewhat hard – the exceptions being three older teens who had completed most of their elementary education in a country where Spanish was the majority language. In fact, the only skill in Spanish rated as very easy by the majority of the youth cohort was understanding Spanish, followed by speaking Spanish, which was rated as very easy by 63% of this cohort. Only one youth reported understanding and speaking Spanish as very hard, and reported not being able to read or write in Spanish.

Comparison of the results for mothers and teens corroborates youth self-perceptions as linguistic brokers between their mothers and the larger community: they had greater ability to communicate in English, and still perceived themselves as able to understand and speak Spanish. These results also tell us a lot about the children's socialization to English literacy, about successful acquisition of English at school and about reduced opportunities for the development of Spanish. Over a longer time frame, these results sketch out what might have been a point in the families' overall language development characterized by household shift to English.

Project data are insufficient to clarify why four US-raised teens who had not received formal schooling in Spanish ranked Spanish literacy as somewhat hard – as opposed to very hard – or reported not knowing how to read and write in Spanish. The simplest answer is that they were trying to save face in front of the interviewer. Other possible answers are: (a) that they had learned to read and write in Spanish in church (their mothers reported that they had all had received religious education in Spanish); (b) that their mothers had taught them to read and write at home; or (c) that they were spontaneous readers, i.e. they learned to decode Spanish words in the print environment of the home and community, and were equating decoding with reading. The intergenerational differences are presented in Table 6.1.

Mothers' Reported Literacy

The last results to be discussed in this chapter relate to reading and writing in Spanish and English as reported by the mothers in this study. The type of texts that the mothers were engaging with at the time of our first interview were recorded as a way to understand the role of literacy in their lives and, by extension, potential household exposure to and

Table 6.1 Mothers' and children's perceptions of language competence (percentage)

Very easy	Somewhat easy	Somewhat hard	Very hard
Mothers			
Speak Spanish 100%			
Understand Spanish 95%			
Write Spanish 79%		Understand English 63%	Speak English 63%
Read Spanish 74%		Read English 53%	Write English 53%
Youth (12–18)			
Read English 87%			
Understand English 75%			
Speak English 75%			
Write English 75%		Read Spanish 50%	
Understand Spanish 63%	Speak Spanish 63%	Write Spanish 50%	

modeling of literacy events for their children. One hundred percent of the mothers recalled having read at least one thing in Spanish during the week of the first interview. Eighty-nine percent recalled writing at least one thing in Spanish. Another 89% reported having read at least one thing in English during the week of the interview, and 68% reported having written something in English.

Examined by type of text, most reported reading in Spanish was religious (e.g. the Bible, church website and church documents), followed by general interest publications (books, magazines, newspapers, texts related to their children's school) and commercial texts. Two things are worth noting here: first, that commercial and school-related texts were translations of texts originally written in English; and secondly, that books were not named by title by the respondents, and that the magazines and one newspaper reported were local publications of limited circulation. Only two mothers reported reading a news item in Spanish on an electronic outlet. There was low reporting of engagement with online publications of either language. The respondents' limited use of the internet represented reduced access to online communities, content and services, as well as the mothers' limited participation in their children's development of electronic literacy.

Differences in function of reported writing in Spanish and English can be observed in the fact that most reported Spanish writing (44%) was intended as dialogue with self or personal reminder, e.g. a list, name and address, entry in daybook, followed by writing intended for a social bonding function (22%), e.g. birthday card, text message, personal email, letter. In contrast, the results for reported reading and writing in English point to their children's school as an important site for the development

Table 6.2 Mothers' reported literacy in Spanish and English

Reported literacy events

Last three things you read in Spanish?		*Last three things you read in English?*	
Bible	6	Sign, message, document at work	7
Book for adults	6	ESL textbook or homework	4
Flyer, ad, store sign, catalog	6	Instructions	4
Note from children's school	4	Child's homework, sports schedule, grades	4
Church publication, site, religious education material	4	Flyer, ad, store sign, catalog	3
Book for children	3	Newspaper	2
Magazine	3	Bill	2
Bill	2	Note from children's school	2
News item on the internet	2	Book for children	2
Child's homework	2	Nothing	2
Insurance document	1	Text from sister in law	1
Recipe	1	Book for adults	1
Internet comment	1	Magazine	1
Address	1	Medical form	1
Map	1	Housing application	1
Text in video	1	Insurance document	1
Newspaper	1		
Greeting card	1		
Last three things you wrote in Spanish?		*Last three things you wrote in English?*	
Grocery list, to do list	6	ESL homework or class notes	10
Name and address	5	Nothing	6
Homemade worksheet or exercise for children	4	Child's homework	2
Birthday card	3	Medical form	2
Text message	2	Email, non-personal	2
Email	2	Application	2
Timesheet, list for work	2	Invitation	1
Personal goals, resolutions, note to self	2	Rent check	1
Recipe	2	Note for child's teacher	1
Nothing	2	Answers to questionnaire at work	1
Daybook	1		
Letter	1		
Child's catechism homework	1		
News	1		
School application	1		
Draft of ESL homework	1		

of English literacy for the mothers. Twenty-six percent of all reading in English and 46% of all reported writing in English reported by the mothers was related to their children's school. Six mothers in this study did not report any writing in English. The results for the mothers' reported literacy are shown in Table 6.2.

A few questions to continue the conversation ...

(1) As discussed in this chapter, mother and adolescent self-perceptions of linguistic competence were a mirror image of each other: while mothers rated all skills in Spanish as very easy and all skills in English as somewhat hard or very hard, most teens rated all skills in English as very easy and reading and writing in Spanish as hard or very hard. These results seem to suggest, first, that the mothers and children in these households were undergoing parallel but distinct processes of language development, and secondly that they were a source of input, evaluation and opportunities for use for each other. How might supporting the mothers' language development help the children's overall bilingual language development? If this is the case, do you think that supporting the children's literacy development helps the mothers' own development?

(2) For the children and mothers in this study, the main space for literacy development was the children's school. Because all the children were attending schools where English was the language of instruction, this meant that the children were socialized to view English as the unmarked language of literacy. What might some implicit messages be about successful readers and about the functions of reading and writing that the children and adults in these families are receiving and reproducing? How do these messages contrast with the maternal attitudes to Spanish reported in Chapter 5?

(3) Look at the list of literacy events presented in Table 6.2, and try to remember all the things that you read and wrote today. Now take a moment to observe the print environment around you, and imagine that you did not know how to read or write the majority language in your community. How would you go about your business? What strategies would you use to accomplish all the tasks that you set out for the day? Would you ask for help? How? From whom?

7 Children: Observed Skills in Spanish

Elena: I'm trying to teach them more words

Today, I bring two prompts to get our conversation started: *These are some difficult things about raising my children in a country that is different from mine.* And also: *These are some difficult things about raising bilingual children in the United States.* Definitely the language, says Carmen from one side of the room. It's difficult to help them with homework. *I know the multiplication tables, but I have to 'say nine times nine is...', like that, real slow, because it's harder.* Juana joins in: *In Mexico children are with you until they're married. Here, they turn 18 and they want to throw them out. And families are closer in Mexico,* she says. You think of family and you think of extended family. *Even the neighbors take care of you, they can tell your mother if you misbehave. Here, you can't get involved.* No, says Carina, the hardest thing is time. *Here, no one has time. You barely have time to think about yourself and your children.* Teresa thinks that the hardest thing is disciplining your children. Everyone nods in agreement. Josefina says that her nephew threatens her sister with calling the police when she scolds him. Magdalena says: *Teaching them Spanish, because they teach them English at school and we don't have a school at home to teach them Spanish.* And also, she says, teaching them moral values. *Yeah, it's hard to teach them values,* agrees Elena. For some now unexplainable reason, I ask her: *Teaching them values or teaching them how to express their emotions?* She corrects me without missing a beat: *Expressing emotions IS a value.* I say that I agree, but she's not too convinced, so she tells a story to drive home her point. When her younger son was in kindergarten, she starts, she was called in by his teacher, who asked her to correct him because he hugged other children too much. *She told me that they could think something that wasn't true, and that I should take him to a psychologist, that it was a psychological problem.* For Elena, who is recreating the scene mid-air with her arms, this was not only a non-problem, but quite a ridiculous idea to forbid a child to express his emotions. *This is what makes children lonesome, isolated*, she concludes. The message was that her son was bad, and he was not a bad boy, he was a normal kid, she says. But her son had to go back to school, so Elena had to tell him not to hug his classmates. *Why? He asked, surprised.* Because they can get mad. *But why?* he asked again. Exasperated because she didn't have a better answer, she told him: *Because they're crazy here.*

In the two preceding chapters, we examined children's and youths' attitudes toward speaking Spanish and English, as well as their perceptions about viability and their self-perceptions of proficiency. We turn now to an analysis of their aural and oral skills in Spanish, as observed during the two interviews we conducted with them. Any attempt to gain a full picture of a speaker's level of proficiency in any language with the data obtained only from two, one-hour sociolinguistic interviews is, at best, an overly optimistic proposition, and much more so in the case of children, who are by definition undergoing the different stages of early language development. Data on oral production in Spanish are presented here, then, not as an exhaustive measurement of proficiency, but as a counterpoint to the children's and mothers' perceptions.

Furthermore, to put these results in context, we would do well to revisit Carmen Silva-Corvalán's (2014) distinction between *dominant language* and level of *language proficiency*. Silva Corvalán understands *proficiency* as 'advancement in the knowledge of a specific aspect of language' (Carmen Silva-Corvalán, 2014: 43), and language dominance as a state of affairs defined by the sum result of language-internal and language-external factors (Carmen Silva-Corvalán, 2014: 20). Among the language-internal factors that determine a child's dominant language she cites: richer vocabulary; more fluency; fewer errors in production; absence or rare presence of constructions unattested in monolingual acquisition; higher mean length of utterance averages; and more advanced syntactic development. As language-external factors that impinge on a child's language dominance she cites: preference for using language X when contextual conditions permit language choice; higher amount of exposure and use of this language; and faster rate of acquisition of language X (Carmen Silva-Corvalán, 2014: 20).

As described in Chapter 3, the *child* group included 11 respondents between the ages of five and ten. The median age for this subgroup was seven. All the children in this group were attending school at the time of our interviews. The youngest one was enrolled in a federally funded early childhood education program, and the eldest was in the fifth grade.

Ability to understand and speak Spanish was tested by asking the child to respond in Spanish to a three-part instrument. The first part of this instrument was a 16-item questionnaire in which the child had to provide their name, age, school routine, preferences and evaluations about school and play, as well as reported language choice and perceptions of the viability of Spanish at home and in school. The second part was a guessing task designed to test the child's ability to understand and follow complex instructions in Spanish, as well as to produce and understand descriptions of household objects. These descriptions included size, shape, color, function and location in space (see Appendix 4). In order to test the stability of the responses, the same instrument was administered at the end of the study. The distance between the first and second interviews allowed us the opportunity to speak retrospectively about the school year with the child, which allowed us to test the child's production of verb forms associated with past events.

The third and last part of this instrument was a storytelling task in which the child was asked to narrate a story in Spanish and another in English. The results of narrative analysis for the 44 stories produced by these 19 children during both interviews are discussed in detail in Chapter 8. Table 7.1 summarizes the results for the children's aural and oral proficiency in Spanish as evidenced in interview recordings.

The results for aural comprehension were high for all the children in this study. All the children understood complex sentences, detailed descriptions, multi-step instructions, and adverbial phrases locating objects in space, as well as vocabulary about family, play, school and neighborhood. In several of our interviews with the youngest children in the group, the mother or father provided the child with a word to fill a lexical gap, or prompted the child to respond. Several of our recordings also include a background of spontaneous responses, comments or interruptions by younger siblings and cousins who were often the very curious observers of our interviews.

Regarding oral production, the children were able to speak about school routines, preferences, friends, games and playing in their neighborhood. They were able to use vocabulary about family, school, play, friends, colors and shapes. Only one neologism was found: 'rectongo' < rectangular, perhaps as an analogy with *oblongo* 'oblong'. All the children provided evidence of use of cardinal numbers in Spanish, but only three used ordinal numbers – in all instances to refer to the school grade they were attending. Overall, the children produced possessives, articles, gender and number agreement, subject and object pronouns – most often *se*. As expected, the older children used greater detail in their descriptions and incorporated more everyday knowledge of the world.

Recordings of the children's oral production provide evidence of a reduced verbal paradigm in Spanish. While all the children produced infinitive and present verb forms, only four produced preterite and only

Table 7.1 Evidence of children's aural and oral proficiency in Spanish

	F11	F12	F15	F17	F19	F20	F21	F22	F23	F24	F25
Age	5	8	9	7	9	6	10	9	6	5	7
Gender	M	F	M	M	M	M	M	M	M	M	F
Aural comprehension											
Understands questions in Spanish	2	2	2	2	2	2	2	2	2	2	2
Understands instructions in Spanish	1	2	2	2	2	2	2	2	2	2	2
Guessing task successful	2	2	2	2	2	2	2	2	2	2	2
Oral production											
Description task successful	2	2	2	2	2	2	2	2	2	2	2
Can say name and age	2	2	2	2	2	2	2	2	2	2	2
Ordinal numbers	0	0	0	0	0	0	1	0	0	2	2
Cardinal numbers	2	2	2	2	2	2	2	2	2	2	2
Colors	1	2	2	2	2	2	2	2	2	2	2
Location in space	2	2	2	2	2	2	2	2	2	2	2
Shapes	1	2	2	2	0	1	2	2	2	2	2
Likes/dislikes	1	2	2	2	2	2	2	2	2	2	2
Can talk about school activities	1	2	2	2	2	2	2	2	2	2	2
Family vocabulary	2	2	2	2	2	2	2	2	2	2	2
Game and toy vocabulary	2	1	2	1	1	2	2	2	2	2	2
Gender agreement	1	2	2	1	2	2	2	2	2	2	2
Number agreement	1	2	2	2	2	2	2	2	2	2	2
Possessives	2	2	2	2	2	2	2	2	2	2	2
Subject pronouns	2	2	2	2	2	2	2	2	2	2	2
Object pronouns	1	2	2	2	2	2	2	2	2	2	2
Infinitive	2	2	2	2	2	2	2	2	2	2	2
Present	2	2	2	2	2	2	2	2	2	2	2
Preterite (not in story)	2	2	0	0	0	0	0	2	0	2	0
Imperfect (not in story)	0	0	1	2	0	0	0	2	0	2	0
Any form of subjunctive (not in story)	0	0	0	0	0	0	0	0	0	2	0
Code-switching	2	0	2	2	2	2	2	2	2	2	2
Calques from English	2	0	0	2	0	0	0	2	0	0	0
Gerund as progressive	1	0	0	0	0	0	0	0	0	0	0
Gerund as infinitive	0	0	0	0	0	0	0	2	0	0	0

Key: 2 = produced during interview; 1 = produced with few errors, some assistance; 0 = not produced during either interview.

four produced imperfect. No uses of the future were recorded – due in large part to the fact that the interviewer did not ask questions about future events. No uses of compound verbs were recorded, e.g. present perfect or pluperfect. Only one child, a five-year-old boy, produced subjunctive verb forms.

Regarding past tense verb forms, however, the fact that most children did not produce them during the question-and-answer portion of the interview does not necessarily mean that they did not know or use them, as most of the children who did not use past verb forms during the first part of the interview produced them when narrating a story in Spanish. In the following passage, for example, a member of the research team is speaking with Juan Carlos Fernández, a nine-year-old boy, about the recently ended school year. Although the interviewer attempts to direct the conversation to past events several times, the boy answers correctly, but produces only one token of a past tense verb form. Moments later, however, he produces the contrast between imperfect and preterite when narrating a story:

Extract 7.1 Fernández family, child, Session 2

Researcher: ¿Y qué grado acabas de terminar?
Child: Tercero
R: O sea que vas para cuarto ¿No?
Child: Uhhuh
R: Ok, ¿Te pareció que la escuela fue fácil o difícil este año?
Child: Un poco, duro
R: ¿Sí, difícil?
Child: Uhhuh [...] Un poquito
R: Un poquito, no mucho, Ok. Y, pero ¿te gustó la escuela?
Child: Uhhuh
R: ¿Sí? ¿Qué tipo de cosas hacían en tu salón? ¿Qué tipo de actividades?
Child: Tarea
R: Uhhuh
Child: Uhm, leer libros y esas cosas [...] Unas cosas, papeles, cosas, XXX
R: Sí, sí
Child: Y tarea for home
R: Y ¿Escribían también, o no?
Child: Uhhuh
R: ¿Sí? Ok. ¿Te dejaban mucha tarea, o poquita?
Child: Sí habían dos o uno
[Later, same interview]
Child: Y el perro se cayó en, en la, en, niño está siendo, y el niño está enojado, y el perro
R: Uhhuh
Child: La rana, y el perro está dando moscos, y el perro quería jugar estas bees abejas, el niño estaba viendo abajo, el se encontró...

Researcher: *So, what grade have you just finished?*
Child: *Third.*
R: *So you're going onto fourth, right?*
Child: *Uhhuh*
R: *Ok, Did you think that school was hard or easy this year?*
Child: *A little hard*
R: *Yeah, hard?*
Child: *Uhhuh [...] A little*
R: *A little, not a very [hard], Ok. And, but, did you like school?*
Child: *Uhhuh*
R: *Yeah? What type of things did you do in your classroom? What type of activities?*
Child: *Homework*
R: *Uhhuh*
Child: *Uhm, reading books and things like that [...] some things, papers, things XXX*
R: *Yes, yes*
Child: *And take home work*
R: *And, did you write too, or not?*
Child: *Uhhuh*
R: *Yeah? Ok. Did you have a lot of homework, or a little?*
Child: *Yeah, there were two or one*
[Later, same interview]
Child: *And the dog fell in, in the, in, the boy is being, and the boy is mad, and the dog*
R: *Uhhuh*
Child: *The frog, and the dog is giving [surrounded by?] flies/mosquitos, and the dog wanted to play [with] these bees, the boy was looking down, and he found...*

Language Contact Phenomena

All the children in this group code-switched during the course of our two interviews. Three produced calques from English and one produced one token of gerund for infinitive. Two examples of semantic extension were found in interview recordings with the same child. During our second interview (see the passage below), Juan Carlos Fernández fills the lexical gap for *grass* < *pasto, pastizal, zacate, grama*, with *grasa* – a word similar in form, but altogether different in meaning: 'fat'. In Extract 7.2 Juan Carlos produces the target form *salón*, and the extended form *cuarto* < 'school room', in the same stretch:

Extract 7.2 Fernández family, child, Session 1

Researcher: [...] bueno algunas veces hablas, ¿algunas veces hablas español con otros niños?
Child: Uhhuh
R: ¿Con quién?

Child:	Mi amigo está, tiene ocho años y va a mi mismo salón
R:	Uhhuh
Child:	Otro, tiene mismo, mismo, mismo cuarto, y [los] mismos años que yo

Researcher: *[...] well, do you sometimes speak, do you sometimes speak in Spanish with other kids?*
Child: *Uhhuh*
R: *With whom?*
Child: *My friend is, he's eight and is in my same class*
R: *Uhhuh*
Child: *Another, [he] has the same, same room, and the same age as me*

Several aspects of the children's proficiency in Spanish are not reported in Table 7.1, such as the type and amount of their interaction with younger siblings and parents during our time in all households. Neither is their knowledge of when/with whom/in what space to switch languages, nor the fact that all elementary-school aged children provided evidence of equal or greater competence in English. Also absent from Table 7.1 is the fact that some lexical choices appeared to be culturally weighted. This is the case with game names, which were marked for English or Spanish according to whether they were linked to the space of home/neighborhood or the school playground. Game names generally marked for Spanish were *futbol, escondidillas* and *atrapadas* versus soccer, hide and seek and tag. Game names generally marked for English were tag, foursquare and dodgeball versus *atrapadas/la traes* and *quemados*.

The last three examples in this section are instances of children describing an object in their immediate surroundings. These examples are worth examining in detail because they illustrate the interplay between the linguistic strategies employed by the children to carry out this task. In Extract 7.3 Emilio Arroyo, a nine-year-old boy, describes the television located at the center of the family's living room. At the beginning of the passage he fills the lexical gap for *audio speaker* with a description: *en donde sale el sonido* 'where the sound comes out'. Toward the end of the passage, he does not know or does not remember the name of the decorative objects placed on the tabletop in front of him, and describes them using circumlocution. Of secondary interest here is the fact that after he uses the borrowing 'screen', the interviewer provides the word in Spanish, even though the child has produced the target form a moment earlier. The article that accompanies the borrowed form agrees in gender with the Spanish word *pantalla*:

Extract 7.3 Arroyo family, child, Session 2
Researcher: Te voy a pedir que me describas un objeto que hay aquí en este, en este cuarto
Child: Uhhuh
R: Voy a pedirte que me describas mmm... tu televisor

Child:	Es grande, la pantalla es negra cuando está apagada, tiene botones, tiene arriba perros y algo para dormir, tiene por abajo de la screen algo que dice Sony
R:	Pantalla
Child:	Pantalla. Algo que dice Sony y botones y como [Sound of train passing by] en donde sale el sonido
R:	Uhhuh. Muy bien. Excelente descripción. ¿Qué hay sobre la mesa?
Child:	Tiene tres bebés chiquitos tiene una agua, una planta no está toda cubierta, tiene [long pause] y lo está sosteniendo las velas y algo para jugar con unas raquetas

Researcher:	*I'm going to ask you to describe an object in this, in this room*
Child:	*Uhhuh*
R:	*I'm going to ask you to describe mmm… your TV*
Child:	*It's big, the screen [in Spanish] is black when it's turned off, it has buttons, it has dogs on top, and something to sleep, under the screen [in English] it has something that says Sony*
R:	*Screen [in Spanish]*
Child:	*Pantalla [In Spanish] Something that says Sony and buttons, and like Algo que dice Sony y [Sound of train passing by] where the sounds comes out*
R:	*Uhhuh. Very well. Excellent description. What's on top of the table?*
Child:	*It has three small babies and [a] water, a plant that's not covered all the way, it has [long pause] and it's holding the [candles/ sails?] and something to play with racquets.*

In this second example, Juan Carlos Fernández provides evidence of knowing vocabulary about animals, colors and nature in Spanish. When he struggles to find a word, he fills one lexical gap by borrowing: *branch* < *rama* and a second one with a semantic extension: *grass* ≠ *grasa*. Unlike the case of *la screen*, the article used with the borrowed form *branch* does not agree in gender with the target form in Spanish:

Extract 7.4 Fernández family, son, Session 2

Researcher:	Bueno, ahorita te voy a pedir el favor que me describas algún objeto de este cuarto, ¿Por qué no me describes esos cuadros que ves allá? ¿Qué ves en esos cuadros?
Child:	¿Esos de ahí?
R:	Sí, en todos o cualquiera, el que quieras. Descríbeme qué ves.
Child:	Este tiene árboles, una casa bonita y muchos árboles, unas vacas…
R:	Sí
Child:	Caballos […] Gallinas

R:	¿Dónde están, en qué lado del cuadro?
Child:	De XXX
R:	Ok. Y ¿De qué color son las casas?
Child:	Una es blanca y otra es roja
R:	Uhhuh ¿y qué más hay?
Child:	Agua [...] Un branch
[...]	
R:	Uhhuh ¿Y cómo está el cielo?
Child:	Rojo [...] El está cielo oscuro [Loud noise, shakes recorder]
R:	Uhhuh, sí. Bueno y, se va a caer... se va a caer el apartamento [Laughs] Bueno y, y, tú que, ¿Qué estación dirías que es? ¿Es verano, es invierno, en primavera o es otoño? En el cuadro
Child:	Primavera
R:	¿Primavera? De pronto. Ok, bueno, ¿y en este otro cuadro de la derecha, qué ves?
Child:	Este de un viejito casa
R:	Sí
Child:	Y mucho viejita árboles, y viejita grass, ¿grasa?

Researcher:	*Well, now I'm going to ask you to describe an object in this room please. Why don't you describe those pictures that you see there? What do you see in those pictures?*
Child:	*Those over there?*
R:	*Yes, in all or any of them, whatever you want. Describe to me what you see.*
Child:	*This one has trees, a pretty house, and many trees, some cows...*
R:	*Yes.*
Child:	*Horses [...] chickens*
R:	*Where are they, on which side of the picture?*
Child:	*On the XXX*
R:	*Ok. And what color are the houses?*
Child:	*One is white and one is red.*
R:	*Uhhuh and what more is there?*
Child:	*Water [...] A branch [in English]*
[...]	
R:	*Uhhuh And what is the sky like?*
Child:	*Red [...] the sky is dark [Loud noise, shakes recorder]*
R:	*Uhhuh, yes. Well, and, it's falling down the apartment is falling down [Laughs] Well, and what would you, what season would you say it was? Is it summer, it's winter, spring or autumn in the picture?*
Child:	*Spring.*
R:	*Spring? Maybe. Ok, good. And in this other picture on the right what do you see?*
Child:	*This is an old house [this is an old man's house?]*
R:	*Yes.*
Child:	*And many old trees and old grass, grease?*

The last description (Extract 7.5) is the most interesting because it is the most complex. In this passage, Felipe García, a seven-year-old boy, is sitting with the researcher in his family's living room. The researcher looks around and asks him to describe a calendar they both see at a distance, hanging in the kitchen. The calendar is a Mexican-style calendar given to clients at Christmas and New Year by a local Latino-owned supermarket. In this passage, Felipe not only describes what he sees, but engages his little sister in the task, gives her instructions, decodes a word in Spanish, uses animal and color vocabulary, uses several adverbs of place, requests clarification, provides information about the supermarket, uses logic to connect the image of a food container depicted on the calendar with his knowledge of the world – i.e. that the supermarket also sold prepared food – and corrects the researcher, providing the correct distance between the supermarket and his house:

Extract 7.5 García family, son, Session 2

Researcher: Okay. Bueno, ahora te voy a pedir un favor [giggles] ustedes también están aprendiendo mucho ¿no? aaahh [at other children in the room] [children giggle] bueno, quiero que me describas algún objeto que veas en la cocina, descríbeme ese calendario, ¿qué ves? ¿qué ves en ese calendario?

Child: Este, ovejas

R: Sí, ¿y qué más?

Child: Y un- y un poco de un arbolito de navidad

R: Eeehh

Child: Al lado de [child screams in background] un lado de los números

R: OOHH aquí abajo okay, veo, sí, sí, sí, sí, okay, ¿qué más ves?

Child: Este: que (diga) Guerrero Market

R: Sí [giggles]

Child: Hmm

R: ¿Qué más? [...] ¿Qué ves en el dibujo?

Child: A Dios [Picture of Jesus]

R: Uh huh, ¿y qué tiene puesto?

Child: ¿Ropa?

R: Sí, ¿y cómo es la ropa?

Child: (2) ¿Qué?

R: ¿Cómo es la ropa?

Child: (1) Blanca y roja

R: Uh huh, bueno

Child: Y también un panadero pequeño debajo de la 'o' de Guerrero

R: Un panade- ah sí, ya lo veo, ¿y qué es eso al lado izquierdo?

Child: No sé bien

R: Yo tampoco, creo que so- creo que es comida ¿no?

Child: Jacquie [little sister] ¿puedes ir a ver qué es eso ahí, debajo de la 'G'?

R: ¿Qué dibujo es? (3) creo que son como: ¿como recipientes de comida?

J: (No hay) ¿cuál 'G'?
Child: Jacquie, en donde dice Guerrero, mira abajo de la 'G'
R: [Stands up and walks over to Jacquie,] mira, mira, éste, ¿esto qué es? [talking to Jacquie]
J: (4) Hmmm, creo que es comida
R: Sí, Jacquie, tiene razón, es comida [talking to Felipe] (2) muy bien
Child: (1) También en la Guerrero (venden) comida
R: Uh huh, ¿queda como a dos cuadras ¿no? (queda cerquitica)
Child: [Una, una cuadra

Researcher: Okay. Well, now I'm going to ask you for a favor [giggles] you're learning a lot too, aren't you? aaahh [at other children in the room] [children giggle] well, I want you to describe something you see in the kitchen. Describe that calendar for me. What do you see?
Child: Mmm, sheep
R: Yeah, what more?
Child: And a little, a little of a Christmas tree.
R: Eeehh
Child: Next to the [child screams in background] next to the numbers
R: OOHH here down below, okay, I see, yes, yes, yes, okay, what more do you see?
Child: Mmm: I mean [it says] Guerrero Market
R: Yes [giggles]
Child: Hmm
R: What else? […] What else do you see in the picture?
Child: God [Picture of Jesus]
R: Uh huh, and what is he wearing?
Child: Clothes?
R: Yes, and what are the clothes like?
Child: (2) What?
R: What are the clothes like?
Child: (1) White and red
R: Uh huh, well
Child: And a small baker under the 'o' in Guerrero, too
R: A bake-ah, yes, I see. And what is that on the left side?
Child: I don't know for sure
R: Neither do I. I think they are- I think it's food, isn't it?
Child: Jacquie, [at little sister] can you see what is that over there, under the 'G'?
R: What picture is it? (3) I think they're like: food containers?
J: (There aren't/isn't any) What 'G'?
Child: Jacquie, where it says Guerrero, look under the 'G'
R: [Stands up and walks over to Jacquie] look, look, this, what is this? [talking to Jacquie]
J: (4) Hmmm, I think it's food
R: Yes, Jacquie is right it's food [talking to Felipe] (2) very well

Child: (1) *They also sell food at Guerrero's*
R: *Uh huh. It's about two blocks from here, isn't it? (it's very near)*
Child: *[One, one block.*

Youth: Observed Skills in Spanish

The youth group included eight respondents between the ages of 12 and 17. The median age for this subgroup was 14.5 years. Data on the youths' aural comprehension and oral production in Spanish were obtained using a four-part instrument (Appendix 5). The first part of this instrument was a 19-item open-ended questionnaire in which youths were first asked general information about age, school, favorite school subjects, spare time and afterschool part-time work. Two items were included in this section to survey the respondents' choice of verbal forms when speaking about imagined situations in the future. These were *¿Qué te gustaría hacer después de graduarte de high school?* 'What would you like to do after you graduate from high school?' and *¿Cuál sería tu trabajo ideal?* 'What would your ideal job be?'. The last 12 items in this section were intended to survey their perceptions of the viability of Spanish with friends, siblings, parents and other adults in the family (Chapter 5).

The second part of this instrument was designed to survey self-perceptions of proficiency in Spanish and in English. In this section, the respondents were asked to rate how hard or how easy was for them to understand, speak, read and write in both languages (Chapter 6).

The third part of the instrument was a narrative production task in which youths were ask to retell a travel anecdote. The first five questions were used as a prompt, and were presented using the preterite to situate the narrated action in the past. This was done to elicit past-tense verbal forms. One question was presented using the pluperfect subjunctive: *¿Te hubiera gustado X?* 'Would you have liked to do X?', in order to elicit responses about hypothetical situations in the past. The last five questions in this section were presented using the conditional as a way to elicit verb forms associated with imagined situations located in the future. The flaws in the design of this part of the instrument, as well as the youth results for this narrative task, are reported in detail in Chapter 8.

The fourth and last part of this instrument was a 6-item open-ended questionnaire intended to survey youth attitudes toward speaking Spanish, speaking English and bilingualism. Table 7.2 summarizes the results for the teens' aural and oral proficiency in Spanish as evidenced in interview recordings.

Results for youth aural comprehension and oral production

All the teens understood the questions and instructions in Spanish presented to them by a member of the research team. Two required minimal clarification before responding. Interaction with the youth respondents was conducted predominately in Spanish during both interviews, with 4/8 of the respondents code-switching between Spanish and English at some point in either interview, and the member of the research team code-switching to follow their lead. The two partial exceptions to this pattern were 16- and 13-year-old girls Gaby Rodríguez and Vanessa Gómez. Overall, Gaby and Vanessa provided evidence of lower proficiency in Spanish when compared with the data for the rest of this subgroup. Regarding language selection, the highest percentage of exclusive use of English was recorded in interviews with Gaby, whose oral production included 10.7% of conversational turns in English during the first interview and 5.7% during the second. Vanessa produced 8.1% of all conversational turns exclusively in English during the first interview and only 0.7% of conversational turns during the second. While 6/8 youth respondents were able to relate an anecdote and to describe in Spanish what happened on the last day of classes, Gaby and Vanessa provided evidence of more limited narrative abilities in Spanish, and could only fulfill one of these two narrative tasks. More details about the youths' narrative production and the design flaws that resulted in the limited data available to measure their narrative competence can be found in Chapter 8.

Other Language Contact Phenomena

Although small in number, the lexical field of English nouns borrowed by teens point to their everyday experience of the functional separation between public and private spaces. A total of 6/8 respondents borrowed the names of school subjects, professions or occupations. The interview transcripts include 12 borrowed tokens with the following distribution: school subjects (6); professions or occupations (3); and the construction 'una movie' (1), 'la movie' (1) or 'llevaron movies' (1). In both cases *movie/movies* were used in reference to a movie that the respondent had watched at school on the last day of classes. The interview transcripts show that the most common strategies employed by the teens to fill a lexical gap were circumlocution and borrowing. It should be noted, however, that borrowing a word in English does not necessarily mean that the respondent did not know or did not use the correspondent word in Spanish in other contexts, as 4/6 teens who produced a borrowed noun in English during the first interview produced the equivalent word in Spanish during the second interview or at a later time during the same conversation.

Analysis of the lexical choices in the interview transcripts provides additional evidence of the differential development of Spanish and English in this group of teens. Unlike their production in English, only 2/8 of youth respondents used ordinal numbers, and then only to refer to their school grade. Examination of transcript interviews for Gaby Rodríguez and Vanessa Gómez points again to their lower overall proficiency in Spanish. The following example was produced by Gaby:

Extract 7.6 Rodríguez family, daughter, Session 1

Child: Mi prima se gomitó de comer tantas chucherías, que salimos un día y ya [...]
Child: *Mi cousin vomited because she ate a lot of junk food, so we went out one day and that was it [...]*

The production of *vomitó/bomitó* 'vomited' as [*gomitó*] is somewhat common in very young children developing the contrast between /b/ and /g/, but would be unexpected in the Spanish production of a 16-year-old. Vanessa Gómez' recorded production includes the neologism (or semantic extension?) 'pender' (*obtener/conseguir*), and the construction *Tiene bien sonrisa* 'has a nice smile', where the adverb *bien* occupies the space where an adjective would be expected. Only one error in number agreement was found in all the youth interview transcripts: *El año que vienes < el año que viene*, produced by Laura Pérez, a 12-year-old girl. Data are insufficient to determine if the plural marking in what is otherwise a formula – *el año que viene* – is due to the respondent misspeaking, if it is a case of reanalysis of agency (i.e. who is coming? the year, the interlocutor or the speaker as a generic *tú*?), or something else.

Calques and semantic extensions

Eighteen tokens recorded in interview transcripts suggest the influence of English on the teens' Spanish production. As summarized in Table 7.2, some were classified as calques and some as semantic extensions. All involve assigning the lexical specification of English to a word in Spanish.

Verbal morphology

Perhaps the most interesting results regarding the teens' oral production in Spanish relate to verbal morphology. Overall, the teens provided evidence of a simplified or reduced verbal paradigm in Spanish. As expected, all youth respondents provided evidence of command of the infinitive, present and preterite. No use of future tenses was recorded (not surprisingly, as neither interview included prompts for the use of the future tense). Most striking, however, is the fact that only two respondents produced any form of the subjunctive, and then only the present subjunctive (Anita Luna) or only the imperfect subjunctive (Lily Aparecido). The interview transcripts do not provide evidence of command of the subjunctive/imperative mood contrast for this group of young speakers.

Regarding compound verb forms, only one teen (Anita Luna) produced the present perfect. Only one token of gerund was found, in the

Table 7.2 Calques and semantic extensions (youth)

Token	Contact feature	Example
Calqued structures		
3	Missing human direct object marking	*Visitamos ø nuestra familia.*
2	Use of article with generic noun	*Quiero ser una maestra*
2	Number agreement in English	*[Quiero estudiar] cerámicas.*
1	Preposition + infinitive	*Para entender* < 'to understand' > *entender*
1	Lexical specification of prep in English	*Estoy jugando soccer para la escuela.*
1	Calque of whole phrase	*Tener un buen tiempo* < have a good time > *divertirse*
1	Calque or semantic extension?	*Para comunicarse dentro de ellos mismos* < 'to communicate among themselves' > *para comunicarse entre ellos.*
Semantic extensions		
1	mejor ≠ better = más	*Me gusta hablar mejor en español*> 'I like speaking in Spanish better' < *me gusta hablar más en español*
1	tiempo ≠ time = vez	*Un tiempo* < 'one time' > *una vez.*
1	papel ≠ school paper = trabajo/ensayo	*Escribir un papel* < 'write a paper' > *escribir un trabajo/ensayo*
1	grados ≠ grades = calificaciones/notas	*Sacaron los grados mejores* < 'They/who got the best grades' > *Sacaron las mejores calificaciones/las mejores notas*

production of Josué López, a 15-year-old boy who, at the time of our interviews, had lived for the shortest amount of time in Lincoln.

When speaking about past events, all the youth respondents produced preterite and imperfect verb forms. Five provided evidence of command of the preterite/imperative contrast when establishing foreground and background action in narration. As exemplified in Extract 7.7, Lily Aparecido's command of the contrast between the preterite/imperfect oscillated between targetlike and non-targetlike, and also her use of the preterite with atelic meaning and use of the imperfect with telic meaning. Only one token of non-targetlike regularization of an irregular verb was found in all the transcripts for this subgroup: 'saber' > *sabo*, produced by Vanessa Gómez.

Extract 7.7 Aparecido family, daughter, Session 1

Researcher: Okay. Bueno ahora quiero que te acuerdes de algún viaje que hayas hecho, cualquier viaje que se te venga a la mente...
Child: [Uh huh
R: Okay, ¿a dónde fuiste?
Child: A Kansas [giggles]
R: Okay, ¿y con quién ibas?
Child: Con las personas de mi iglesia

R: Okay, bueno, cuéntame, ¿cómo fue y qué hiciste?
Child: Um, era [foreground: -telic] como un retiro para los jóvenes de
          mi iglesia [...] Y: (3) había [background: -telic] concursos y
          juegos y (2) pa- así para jóvenes
R: ¿De cuánto, cuánto tiempo fue? O sea, ¿cuánto tiempo en total?
Child: Eran tres días [foreground: -telic]
R: Okay. ¿Pasó algo gracioso o chistoso?
Child: (3) Sí [giggles]
R: [giggles] ¿Qué? (1) ¿Qué fue?
Child: Hmm cuando estábamos [background: -telic] (1) en un (2) era
          [background: -telic] como un lago [...] Y hay como un palo
          así, pero era- [background: -telic] no lo puedo decir en español
          [laughter] (1) uuh, era [background: -telic] así como un palo
          bien grandote y- todas todas mis amigas estaban [background:
          -telic] ahí y mis amigos y (3) entraron [foreground: +telic] dos
          muchachos y [laughter] y (1) no los conocíamos [background:
          -telic] y mi hermana habló [foreground: + telic] con ellos [...]
          Y de ahí nosotros fuimos [foreground: + telic] al- a otro
          campamento que tenemos [background: present] con toda la
          iglesia y- mi hermana se conoció [foreground: + telic] con
          (1) su novio que tiene [present reference: present] ahora,
          entonces- [...]

Researcher: Okay. Well, now I want you to remember about some trip that
          you've taken, any trip you can remember...
Child: [Uh huh
R: Okay, where did you go?
Child: To Kansas [giggles]
R: Okay, who did you go with?
Child: With the people from my church
R: Okay, well, tell me, how was it and what did you do?
Child: Um, it was like a retreat for youth in my church [...] And: (3)
          there were competitions and games and (2) pa- like that, for
          teens
R: How long, how long was it? I mean, how much time in total?
Child: It was three days
R: Okay. Did something amusing or funny happen?
Child: (3) Yes [giggles]
R: [giggles] What? Whaat was it?
Child: Hmm when we were (1) in a (2) it was like a lake [...] And
          there was like a stick [pole?], like that, but it was- I can't say
          it in Spanish [laughter] (1) uuh, it was like a huge stick and all
          my [female] friends were there and my [male] Friends and (3)
          two guys came in and [laughter] and (1) we didn't know
          them, and my sister spoke with them [...] and from there we
          went to the other camp that we have with the whole church
          and- my sister met her boyfriend, the boyfriend she has now,
          so- [...]

¿Qué te gustaría hace después de graduarte? ¿Te gustaría hacer algún viaje?

As has been described above, the last five questions in our instrument were presented using the conditional as a way to elicit verb forms associated with imagined situations located in the future. Fifteen responses were collected. As presented in Table 7.3, the most common structure used to respond to a conditional was a prepositional phrase. This was followed by the use of an infinitive. The canonical use of the conditional was only found once in all transcripts. No examples of the imperfect subjunctive – common in adult informal speech, were found.

In sum, examination of the children's and youths' oral production in Spanish provides us with evidence of high levels of aural comprehension and oral proficiency. Children between the ages of five and ten were able to understand interviewer questions and instructions, and were able to speak in Spanish about school routines, preferences, friends, games and playing in their neighborhood, using vocabulary for family, school, play, friends, colors and shapes. Additionally, they provided evidence of the use of possessives, articles, gender and number agreement, and subject and some object pronouns. By the same token, all the youths aged 12–17 understood the questions and instructions in Spanish presented to them and, with two exceptions, were able to relate an anecdote and to describe in Spanish what had happened on the last day of classes. Although small in number, the lexical field of English words borrowed by the teens points to the functional separation of Spanish and English in their everyday lives, as most borrowings referred to school subjects, professions and occupations. No examples of borrowings belonging to the home or family were found in transcripts of our interviews with the youths.

Importantly, regardless of their high oral proficiency, all the children and teens in this study provided evidence of a simplified or reduced verbal paradigm in Spanish. Determining how much of this system simplification is related to incomplete acquisition, how much is the result of linguistic

Table 7.3 Response to a question with conditional (youth)

¿Qué te gustaría hacer después de graduarte de high school?/¿Te gustaría hacer algún viaje?
'What would you like to do after you graduate from high school?/Would you like to take a trip?'

Token	Structure used in response	Examples
7/15	Prepositional phrase	*Para México, A Rome, A otros países*
4/15	Infinitive	*Ir al college, Ser jugador de futbol profesional*
1/15	Conditional	*Sí, me gustaría ir a España*
1/15	Prepositional phrase missing prep	*¿Con quién te gustaría ir a Hawaii? ø mi amiga*
1/15	Noun phrase in Spanish	*Doctor, una doctora*
1/15	Noun phrase in English	Social work

Table 7.4 Evidence of aural and oral proficiency in Spanish (youth)

	F1	F2	F3	F6	F7	F8	F10	F14
Age	16	15	17	13	16	13	12	14
Gender	F	M	F	F	F	M	F	M
Aural comprehension								
Understands questions in Spanish	2	2	1	1	2	2	2	2
Understands instructions in Spanish	2	2	2	2	2	2	2	2
Oral production								
Anecdote task successful[a]	0	2	2	0	2	2	2	2
Can say name and age	2	2	2	2	2	2	2	2
Ordinal numbers	0	0	0	0	0	2	0	2
Cardinal numbers	1	1	1	0	1	1	1	1
Can talk about likes/dislikes	2	2	2	2	2	2	2	2
Can talk about school activities	2	2	2	0	2	2	2	2
Family vocabulary	1	2	2	2	2	2	2	2
Gender agreement	2	2	2	2	2	2	2	2
Number agreement	1	2	2	2	2	2	1	2
Possessives	2	2	2	2	2	2	2	2
Subject pronouns	2	2	2	2	2	2	2	2
Object pronouns	0	2	2	0	2	2	0	2
Infinitive	2	2	2	2	2	2	2	2
Present	2	2	2	2	2	2	2	2
Preterite	2	2	2	2	2	2	2	2
Imperfect	2	2	2	0	2	2	0	0
Present perfect	0	0	0	0	2	0	0	0
Subjunctive	0	0	2	0	2	0	0	0
Gerund as progressive	0	2	0	0	0	0	0	0
Gerund as infinitive	0	0	0	0	0	0	0	0
Conditional	0	0	0	2	0	2	0	2
Code-switching	2	2	2	2	0	0	0	0
Calques from English	2	0	2	0	2	2	0	0
Borrowing[b]	2	2	2	2	2	0	2	2
Circumlocution to fill lexical gap	2	0	2	2	0	0	0	0
Semantic extension	0	0	0	0	2	2	2	0

Key: 2 = feature produced during interview; 2 = produced with few errors, some request for
    clarification; 0 = not produced during either interview.
[a]Anecdote: 2 = related two anecdotes in Spanish; 1 = related only one anecdote, or one in Span-
    ish and one in English; 0 = no anecdote in Spanish produced in either interview.
[b]Borrowing: 2 = use of at least one word exclusively in English; 0 use of one word in English and later
    produced same word in Spanish in different interview or different segment of same interview.

attrition in the older children, and how much is a snapshot of emerging linguistic abilities goes well beyond the scope of this study. It must be mentioned here, however, because the development of verbal morphology is a strong predictor of language development (Montrul, 2002).

Further indirect evidence of the functional separation of Spanish and English for the children and adolescents in this study is provided by the fact that only 5/19 respondents aged five to 17 produced ordinal numbers in Spanish. This is means, for example, that 14/19 replaced them with cardinal numbers when speaking about their grade in school. Children as young as two are able to make numerical discriminations and represent ordinal relations as large as six (Brannon & Van de Walle, 2001), but larger ordinal relations and related vocabulary are generally introduced in school at around age five (Fernández & Alfonso Ortiz, 2008; Hernández Gutiérrez, 2013).

Analysis of the children's observed skills in Spanish suggests, then, that most of the children and adolescents maintained high levels of oral proficiency in Spanish, but that the dominance of English was greater as the number of years in school increased. In the following chapter the reader will find a detailed analysis of the children's narrative abilities in Spanish.

A few questions to continue the conversation ...

(1) As in many other bilingual communities in the United States, most children and teens in these families maintained high levels of oral proficiency in Spanish, but their everyday use of English was greater as the number of years in school increased. Is this the only possible outcome? How might schools, parents and the rest of their community help them develop both languages?

(2) Montrul (2002) posits that verbal morphology is a strong predictor of language development. If you had to draw a schematic with the verbal paradigms described in this chapter, what verbal forms would be absent? What may be the reason(s) for this?

(3) Two very different ways to look at the language proficiency reported in this chapter are from a deficit or a strength perspective. What did you learn in this chapter about what teens and children can do in Spanish? What strengths (in both languages) can you identify? Would your perceptions of the oral production described in this chapter change if the children were identified as second-language learners of Spanish?

8 Tell Me a Story: Analysis of Children's Storytelling in Spanish

Rosario: Between making rent and paying the gas bill

Quick to judge. So, so quick to judge. Rosario applied to the workshop, said she wanted to come, called to confirm her attendance one week prior. She had a place reserved and didn't show up. Week one: no show. Week two: no show. The little authoritarian in my head nags: *What's wrong with this woman? How rude to take a spot from someone else if she wasn't planning on showing up. I planned, I prepared, I came, I took time from other things to be here. I made an effort, dammit!* And so on and so forth, repeat as needed. All variations on the same theme: Why is this happening to ME? I learn today that Rosario has bronchitis. The heating in her home has been shut off for some weeks for lack of payment. Her family has an electric heater, but they avoid turning it on as much as they can because they are out of work and they don't want to run up the bill. So, Rosario is nursing her bronchitis in a home with no heat, in the tail end of a Nebraska winter. A week later I will find out that her brother passed away. The grief and the challenges compounded. The ebb and flow of an ordinary human life, exponentially complicated by economic circumstance.

Was it worth it? – to leave your country, to leave your loved ones, to leave what you know and start over somewhere else with the promise of better times to come. This question is not mine to answer. Or better yet, it is mine to answer only as it pertains to me. Rosario, and all the women who have allowed me to learn from their experience over the past months, will arrive at their own conclusions. But there is something alive, something pulsating. Something that survives over distances and troubles. Something that makes Rosario come to our sessions when the weather improves (even if she stops coming a few weeks later). Something that these mothers find of value and worth preserving. Something that is about language and more than language.

As I am gathering my things and thinking about all of this, Carina comes to say goodbye after our session and to gift me with this truth: that when you hear your kid speaking in English, you get a bittersweet feeling at the center of the heart. That you feel pride, a lot of pride, because he's learning English. But also, guilt, because he's not using Spanish. That you get a secret tinge of anger, or frustration because you've spent four years trying to learn what your kid picks up in the playground by the middle of the summer vacation. A mixture of feelings. I jot this down as quickly as I can. I add: that when we feel frustrated, angry, guilty when/if our kids don't use Spanish, they feel the same. That they feel they disappoint us, that they feel they fail to live up to our expectations if they don't speak Spanish when/how we expect them to do. A sense of falling short. Frustration.

In Chapters 5 and 6 we focused on children's and adolescents' attitudes toward Spanish, as well as their perceived viability of the family language. We also examined their self-perceptions of proficiency in both English and Spanish. In the preceding chapter we also presented the results of an analysis of their language skills as observed by the members of the research team. We now turn to the task of storytelling. To be sure, the Spanish language competence of all the children and adolescents interviewed for this study was evidenced by the fact that they were able to participate in two semi-structured interviews in Spanish; they were able to follow instructions and provide information about themselves, their family, their school and their preferences, and provide age-appropriate metalinguistic insights into the ways in which they navigated the use of both languages in their everyday lives.

Our focus on the children's ability to tell a story in Spanish and English was an attempt to understand their level of linguistic and cognitive development, as well as any interlanguage and intra-group differences. The literature on children's emergent narrative abilities in first and second languages is vast and is motivated by both theoretical and instrumental concerns, most notably because of the fairly robust finding that children's narrative development can be used as a predictor of literacy development and academic achievement later in life (Feagans, 1982; Kao, 2015; Muñoz et al., 2003; Reese & Cox, 1999; Snow, 1983; Snow & Dickinson, 1990; Wishard Guerra, 2008). According to Kao (following Hedberg & Westby, 1993), through the act of narration a child transforms the highly contextualized and concrete environment of early childhood into abstract concepts and remote events (Kao, 2015: 40). This leads this author to argue that data on children's emerging narrative abilities are a good source for documenting the different stages of development (Kao, 2015: 62).

In many ways, the act of recounting a story was the most complex task presented to the children in this study. Compared to answering interview questions, telling a story exerts greater cognitive demand, requires greater control of linguistic structures and necessitates awareness of sociocultural schemata. Reilly *et al.* (2004) describe the interaction of linguistic, cognitive and affective/social abilities involved in children's narration. They explain that in telling a story children must make appropriate use of morphosyntactic devices to situate characters and events in temporal sequence. Concurrently, they must make inferences about the protagonist's actions, about the theme of the story and about the relationships between events. Finally, children must show awareness of their audience and the social-evaluative devices related to the social activity of telling a story (Reilly *et al.*, 2004: 230).

Reilly *et al.* (2004) argue that documenting emerging narrative abilities is a good way to measure cognitive and linguistic development, because although children generally have command of the morphosyntactic structures of their language by the age of five, the process of learning to use complex structures and different discourse genres continues well into adolescence. More recently, researchers have begun to examine the specific features of narrative development in bilingual children (Gutiérrez-Clellen & Goldstein, 2004; Pearson, 2002; Uccelli & Páez, 2007). In this chapter we examine whether the children and adolescents interviewed in these households were able to produce age-appropriate narrations in Spanish and English when prompted, what the structural features of these narrations were and, finally, what these features tell us about their productive ability in the family language.

Description of the Data

Nearing the end of each of the two interviews conducted in each household, the children and adolescents in this study were asked to tell a story. Eleven children between the ages of five and ten were asked in Spanish to find and fetch two wordless picture books (which the interviewer had placed in a semi-conspicuous place before the start of the interview). They were then asked to recount in Spanish the story of *Frog, Where Are You?* (Mayer, 1969). After being praised for their effort, they were then asked to recount in English the story of *A Boy, a Dog, and a Frog* (Mayer, 1967). Appendix 4 includes the script used by the researchers at the beginning of this task. Mayer's *Frog* books have been used extensively to elicit children's narratives in studies of typical and atypical L1, L2 and L3 development (e.g. Berman & Slobin, 1987; Cenoz, 2001;

Gutiérrez-Clellen & Goldstein, 2004; Guitiérrez-Clellen & Kreiter, 2003; Kremser, 2011; Muñoz *et al.*, 2003; Pearson, 2002; Schecter & Bayley, 2002; Takemoto, 2010).

In the present study, the *Frog* books were used only with 11 children between the ages of five and ten, because it was determined that they were not age appropriate for use with adolescents. In light of this, eight participants between the ages of 12 and 17 were instead asked to recount a trip that was memorable to them because of something funny or exciting. Appendix 5 includes the script used by the researchers to elicit the adolescent narratives. Appendix 6 includes an example of the youth travel narratives. Data on the children's narratives were considerably richer than those gathered from the adolescents. This is due in large part to the different methods employed for the elicitation of narratives, and constitutes a major flaw in the data collection process. Because of this, the present chapter focuses on the stories produced by the children between five and ten. Narrative production for all children and adolescents was audio-recorded and transcribed by bilingual research personnel.

A total of 525 unique words were collected from the children (aged five to ten) during the first iteration of the storytelling task in Spanish. Of this total, 9% were words in English. In comparison, 384 unique words were collected during the first storytelling task in English (of these, 7% were words in Spanish).[1] Several months later, the children were asked to retell the same stories during a second sociolinguistic interview. In this second iteration, an overall total of 482 unique words were collected when children recounted the story in Spanish (4% were words in English). A total of 360 unique words were collected during the second iteration of the storytelling task in English (4% of these were words in Spanish).[2]

It seems relevant to caution the reader here that the results for both iterations of the storytelling task must not be interpreted in a linear fashion (i.e. more Spanish words in the second story would mean that children were using more Spanish in their daily life, fewer would mean less use, etc.). This is, first, because the time elapsed between the beginning and end of the study was too brief to truly measure changes in language use and, secondly, because much like in the case of everyday household interactions, the conditions surrounding the child's telling of these stories was not reproducible in exactly the same way. What these stories do offer us is a layered picture of their narrative abilities at two different points in time, as well as their language production in Spanish and English.

Finally, it will be argued here that used in isolation neither of these measures was by itself a reliable gauge of the linguistic and communicative competence of these children. This picture, however, affords us a crucial point of comparison between their own (and their mothers') perceptions of their own proficiency and their actual language use.

Measures of Analysis

Lexical density and lexical diversity

Three features in the children's stories were examined: lexical density/ lexical diversity, narrative structure, and verbal system. A measure of *lexical density* was employed in this study as a way to compare productivity in Spanish and English as evidenced in the stories told by the children at the same point in time and, later, between the two stories in Spanish produced by the same child several months apart. *Lexical diversity* was examined to ascertain the richness of vocabulary in both languages.

For short texts, lexical density is generally understood as a good index of vocabulary development (Johansson, 2009), and also as a measure of the richness of information contained in an oral or written text (Halliday, 1985; Ure & Ellis, 1977). Broadly defined, lexical density can be understood as the ratio of content words to function words (Johansson, 2009). Content words were understood here as words belonging to an open set (nouns, adjectives, most verbs and most adverbs). Prepositions, interjections, pronouns, conjunctions and count words were understood as function words (Johansson, 2009). Thus, lexical density was determined using this formula:

$$L_d = (N_{lex}/N) * 100$$

where L_d = lexical density, N_{lex} = lexical words, and N = all words in text (token).

Johansson (2009) distinguishes between two measures of vocabulary development: lexical density and lexical diversity. While the measurement of lexical density provides the proportion of lexical words used in a text, lexical diversity is a measure of how varied a vocabulary it contains. It is most commonly measured by establishing the type/token ratio[3] (Johansson, 2009: 62). This author is careful in pointing out, however, that neither lexical diversity nor lexical density are by themselves enough to judge the complexity of a text (Johansson, 2009: 62). Indeed, Muñoz *et al.* (2003: 332) argue that 'measures of language productivity (such as total number of words and number of different words) that reflect developmental differences in monolingual mainstream preschoolers may not be sensitive indicators of narrative language development in young Latino children from low-SES environments'. They argue that measures of syntactic accuracy and episodic structure are better indicators of developmental changes in these children's narrative abilities. Similarly, Uccelli and Páez (2007) found, in their longitudinal study of narrative skill development in a group of 24 Spanish/English bilingual kindergarteners, that the total number of different words was a indeed a sensitive measure of the development of English narrative productivity, but not so for Spanish (Uccelli & Páez, 2007: 225).[4]

Narrative structure

The second measure of analysis was an examination of the structural organization and coherence of the stories told in Spanish by the five- to ten-year-old children in these families. We used an adapted version of Schecter and Bayley's *Narrative Assessment Scale* (2002: 129),[5] as well as the measure for narrative coherence adapted by Wishard Guerra from Peterson and McCabe (1983). Both scales are based on Labov's framework for narrative analysis (Labov, 1972; Labov & Waletsky, 1967/1997).

Verbal system

Analysis of command of tense/aspect/mood distinctions in Spanish was included as a way to gain a more reliable picture of the children's development in the family language. This decision follows Schecter and Bayley's observation that the preservation of tense/aspect distinctions (or the acquisition of such distinctions) is tied to the amount of Spanish used in the home (Schecter & Bayley, 2002: 115).

For each child, the total number of verb forms was tallied for the first story in Spanish. The verb forms were then classified as Spanish, English or hybrid. The verb forms in Spanish were analyzed for person and number agreement. One point was awarded for each person and one for agreement, with a maximum possible of 2 points per story (points were subtracted if any error in agreement was present in the story). Finally, we focused on those features of Spanish verbal morphology that could be understood as evidence of the children's command of temporal relations in narrative (Reilly *et al.*, 2004: 230).

Tense

One point was awarded if events were correctly located in time, and narrated in logical temporal sequence.

Aspect

One point was awarded for use of the preterite to encode the past perfective aspect, and one point for use of the imperfect to encode the past imperfect aspect. One point was awarded for use of *estar* + gerund to encode progressive events.

Mood

One point was awarded for use of the subjunctive to encode irrealis clauses, and one point for use of a modal verb + infinitive to encode modality. The table used to perform this analysis is presented in Appendix 10.

Results

Were the children in these families able to tell a story in Spanish? Were they able to do so in English? The answer is yes in both cases, but with important differences between children and between languages, as will be described in the coming pages. We will first examine the features of productivity and richness of vocabulary. Worth highlighting here is the fact that, for the most part, lexical density and lexical productivity measures remained stable in both iterations of the storytelling task. The results are summarized in Table 8.1.

Lexical density, understood as the ratio of content to function words, was measured as a way to compare productivity in Spanish and English at the same point in time, and for the same story, told by the same child in the same language, several months later. For our purposes, nouns, adjectives, verbs and most adverbs were counted as content words, while prepositions, interjections, pronouns, conjunctions and count words were counted as function words. The proportion of lexical words employed in a story was understood here as a measure of vocabulary development (Johansson, 2009). In other words, in Table 8.1 a score closer to 100 indicates higher lexical density.

The results for lexical density presented above must be interpreted bearing in mind the method that was employed to perform this analysis. All words in all stories told in Spanish and in English by the children in this study were analyzed using *Voyant Tools*, a web-based analysis environment for digital texts. Lexical density was measured only for unique words, and after removing stop words for Spanish (which would, by definition, be non-lexical).

With this caveat, we can report that most of the unique words employed by the children when telling a story in Spanish were lexical. Nine of the 11 stories in Spanish received a score of 85 and 96 (i.e. between 8.5 and 9.6 words out of 10 were lexical). The results for lexical density in Spanish remained stable for both iterations of this narration task, with two exceptions: Tomás Lara (a five-year-old boy) and Jesús Martínez (an eight-year-old boy), whose stories show a considerable increase in vocabulary density scores between the first and second iteration of their stories. Data are insufficient to ascertain whether this is a result of normal linguistic development or of an unnoticed change in the conditions in which the stories were told for the second time. What they do tell us is that the Spanish story with the lowest score for lexical density and lexical diversity (Tomás Lara) is also the story with the least structural complexity and the most use of English, even (or particularly) when compared with the stories told in Spanish by Luisito Quiñónez, the other five-year-old boy in the group.

Lexical diversity was understood as a measure of how varied the vocabulary was in these stories, and was calculated by dividing the total

Table 8.1 Lexical density and lexical diversity in children's narratives (organized by age)

Narrator			Iteration #1				Iteration #2			
			Lexical density (lexical words/ all words)		Lexical diversity (token/type)		Lexical density (lexical words/ all words)		Lexical diversity (token/type)	
Child	Age	Gender	Spanish	English	Spanish	English	Spanish	English	Spanish	English
F11	5	M	47	94	2.8	2.1	90	87	2.1	2.4
F24	5	M	93	100	3.8	7.5	92	98	3	2.5
F20	6	M	88	98	2.8	4.8	90	98	3	3.2
F23	6	M	88	97	2.2	3.7	88	96	2.5	4
F25	7	F	92	95	2.9	2.7	90	98	3.2	4
F17	7	M	89	99	2.7	2.1	88	95	2.9	2.3
F12	8	M	59	100	2.9	3.6	94	98	2.9	3.6
F15	9	M	85	96	3.2	3.5	82	98	3.2	3.6
F19	9	M	86	94	2.4	2.9	93	97	2.8	3.4
F22	9	M	86	96	2.6	2.8	87	96	2.1	3
F21	10	M	96	99	2.7	2.8	95	96	3	2.7

number of words by the total number of unique words (i.e. token/type ratio). Vocabulary diversity measures remained stable overall for both iterations of the storytelling task in Spanish.

Overall, lexical density and lexical diversity scores were higher in English than in Spanish, even for those children who spent most of their days around Spanish-speaking adults and who were receiving higher amounts of input in Spanish. This result, which suggests lower lexical productivity in Spanish than in English for these children, is not enough to understand these children's narrative abilities in Spanish at the time of interview.

Comparison of the results on vocabulary and narrative structure lends credence to Muñoz *et al.*'s (2003) observation that lexical productivity measures are not sensitive indicators of developmental differences in bilingual development. Examples of this include the two stories told in Spanish by Luisito Quiñónez. Examined in isolation, his scores for lexical diversity would suggest some of the lowest vocabulary development levels in the group (which would perhaps be consistent with the fact that he was one of the two youngest respondents). This, however, would belie the structural richness of his stories. In the following passage taken from the first story told in Spanish by Luisito, for example, the word *búho* (owl) is used three times. This repetition, which would in isolation suggest less diversity in vocabulary, functions as a narrative device that helps to set the rhythm of the story:

Extract 8.1 Quiñónez family, son. Storytelling task. SPANISH. Iteration #1

Porque ahí adentro había un búho y el perro corrió, porque se espantó (...) Porque el búho era más grande que él (...) Y el búho no vio al niño (...) Y él, luego el búho se subió a un árbol y uso sus ojos para ver el niño, y el niño estaba llamando a la rana y el perro estaba caminado solito...

Because inside there there was an owl and the dog ran, because he got scared (...) because the owl was bigger than him (...) and the owl didn't see the boy (...) And he, then the owl climbed a tree and used his eyes to see the boy, and the boy was calling the frog, and the dog was walking alone...

Despite the fact that they are not very long, analyses of these narratives yield other features worth discussing here, as they relate to the children's overall linguistic competence. These can be organized into three broad categories: command of gender and number agreement in Spanish; syntactic structure; and language contact phenomena. An important finding, for example, is that in retelling these stories, the 11 children in this study provided evidence of stable number/gender agreement systems in both Spanish and English. Only 18 errors of agreement were found in the 22 stories collected, and 100% of these were produced by four children.[6] These are presented in Table 8.2.

Table 8.2 Errors in gender/number agreement (type, per story)

Narrator	Iteration #1		Iteration #2	
	In Spanish	In English	In Spanish	In English
Tomás (5-year-old)	un rana	un rana	el rana el bejas el rock la tree a la niño	Ø
Juan Carlos (9-year-old)	los cosa	Ø	Ø	Ø
Emilio (9-year-old)	con otro rana	Ø	Ø	en la bosque
Toño (9-year-old)	los abejas el rana un roca al casa un bota	Ø	Ø	Ø

Importantly, as illustrated in Extract 8.2, the children who produced 'un rana', 'el rana' (i.e. masculine article + feminine noun), also produced 'una rana', 'la rana' (feminine article + feminine noun), within the same story. By the same token, Juan Carlos Fernández, the nine-year-old who produced 'los cosa' (plural, masculine article + singular, feminine noun) also produced the target 'las cosas' within the same stretch of discourse.

Extract 8.2 Navarro family, son. Storytelling task. SPANISH. Iteration #1

El niño está mirando la ran [...] la rana, se salió [...] y (buego) el próximo día XXX (perro) miró el- la (jarrón) y el jarrón [...] la rana se XXX y miró (un) bota [...] el niño XXX [...] buscar para buscar el, el rana, esto es un, un roca [...] Y se XXX (buego) oyeron algo [...] ¿Podría ser el rana?

The boy was looking at the fr... [...] the frog got away [...] and then the next day XXX (dog) looked the – the (jar), and the vase [...] the jar XXX and he saw a boot [...] the boy XXX [...] look for to look for the, the frog, this is a, a rock [...] And it XXX (then) they heard something [...] Could it be the frog?

Structurally, the most common syntactic mechanism was coordination (i.e. two syntactically independent clauses joined by a nexus); 100% of stories included coordinated sentences.

Eighty-two percent included some form of subordination (i.e. two or more conjugated verbs organized in a main and a dependent clause), and 73% included juxtaposed structures (i.e. two semantically related but syntactically independent clauses that appear side by side).

Code-switching

We turn now to the issue of switching between languages within one story. Only three of the 22 stories in Spanish produced by these children during both iterations of this task include English segments larger than a word.[7] That is, 86% of all child narrators stayed entirely on task and on language during their retelling in Spanish. Four of the 22 stories narrated in English include at least one segment in Spanish larger than a word. That is, 64% of child narrators stayed entirely on task and on language during their retelling in English.

Indeed, of the six stories that included code-switched stretches in either language, four were produced by the same child: Tomás Lara, a five-year-old boy who was one of the two younger narrators in the group. Extracts 8.3 and 8.4 illustrate the type of code-switching produced by Tomás during the first iteration of this task. Aside from the switched segments, Extract 8.3 includes the morphologically adapted borrowing *jumpó* (i.e. the English verb to jump + Spanish flexive morpheme for preterite, third person singular).

Extract 8.3 Lara family, son. Storytelling task. SPANISH. Iteration #1

La rana jumping y- y tha boy no looking (it) [...] He- tha dog is looking him [...] Feliz [...] Feliz [...] El niño no vio, jumpó, y el perro [...] solito no vio el XXX triste [...] (I)- rana XXX brincó ahí [...] Y no (pudo) cacharlo- el- el niño ta mal, ta mal [...] El (búho- el niño digo) es that way [...] is that way [...] Para (brincarlo) [...] El frog is- i- i- [...] sad, the frog is sad.

Extract 8.4 Lara family, son. ENGLISH. Iteration #1

(I)- the kid is cl- climbing tha thr- uuhh [...] The rock [...] (He climbed there) the- the- rock, there's a moose [...] Tha moose runs and the dogs run [...] And the kid XXX the- [...] Yeah [...] A- the- the moose (horita dejó el kid que se cae) and his dog is falling [...] (The fall and) now, you see the puddle, the rock- [...] The frog jump in the puddle.

In order to understand the relevance of finding a very small amount of code-switching present in these 22 stories, the reader must bear in mind the conditions of the storytelling. During the course of the interview, the children were prompted by a stranger – with tape-recorder on hand – to switch from Spanish to English and back again. Often, they did this in household spaces that were noisy, with the TV on, other adults speaking in the background, and siblings or other children present. And, at least during the first interview, they were retelling a story from pictures in a book that they were seeing for the first time.

Borrowing

Borrowings from either language were greater in number than instances of code-switching, but still small, considering the total number of words produced. Only seven examples of borrowing from English to

Spanish (*el* frog, *su* net, *un* branches, *el* moose, *un* lake, so, *como en* silent) and three from Spanish to English were found during the first iteration of the task. Stories collected at the end of the study include nine examples of borrowing from English to Spanish (*un* squirrel, *está buscando* anywhere, *el* bee, *el* ribbit, *el* rock, *la* tree, *estas* bees, *la* bee, *los* tracks) and one from Spanish to English. As in the case of code-switching, 90% of the borrowings in either language were produced by Tomás Lara. Eighty-nine percent of all borrowings were from English, and the type of word most often borrowed was a noun – 78%. The only two examples of borrowing from Spanish to English were produced by Tomás Lara (the *rana*, a *búho*).

Calques

Also present in these stories were calques (understood here as the production of a structure from language A with vocabulary from language B). A total of 28 examples (tokens) were found. Calqued structures are listed in Appendix 7. Of these, 79% were English structures calqued into Spanish – e.g. *y atraparon al perro en vez*. The most commonly calqued structure from English involved a prepositional or adverbial phrase – e.g. *está preocupado con la rana, estaba llamando para su rana*; these were 59% of all calques into Spanish. These were followed in number by adjective placement, e.g. *Tenían una grande familia*; these were only four tokens, or 18% of all calques, into Spanish. Considerably smaller in number were calques from Spanish into English. These represent only 21% of all calqued structures, and were produced by only five children in the group. Of these six calques into English, five were non-target verbal phrases. Only one example of Spanish adjective placement was found – i.e. *the boy saw the jar empty*.

Although small in number, an examination of the calqued structures in these stories provides us with insights into the pressure from English upon Spanish, on the one hand, and about their stage in the acquisition of English on the other. Seventy-eight percent of calqued structures were produced by children who were six years old or older, that is, children who were attending school and spent a large part of the day receiving intensive input in English – with no concomitant increase in Spanish input. Finally, the last feature to be discussed here is the children's strategic use of semantic extension, circumlocution, metaphor and metonym to fill a lexical gap in Spanish, or to conceptualize relations between characters. Three of these strategies are presented in Appendix 8. The first set of examples involves the anthropomorphization or near-anthropomorphization of a group of frogs, which were described by several of the children (in both Spanish and English) in human relational terms (e.g. wife, husband, children). These examples are presented in Appendix 8 with Image A. The second and third set of examples involve strategies used by the children to circumvent an unknown or forgotten word in Spanish. In the examples that accompany Image B, the word *venado* 'deer' is rendered as *venado* and also, by semantic extension and code-switching, as *reno, deer, mus* and *burro* 'reindeer', 'deer', 'moose' and 'donkey'. The last set of examples is related to Image C, whose description would necessitate the production of the low-frequency word *panal* 'beehive'. The word *panal* was not produced by any of the children in either iteration. Instead, several of the children resorted to circumlocution, metaphor or metonym. Stories in English yielded only three tokens of the word *beehive*, and one of *hive*.

Results for Narrative Structure

Narrative coherence

The results show that all the children in this group possessed the narrative abilities to produce a story in Spanish and in English, with events successfully narrated in the past or in the present, and in chronological sequence. In the case of Spanish, 64% of the stories told during the first iteration of this task included more than two events narrated in the past, a highpoint and a resolution. The other 36% of the stories in Spanish included more than two events narrated in the past, and a highpoint but no resolution. During the second iteration of this task, 100% of the stories in Spanish included more than two events narrated in the past, a highpoint and a resolution.

Organization

Two of the stories in Spanish collected during the first iteration of this task (Quiñonez and García households) included detailed action, evaluation and resolution of the narrative conflict. Four more (Lara, Fernández, Arroyo and Gallegos families) included detailed action, and some evaluation and resolution. One story (Villarreal family) had minimal detail, evaluation and a resolution, and three more (Martínez, Navarro and Molina households) were narrations with minimal action. All the stories in Spanish produced by these 11 children during the first iteration of this task included a *who, when, where*, complicating action and some form of resolution. All included inferences about the protagonist's actions. Five included evaluation of the characters' mental states.[8] Only two of these included additional information that was not part of the storyline, and only one included a summary of the action.

Most of the stories produced in Spanish during the second iteration of this task were of equal or greater complexity than the stories produced at the beginning of the study (seven out of 11 stories). All the stories produced in Spanish during the second iteration of this task included a *who, when, where*, complicating action and resolution. Seven included some evaluation of the characters' mental states, and six included minimal information that was not part of the storyline. Only three included a coda signaling the end of the story.

Comparison of the narratives in Spanish and English collected from the same child at the same point in time shows higher overall story organization scores for narratives in English. The following examples illustrate some of these interlanguage differences. The stories in Extracts 8.5 and 8.6 were produced by Toño Navarro, one of the oldest children in the group. As seen in Extract 8.5, the Spanish narrative produced by this nine-year-old boy includes only minimal narration, with orientation, complicating action and resolution, but no details, evaluation, or coda. In contrast, Toño's English narrative signals the beginning of a story – 'There once was a kid and a dog...', includes greater structural complexity and more detail. More importantly, the narrative in Extract 8.6 includes insights into character's motivations and mental states that are absent from his story in Spanish – 'He wanted to get the frog [...] But the frog jumped up then he thought for a moment how to get the frog', and his own evaluation about the outcome of the story and the images on the page – 'The boy saw him and the dog did too- then the fro jumped in the tub [...] And the boy was happy- THAT'S HIS BUTT [...] Hmmm he's NAKED'.

Extract 8.5 Navarro family, son, Storytelling task. SPANISH. Iteration #1

El niño está mirando la rana [...] Y el- p- pone XXX este XXX la rana, se salió [...] Y el XXX y buego el próximo eh- el y buego el próximo día [...] XXX XXX perro miró el- la jarrón y el jarrón no XXX XXX la rana se XXX y miró un bota [...] Y el perro (metió) su cabeza [...] Y buego el se miró XXX miró fuera XXX él pensó que se escapó [...] Bu- buego un- el perro se cayó [...] El otr- y buego el niño XXXX con la botella XXX XXX rompió [...] Buego fueron a buscarlo En el bosque [...] Y, y buego él miró [...] Hmm el miró en uno- en un hoyo [...] Pero un anim- un animal salió [...] E- el XXX perro salió a mirar las XXX que se fueron [...] BUEGO XXX él, el- los XXX abejas [...] Es- pasa XXX las abejas se enojaron [...] Y, y el niño siguió mirando otro [...] Hoyo en el árbol (1) pero no XXX ahí, uuh no vio (ningún) perro en el hoyo sólo un búho [...] Y las abejas seguían, se- persiguiendo (1) el perro [...]El búho se XXX, el niño XXX [...] XXX buscar para buscar el, el rana, esto es un, un roca [...] Y se agarró de- de unas hmm [...] Uh huh [...] Ramas [...] Este no eran ramas, era un venado [...] El venado se llevó al niño, el perro quería ir al niño [...] XXX XXX y buego XXX cerca de- le quitas la XXX [...] Eh el- el venado XXX XXX se cayeron [...] Hmm, en- en un lago [...] Buego se es- se cayeron en el agua SPSSSSHHH [...] Y se XXX buego oyeron algo [...] ¿podría ser el rana? [...] El ni- el niño dijo ssshhh al perro para no s- hacer ruido [...] Pero XXX del otro lado se- del árbol que ha caído y buscaron el rana con o- un- eh- un-otra rana [...] Con bebé- y ten- y tenían bebés [...] Buego el niño se levó una beb- una bebé para llegar al casa. El (dejó) los otros a- [...] Buego el niño se fue [...] A la casa [...] Uh huh [...] Huh okay.

Extract 8.6 Navarro family, son, Storytelling task. ENGLISH. Iteration #1

Once- once there was a kid and a dog, the kid got his net and pail to go s- to the lake and get something [...] He looked huh- he looked between trees XXX the lake [...] And and his dog- and then he found a lake [...] And a frog [...] The kid ran [...] then he tripped over [...] The root of a tree [...] The kid threw (his) things up and t- dog jumped up [...] And- then they made a big splash [...] And they all got wet [...] Ah- then he (saw) the frog [...] and he had the pa- the pail on his head [...] he wanted to get the frog [...] But the frog jumped up then he thought for a moment how to get the frog [...] He swam XXX (1) then he got his net [...] And the dog was on the (other) side, they stepped- on- the- root [...] climbed (2) the- the dog scared the fr- XXX tried to get the frog but- and then the kid tried to get it [...] BUT the frog fell down [...] And the kid got the dog [...] The- eh- the fr- the frog swam away [...] and he got XXX [...] And the- (1) the kid (1) wa- thr- was XXX or something [...] And XXX frog sad- became sad [...] Uh huh [...] Then the kid went away the- the frog stayed at the pond [...] Sure) [...] and the boy went back home [...] All soaking WET [...] The (frog) was sitting- on the- rock, he (wasn't) eating, not XXX [...] He was just sitting (1) and he was sad [...] Then he followed the tracks [...] He followed them in the house [...] the b- and the boy was taking a bath [...] Then the frog got- XXX and saw them [...] The- frog XXX, the boy saw him and the dog did too- then the fro jumped in the tub [...] And the boy was happy- THAT'S HIS BUTT [...] Hmmm he's NAKED

The example in Extract 8.7 was one of the two stories with the highest score for narrative organization. It was produced by Felipe García, a seven-year-old boy who was attending a school where English was the only medium of instruction.

Grammatically, the story in Extract 8.7 exhibits several non-standard features that suggest either a lack of acquisition of structures that would be expected in a child of this age exposed to sufficient Spanish input, or an erosion of structures that the child acquired and later lost. The first is use of the third person subjunctive *traiga* to set the background action of the story – where the imperfect *traía* or the present *trae* would be expected. The second is the non-standard *trompezó* for third person singular indicative of the verb *tropezar* – to stumble.[9] Consistent with writing in Spanish produced by college-aged heritage speakers (Beaudrie, 2012), the use of the preposition 'a' in this story is unstable – i.e. it is produced in some contexts where it would be expected, and absent in others. Also unstable is the use of the 'a personal' to mark human direct objects – e.g. *Miró al niño* = human direct object, but *persiguió a las huellas* ≠ non-human direct object. Finally, an interesting feature in Extract 8.7 is the semantic extension of the word *gorra* 'a soft cap/hat', with the meaning of hardhat or helmet. The bilingual reader will of course notice the lexical difference but morphological similarity between the English words 'hat'/'hardhat', which in monolingual Spanish would be rendered using two different words: *gorra/casco* – i.e. a 'hard hat'.

Despite these non-standard features, however, the action in Extract 8.7 is detailed and clear. The narrator provides insights into the characters' mental states and offers a coda to signal the end of the story – notice, however, that this coda is a calque of the English 'The end'.

In contrast, the story produced in English by Felipe (Extract 8.8) exhibits some non-standard features that would be consistent with a child of this age acquiring English as a second language, but is also constructed with greater complexity and greater command of narrative devices. For example, the narrator takes on the voice of the main character, adopting a first person point of view: 'I am Jim and I have a frog.' He incorporates the title of the book in his narrative, 'I looked outside and yelled oh frog, where are you?', and uses a structure most commonly found in literature: 'Down he fell in a pond.' This story also suggests a command of adjective placement in English, 'And little baby frogs'; irregular verbal morphology, 'I caught him'; and semantic distinctions of two verbs within the same lexical field, 'my frog saw some bees- [...] he looked under the log and he saw ...'. One non-standard feature of this story is the semantic extension which allows the narrator to use a word within the same lexical field to describe an action, e.g. 'They started to poke me' < *They started to sting* me; 'the bees fell down' < *the bees exited/left/flew away through a hole located at the bottom* of the honeycomb. Another was the creation of the structure 'left away', which combines the structures 'to leave' and 'go away'. The results for narrative organization and narrative structure are summarized in Appendix 9.

Extract 8.7 García family, son. Storytelling task. SPANISH. Iteration #1

> El niño traiga una red [...] Para atrapar un sapo, y luego entró un árbol y miró un sapo [...] se fue corriendo y se trompezó, ya- casi se cayeron a agarrar el sapo [...] el sapo le sonrió [...] Y la cubeta estaba en la ca- beza como una- como una gorra [...] trató de agarrarla pero se fue brincando [...] el niño estaba enojado [...] El- perro le dijo al niño que se sali- que el perro vaya por un lado y el niño por el otro [...] Y en vez de atrapar el sapo el sapo se cayó y atraparon al perro en vez [...] Y el- perro estaba triste entonces el niño lo sacó [...] y el- y el sapo estaba enojado [...] Y el niño se enojó con el sapo y el sapo se puso triste y el niño se fue [...] El sapo todavía quedaba triste mirando al niño [...] y el niño y el perro se fueron a la casa [...] Entonces dejaron al sapo en paz [...] el sapo estaba allí todavía en la piedra, todo triste en su [...] tronco [...] el sapo persiguió a las huellas, y entró a la casa del niño [...] y entró- y entró al baño y miró a- que es- que estaban en el bathtub se vin- el sapo estaba allí a un lado y el niño y el perro lo miraron [...] Entonces el sapo brincó y entró, [...] splish splash splush [Giggles] El fin.

Extract 8.8 García family, son. Storytelling task. ENGLISH. Iteration #1

I am Jim and I have a frog [...] I went to sleep [...] Then in the morning I woke up and my frog was gone [...] I looked in my boot [...] I looked outside and yelled oh frog, where are you? [...] my dog fell down, I caught him. [...] I went towards the forest and yelled, frog, where are you? [...] my frog saw some bees- I mean, my dog [...] Umm, [...] startled some bees [...] They started to poke me [...] the bees fell down [...] there they were sliding towards the dog, the boy looked in a hol- tree hole [...] An owl startled him and he fell [...] he looked [...] and saw a rock and looked around and got up [...] and climbed on it and [...] Yelled frog, where are you? [...] He didn't see the horns of a deer [...] That's [...] that he star- that a deer started running towards a cliff [...] S- the deer stopped, the boy fell off with his dog [...] Down he fell in a pond [...] and he splashed [...] he hear- he heard a croak from a frog, he looked under the log and he saw [...] TWO FROGS [...] And little baby frogs [...] So he just took a baby and left away [...] [Giggles]

Results for Verbal System

A total of 491 verb forms were collected from the 11 Spanish stories produced by the children during the first iteration of this task. Of these, 441 (90%) were in Spanish and 49 were in English. Only one hybrid verb form was found: *jumpó*, produced by Tomás Lara, and discussed above. Additionally, only one error in person and number agreement was found: *salió unos búhos*, produced by Ramón Villarreal. With the exception of two examples in which the narrator jumps from the present to the past without a trigger in the story, temporal relations were effectively articulated in all the stories.

All the children produced evidence of command of the preterite to encode the perfective aspect, and all but one produced the verb *estar* + gerund to encode progressive events; i.e. they were able to advance the action of the story. Nine children in the group (82%) produced evidence of use of the imperfect to encode the past imperfect aspect; i.e. they were able to distinguish between narrative foreground and background. Only four children in the group produced the subjunctive to encode irrealis clauses, a fact that is consistent with the context in which they were acquiring Spanish and with the stage in their linguistic development. As expected, three of the four children who provided evidence of subjunctive use were among the oldest in the group (aged seven, eight and nine). Only two stories include use of a modal verb + participle. Only one token of the pluperfect was found – *se habían caído*.

The most common errors involving verb forms include six tokens of non-target verb choice, e.g. *buscaron < encontraron* (to look for versus to find) and *perseguir < seguir* (chase versus follow), as well as elision or non-target choice of preposition, e.g. *van correr < van a correr* and *se asustó* *de ése < se asustó con ése.* Other errors, with less than two tokens each, were: use of the preterite to encode the past imperfect aspect; use of the imperfect to encode the past perfective aspect; and one example of the present subjunctive to encode the past imperfect aspect.

The results show that the children in these families possessed the narrative abilities to produce a story in Spanish and in English, with events successfully narrated in the past or in the present, and in chronological sequence. As Kao (2015: 35) reminds us, 'age is one of the primary factors affecting the general structures of children's narratives'. With the exception of one of the two youngest children in the group, the children whose narratives were included in this analysis were able to produce an age-appropriate story in Spanish despite the fact that they were living in environments with limited input beyond the immediate space of the home.

Examined as a group, the children's stories provide us with several indicators of lexical and structural pressure from English on Spanish. A deeper analysis, however, invites us to see beyond what features these children had lost – or had yet to develop – in order to fully appreciate what they did possess: stable gender, number and verbal systems; the ability to stay on task and on language while telling a story; as well as the strategic use of semantic extension, circumlocution, metaphor and metonym to fill a lexical gap, or to conceptualize relations between characters.

The preceding chapters have been an attempt to understand the language experience of 19 first-generation Latino families in the US Midwest. We have undertaken this endeavor by examining household language dynamics, as well as maternal self-perceptions, attitudes, motivations and strategies for intergenerational transmission of the family language. In a second stage, we have compared these perceptions with the children's language use, as well as their own attitudes and views about the viability of Spanish. In the next and last chapter, we take a step back from the finer grained, household-level analysis, and present a theoretical model of maintenance in communities with LEV for Spanish.

A few questions to continue the conversation ...

(1) From a very young age, we learn to tell stories through interaction. While hearing others' stories we learn implicitly about the features of good narrative structure (e.g. a hero, an antagonist, a climax, conflict resolution). Aside from fairytales, TV watching and reading of children's books, can you think of other common household practices in which children are exposed to and can participate in storytelling?

(2) What are some contextual and formal differences between stories told at school and stories told at home? What about stories told in

other public spaces? (Think, for example, of stories told during religious services.) What do these differences tell us about children's exposure to language(s) and about their opportunities to use it/them?

(3) Reilly *et al.* (2004) argue that documenting emerging narrative abilities is a good way to measure cognitive and linguistic development because, although children generally have command of the morphosyntactic structures of their language by the age of five, the process of learning to use complex structures and different discourse genres continues well into adolescence. Considering that the children in this study were attending schools where English was the medium of instruction, what type of influence might you expect on the way they told stories in Spanish?

Notes

(1) The total number of tokens for the first iteration of the children's storytelling task in Spanish was 3008. Nine truncated forms plus 'hmm', 'uh huh', 'ahm', 'ah' and 'oh' were excluded from the analysis.

(2) The total number of tokens for the second iteration of children's storytelling task in Spanish was 2945 (482 types). Twelve truncated forms plus 'hmm', 'uh huh', 'ahm', 'ah' and 'oh' were excluded from the analysis.

(3) For a more detailed explanation of why type/token ratio is not a good way to measure lexical diversity in a long text, and why it cannot be used without significant modification to compare two texts of different lengths, see Johansson (2009: 62). In essence: samples containing larger numbers of tokens give lower type/token values and vice versa.

(4) Mean length of utterance (MLU), which is a common measure of language productivity in monolingual children (Williamson, 2009), was not used here, heeding Wishard Guerra's (2008: 154) concerns about the difficulties of accurately comparing MLU across languages. For an elaboration of these difficulties, as well as several alternative measures of narrative production in bilingual children, see Muñoz *et al.* (2003).

(5) This scale, developed by two members of Schecter and Bayley's research team, was originally employed to analyze written stories.

(6) The following example was produced by Felipe García, a seven-year-old boy, during the second iteration of the storytelling task in Spanish. He correctly assigns grammatical gender and biological sex of the character as male but incorrectly marks the adjective as masculine. Notice *un rana*. The word *rana* presents the added difficulty of not being marked for gender, and thus requires the addition of *macho* 'male' or *hembra* 'female' to mark biological sex.

> Iban a atrapar a la eh- a-la-tor- ay [giggles]
> LRP: °A la rana°
> L17: Rana
> LRP: Uh huh
> L17: Que iban corriendo para atraparla
> [...]
> El niño y el perro se fueron pa la casa [...] Ahí estaba la rana todo solito [...] entonces se iba brincando a atraparlos, boing, boing, boing, entonces llegó a su casa.

(7)   Code-switching is understood here as a segment, larger than one word, produced in language A and inserted inter- or intra-sententially within the context of language B. Borrowing, by contrast, is understood as the use of a single word in language A within a clause in language B. Most often, the borrowed word is preceded by a determiner in the borrowing language, or agrees in gender and number with a noun or adjective adjacent to it, e.g. estas *bees*, *un* net.

(8)   In Schecter and Bayley (2002), evaluation is understood as the point of the narrative, or an answer to the question 'so what?' This form of evaluation about the purpose of telling this story was not found in any of the stories produced by the children either in Spanish or in English. Evaluation is understood here as the child's assessments of characters' mental states. The children's evaluation about the point of telling these stories may not be present in the data because they were prompted to tell them. Investigating this, however, is irrelevant to the purposes of the present study.

(9)   The insertion of /m/ between the root and the flexive morpheme in the verb *tropezar* – e.g. *trompezó, me trompiezo, se trompiezan* – is not a neologism, but is frequently produced in younger children exposed to informal registers of Mexican Spanish. In adult speakers of Mexican Spanish it is a linguistic stereotype signaling an uneducated, and most often rural, speaker. In this case, the data are insufficient to ascertain if the child knew both *tropezó* and *trompezó* but used the latter, if he acquired both and lost one, or if he was only exposed to *trompezó* at home and in the community. What is relevant for the purposes of ascertaining his level of competence in Spanish is that this form would not be expected in the oral production of a seven-year-old with a sufficient quality and amount of exposure to the family language.

9 Toward a Theoretical Model of Language Maintenance in Low Vitality Settings

Gabriela: Almost there

M. visited our workshop today and spoke about her work as a linguist, about her own experience as an immigrant from Eastern Europe and about raising two bilingual daughters. Every mom but one prepared a question for her. The conversation was frank and generous. M. spoke in English and a little Spanish. The moms took their English out for a test drive and switched to Spanish when they got more excited. All and all, it was a great session. However – not however, AND – we were all sad and worried. Carina was absent because she had been taken to the emergency room two days prior and was in intensive care.

Our session ends and Gabriela comes in with updates and a to-do list. Her official job description is bilingual liaison. If I had to describe her work, I would add: counselor, social worker, advocate, voice of reason, cheerleader. She speaks English with an accent, and when she speaks in Spanish she can switch vocabulary into three different dialects to accommodate her interlocutor. She is brave, hardworking and committed to this community when things look up and also when they're not looking pretty. She too is an immigrant, and raised her children mostly on her own. She knows. She takes out her list and begins asking questions. The women in the group start organizing. *Who is going to look after her son? What hospital is she in? Who is going to visit her? Should we take turns? Who has a car?* It is thus that I find myself adding my name to the list of potential babysitters for Saturday morning. The same with L., the second member of our research team, who is playing at a show that night, but writes down her name anyway. And this is the lesson: either you're in or you're out, but you can't do both. Either you want to learn about these women's experiences and you roll up your sleeves and get up close, or get out of town.

It is then that I receive a lesson in feminism and research protocol. As they organize visiting Carina, these women teach me that respect is walking with someone, not purporting to analyze their life from ten feet away. *How can you write about these networks of solidarity from the outside?* Feminism is, no more, no less, the recognition of the struggle, the fears, the talents, the joys of women at every stage, every condition. Seeing all women for what they are, regardless of socio-economic standing.

This chapter begins with what should be understood by now as the central claim of this book: that any model that attempts to account for minority language maintenance in LEV environments must take as a starting point the fact that intergenerational transmission is a gendered endeavor. Two important questions arise: (1) Is this too strong a claim? (2) Does this claim reify negative stereotypes about Latino fathers' engagement in their children's education and overall wellbeing? The simplest answer is no in both cases. A more thorough answer requires some clarification.

To begin with, we need a clarification about what this assertion is not. To state that mothers were key for the intergenerational transmission of Spanish in these 19 households – just as in most first-generation, two-parent households, where both parents are native speakers of the family language, is not an effort to erase Latino fathers' contribution to the health and development of their children. It is, rather, a description of the gendered distribution of childrearing tasks, in which the bulk of the children's socialization to language as well as the emotional and practical weight of household management and, more importantly, of maintaining bonds of kinship and affection, rest more heavily on the mother.

For a compelling example of Latino fathers' involvement in their children's educational and emotional development, the reader is invited to read Gallo's (2017) ethnography of first-generation Mexican fathers' engagement in their children's education in a LEV context. Although Gallo presents examples of fathers modelling linguistic appropriateness and evaluating their children's oral production in Spanish and in English (Gallo, 2017: 67), she does not offer counterevidence to the present argument. This is significant because the author's goal was not to describe household language dynamics, but to examine 'fathers' engagement in their children's educational lives to advance the goal of helping educators develop humanizing school policies and practices that create spaces to recognize and build upon students' and families' contributions to meet educational goals' (Gallo, 2017: 18). Careful examination of Gallo's data does not yield evidence of a New Latino Diaspora community where language transmission is not a gendered endeavor, but quite the contrary – first-generation households, very similar to the ones described here, in which both parents are engaged in a differential distribution of childrearing tasks.

Further, claiming that mothers in first-generation households are overwhelmingly responsible for the childrearing tasks related most closely to the intergenerational transmission of language is not the same as claiming that they are exclusively responsible for household language maintenance. As described in Chapter 1, language maintenance is a dynamic, long-term, three-component process in which all household members participate differentially over the family's lifespan. In other words, the mothers in these 19 households were central for language maintenance not because – or not exclusively because – of what they believed, but because what they did facilitated, or impeded, the conditions for maintenance. Why, in what ways, and under which conditions will be described below.

The centrality of mothers' engagement and beliefs in the early language development of monolingual children (Bojczyk *et al.*, 2016; Deckner *et al.*, 2006; Weigel *et al.*, 2006), bilingual children (Quiroz *et al.*, 2010; Yu, 2013) and monolingual children with a language impairment (Skibbe *et al.*, 2008) has been well documented. Outside of the context of the United States, mothers and grandparents have also been identified as the driving force behind the maintenance of different Indian languages by elementary school-aged heritage speakers in Australia (Bissoonauth, 2018). In their study of the effects of mothers' and fathers' play on early vocabulary development in mono- and bilingual families in Finland, Lundén and Silvén (2011: 551) find that 'mothers often play an important role in supporting paternal involvement by encouraging certain levels of participation based on cultural values', and that very early on, 'the combined effects of the mother and father are essential ingredients in creating a path of adaptive language development for the child' (Lundén & Silvén, 2011: 554).

The fact that the mothers in this study were influenced by, and drew material and emotional support from, personal networks of interaction that were overwhelmingly characterized by gender segregation, locality, multiplexity and Spanish language dominance is, for me, a second and equally pertinent reason to argue that intergenerational language transmission in LEV environments is a gendered endeavor. As described in Chapter 2, these networks were important sources of language input and opportunities for use and socialization for the children and teens in these families.

One contribution of the present study is the claim that this maternal influence extends well beyond early childhood. If, as argued in Velázquez

(2013), intergenerational transmission depends on the *quality and amount of exposure, children's opportunities for use* and *relevance*, in first-generation working-class households the first two factors are deeply entwined, conceptualized and evaluated as one of many childrearing duties performed primarily by the mother. In other words, I argue here in favor of an understanding of intergenerational transmission (e.g. the *sine qua non* condition for maintenance at the level of the family and the community) as a form of mothering.

Mothering, of course, is not, and need not be, the exclusive purview of women. The fact that the families in this study lived in households with two heterosexual parents owes more to the researcher's need for comparison among households than to the universality of this family arrangement. Indeed, in other language minority households, childrearing may by carried out by a single parent, two parents of the same gender, two parents who speak different languages, or by other adults such as grandparents or other members of the extended family. We will do well, then, to refine our argument: *mothers* will be understood here in its narrow sense, to refer specifically to the mothers in the 19 households in this study. When used in a broader sense, *mothers* will be understood as *primary caregivers*, in order to include other family arrangements.

It is important to remember at this point in our discussion that the cases presented in this book represent the most common pattern of parenthood (that is, of heterosexual couples). As such, the gender dimension of our analysis arises as especially significant. The future study of families with two parents of the same gender, for example, could potentially offer a different portrait; that is, a distribution of childrearing tasks not based on expectations of gender, but a distribution nonetheless.

A fruitful question, then, might be this: If we concede that, just like the idea of motherhood, the idea of gender is socially constructed, how can a man (socially constructed as a man) expect to fulfill the social expectations embedded within the concept of motherhood? That is to say that the very idea of parenthood is not based on the biological characteristics of the parent, but is rather an idea based on the roles, constructs and practices assigned to different genders. In this light, childrearing is a gendered endeavor *precisely* because it is socially constructed.

Care, affection and intergenerational transmission are related to a particular idea of motherhood centered on a specific set of social expectations of women. What is important for the intergenerational transmission of a minority language, then, is not maternal engagement conceived simply as women's work, but rather the household presence of an adult figure who fulfills the expectations socially attributed to women.

We arrive now at our second point of clarification. To paraphrase Raymond Carver: what we talk about when we use the words *parental* and *padres de familia* when describing the constellation of attitudes, motivations and practices related to the intergenerational transmission of a minority language. A review of the literature on attitudes toward children's development of bilingualism reveals an abundance of studies whose conclusions are presented under the umbrella term of *parental* attitudes, but whose methods sections reveal that mother respondents outnumber fathers, often in a 3:1 proportion (Endo, 2013; Gerena, 2011; Giacchino-Baker & Piller, 2006; López, 2013; Park & Sarkar, 2007; Phinney *et al.*, 2001; Rodríguez *et al.*, 2017; Yu, 2013; Zhang, 2009; Zhang & Slaughter-Defoe, 2009). Other studies make assumptions about parental attitudes but quote only mothers (Guardado, 2008, 2009), or make generalizations about language maintenance and loss in minority language households based on interviews conducted in middle-class families and a sample smaller than five (Endo, 2013; Guardado, 2008, 2009). An exception to this is Schecter *et al.* (2013), in which both mothers and fathers were interviewed about the reasons behind their personal decisions regarding home language use.

A third group of studies on parental attitudes include data on both fathers' and mothers' perceptions about their children's language development, but are based on surveys without verification of who completed the instrument or details about the respondents. See, for example, Young and Tran (2013) for Vietnamese as a heritage language in California, and Oladejo (2010) for EFL in Taiwan. An illustrative example of this is Shannon and Milian (2002), who report on the results of a survey intended to collect parental attitudes regarding bilingual education in Colorado, and about their children's participation in a dual language program. The authors present an analysis of the 1043 surveys that were completed and returned, but fail to address in their discussion the fact that the study itself was born of a meeting primarily attended by mothers (italics are mine):

All bilingual programs in Colorado would be extremely vulnerable if such an initiative passed, including dual language programs. At the time, there were 10 programs in the Colorado Consortium of Dual Language Programs. In April, the consortium met at their monthly meeting and the claims made by the proponents of the initiative were brought up for discussion by parents and teachers. *The parents present at the meeting, mostly Mexican mothers,* knew that these claims did not reflect their reality of parents who had willingly chosen to place their children in a dual language program, who understood the purpose of these programs, and whose children were becoming both bilingual and biliterate. These parents attended the meeting precisely to find out how they could counter the anti-bilingual initiative and preserve the programs they had chosen for their children. *Those attending the meeting, including this group of mothers, suggested that a study could help clarify how parents who send their children to dual language programs view the topic of choice, their understanding of the purpose of these programs, and their opinions on the effectiveness of these programs in teaching the two target languages.* (Shannon & Milian, 2002: 685, italics added)

Data on fathers' attitudes and fathers' social networks were not collected in the present study: not because they were less important to their family's wellbeing; not because they don't have an opinion about bilingualism; not because they don't participate in family language planning; but primarily because the everyday tasks of socialization to Spanish and the bulk of participation in social networks where children were exposed to Spanish were performed by the mothers. Much could be gained by a secondary stage of research, ripe for investigation – male communities of practice in LEV communities (Eckert & McConnell-Ginet, 1992), male forms of interaction in Spanish that could foster children's exposure to and opportunities for use. I recognize, however, that this is one of my limitations as a researcher. As a female, middle-class speaker, my participation in these intimate male spaces would either be precluded or would change the interaction altogether.

The decision to transmit or not transmit one's family language, the ways in which our intentions may collide with our actions and/or with the material conditions in which we raise a family, and the potential tensions between partners, between parents and children or between parents and other adults do not, of course, happen in isolation.

Ultimately, language maintenance is part of a broader power struggle, which is mostly fought through discourses around language. These discourses shape the ensuing actions, thus altering the nature of maintenance itself. The bilingual household may indeed be understood as a speech community with members who plan, manage and evaluate other family members' language practices. And, as explained in Chapter 1: larger, community-wide language ideologies fuel parental language choices; these choices result in sustained language practices; these practices result in language socialization; and this socialization sets the basis for the longer-term maintenance or loss of the family language.

I have argued here that language experience takes place along at least five dimensions: the materiality of language and its use; the perception of the speakers about these conditions; their beliefs about self and others in the speech community; their emotional responses about language; and their emotional responses about language users. It follows, then, that speaking about the mechanisms of maintenance is per force speaking as well about the mechanisms of loss. For, despite linguists' affinity for discrete categories and linear processes, language in the real world is neither discrete nor static.

As illustrated by the experience of these 19 families, household language dynamics and parental language use strategies change as the family's life cycle changes. This in turn has direct implications for the construction of an explanatory model. A model of this kind – which is to say, a model that is based on an honest intellectual curiosity about minority language use and transmission from the perspective of the household – will describe, explain and operationalize these mechanisms, but will not purport to predict ultimate language use outcomes.

Should we mourn for the need to forgo this predictive power? In describing the language experience of Mexican Americans in the US Southwest, Martínez (2009) presents an alternative view – an emphasis, he argues, not on a prediction of what language use will look like, but an exercise in imagination about the ways in which maintaining the family and community language can serve to support the overall socio-economic health of the speakers:

> The sociolinguistic study of Spanish in the Southwest has been, from its inception, a highly speculative task. The main motivation of these studies seems to be the prediction of the future viability of the language. Like the weather forecaster predicting a downpour or a hurricane, the sociolinguist attempted to offer a clear and precise vision of the future. But the type of future projection that I see as urgent these days is not necessarily that of speculation. Just like weathercasters can err in their predictions, so too sociolinguists fail in their speculative endeavors. [...] The projections into the future that I have in mind have to do with the implications of maintenance for the overall development of Spanish speaking communities. [...] Not independent of language maintenance, but precisely because of language maintenance. (Martínez, 2009: 128)

In the preceding chapters I have operationalized the concept of LEV in Spanish/English bilingual communities in the New Latino Diaspora. I have also argued that in these communities language maintenance and loss happen in what I have called *the small spaces*: household interactions that are by definition iterative, informal, intimate, hard to access for researchers, and in constant tension and negotiation by actors within and outside the nuclear family. That is, although perceptions are important and fuel much of our efforts as social actors, they are not enough to explain patterns of household language maintenance. It is important to distinguish in this matter and all others the line between *the way we think* – about ourselves, and others – and *the way we do*. It is also important to contrast the unruly beast called *parenting* – in equal parts messy and beautiful and frustrating and obstreperous – with the slick, shiny, orderly creature called *giving an opinion*, which is a controlled performance of self.

A final *what if*: What if there is a yet unknown, unresearched community in the Midwest or in another New Latino Diaspora community, where the distribution of childrearing and household tasks falls primarily on the fathers, so that the maintenance of the practices and spaces conducive to children's exposure to and development of Spanish falls primarily on the father? What if, for example, there is a community in the Midwest or beyond where children's lack of acquisition of the family language is evaluated by other adults as a failure of the father's parenting duties, instead of the mother's? The existence of this hypothetical speech community is of course, possible, but not without recourse to several assumptions that cannot as yet be verified. We are left, then, in Ockham's razor territory: between two competing theories, the one requiring the fewest assumptions is most likely to be correct.

I have argued here that language dynamics in immigrant households differ from those in language majority households in at least four distinct ways: participation in different (local, national, transnational) speech communities; the physical and social dislocation of household members; the power imbalances that result from these dislocations; and differences in the acquisition of and socialization to language(s) and language varieties. In first-generation minority language households, children and parents are undergoing different but intersecting processes of language acquisition and, while parents in these households (much like their language-majority counterparts) are socializing their children to and through their family language, in language-minority households children are also socializing their parents through implicit and explicit attempts to select the language of the environment, through cultural and linguistic brokering, and sometimes through explicit instruction, correction and evaluation of parental L2 speech.

Starting from this context, I have maintained the centrality of maternal perceptions of the benefit/cost of language transmission and agency, because these mothers must negotiate transnational and local pressures either to foster bilingualism in their family or to encourage subtractive assimilation to English. Additionally, because they bear the primary responsibility for daily childrearing tasks and because they regulate much of their children's schedules, activities and opportunities for interaction outside the home, the mothers play a fundamental role in family language planning and language management.

While both the mothers and teenagers in this study reported positive attitudes toward Spanish, comparison of mother and youth language motivations for use and self-perceptions of proficiency presents us with a compelling household pattern. For the mothers, the motivations to use and transmit Spanish clustered around religion, cultural transmission and maintenance of kinship and affection ties. For several mothers in this study, intergenerational transmission of Spanish was also verted with instrumental value, in that it could accrue professional advantages to the second generation. For the teens in this study, the strongest motivation to use Spanish was to serve as language brokers between adults who were dominant in either language. Regarding self-perceptions of proficiency, the mothers rated all skills in Spanish as very easy and all skills in English as somewhat hard or very hard, whereas most of the teens rated all skills in English as very easy and for 50% of them reading and writing in Spanish as somewhat hard. In fact, the only skill in Spanish rated as very easy by the majority of the youths was aural comprehension.

A major axis of family language dynamics was the distribution of household duties and the amount of interaction between each child and each parent. In the overwhelming majority of these households, the mother was responsible for the day-in-day-out tasks of childrearing,

because the father worked outside the home most of the day and interacted with the children primarily in the evenings and on weekends (this
included those households in which the mother held part-time employment in the service sector).

The experience of the 19 families in this study provides us with important insights into the processes of language maintenance and loss. The
children in these families lived in home environments that favored direct
and indirect exposure to Spanish, but that it was not equally viable for all
activities in which the parents and children interacted. Because of their
limited exposure to adult bilinguals in both household and public spaces,
language choice for the children and teenagers in these families was compartmentalized along the axes of diglossia and generational cohort. While
the mother was the de facto source of Spanish input and opportunities for
literacy development, the father played a key function in the children's
language development both in families in which he refused to switch to
Spanish, and in families in which he addressed them in English.

In these households, both the parents and children engaged in efforts
to manage household language dynamics. Compared to their parents,
however, the language management strategies employed by the children
and adolescents in these families involved greater sensitivity to context
and communicative goals, and most commonly related to language brokering, and evaluation/monitoring of their parents' use of English.

In first-generation Latino families in LEV communities in the
Midwest, adults with the potential to influence the family's linguistic environment may or may not be the parents and may or may not reside within
the same household. This influence can take place through: increased
exposure to either Spanish or English for the children; criticism or praise
of parental strategies; shared caregiving; modeling of parenting behaviors;
access to resources through the medium of the family language; offering
of advice; providing expressed evaluations of language, language varieties
and language users; and generally providing (or failing to provide) a
speech community where children can develop the linguistic and pragmatic skills that will potentially allow them to use their family language
with someone other than their parents.

Despite the lexical and structural pressure of English on their Spanish,
the children interviewed in these 19 families were able to tell stories,
respond and engage in Spanish with the members of the research team.
They were part of larger extended families and communities of practice
in which adults provided them with abundant input in the family language. On the other side of the equation, not all children in these households showed the same level of linguistic competence and, as reported by
their mothers and themselves, Spanish was not the most viable language
for several household interactions. As expected, a greater use of Spanish
was reported and observed in the parents than the children. None of the
school-aged children was receiving instruction in Spanish.

In the preceding chapters I have argued that the experience of Spanish speakers in Nebraska shares features with that of speakers in other communities within and beyond the Midwest. At the household level, some of the features shared with bilingual households elsewhere include: the importance of birth order for language exposure; parents' and teachers' overestimation of exposure to Spanish input and underestimation of the time and effort needed to develop literacy in the family language; and, in general, positive attitudes toward Spanish. At the level of the community some of these shared features include: limited institutional support; limited opportunities to develop literacy; diglossia; language brokering by the second generation; language loss at the individual level and maintenance at the level of the ethnic community; and discursive construction of the minority language as the marked 'other'.

Are we then observing what maintenance looks like at this point in each family's life cycle, or a stage in a process of language loss? And if we cannot know for sure, is it worth examining their experience? Yes, it is. And with this yes we arrive, finally, at the issue of social class. For we cannot examine the experience of immigrant families in the United States without problematizing the fact that, in public discourse as well as in many institutional interactions, the use of languages other than English by working-class speakers is seen as a problem, while it is seen as an asset for those in middle- and upper-class families. At the beginning of this book the reader was presented with the following notation to describe the situation of Spanish in LEV communities in the New Latino Diaspora:

$$\frac{P}{n-P} : \frac{E/S2}{S1/E'}$$

This notation describes a situation of diglossia where prestige functions and much of the language policy and language planning are conducted by monolingual speakers of English, by L2 speakers of Spanish and/or by speakers of exocentric varieties of Spanish. Two features follow from this state of affairs: first, that in LEV communities in the New Latino Diaspora middle- and working-class speakers of Spanish can be members of the same language community without necessarily being members of the same speech community; and secondly, that for members of the local speech community Spanish is vested with social capital, while for middle-class L2 speakers and speakers of exocentric varieties it is often a source of personal capital.

Contra previous models of language vitality, I will end this chapter by claiming that in New Latino Diaspora communities Spanish is not maintained at the level of the community because of demographic density, historical precedent or institutional support, but because it is vested with social capital which allows its speakers to access local networks of solidarity.

One of the main strands in the discussion presented here has been that speakers do not choose a language or language variety purely because of emotional or aesthetic reasons; they do so because they find it to be the most viable option to access and share social capital. Thus, if we truly understand sociolinguistic competence as a source of personal and social capital – with emphasis on both the linguistic *and* the social – it becomes clear that we cannot afford to see minority language maintenance as an all-or-nothing proposition, because in this, as in so many other instances, all or nothing propositions are easier to predicate on other people's capital. Exocentric perspectives of family and community language use allow us to discount practices, bonds and resources accrued through participation in social networks where the minority language is vested with social capital. The perspective presented in the preceding chapters, however, entails an understanding of the maintenance of language as the maintenance of social bonds. The maintenance of these bonds is fundamental for the overall health and viability of families and communities.

A few questions to continue the conversation ...

(1) Other than the examples mentioned in this book, can you think of any other gendered social practices common in your community?
(2) How does changing the material conditions of the household change the conditions for language maintenance?
(3) Think about your own childhood. Remember one or two family activities closely related to language socialization (for example, religious services, birthday celebrations, storytelling, scolding, etc.). Who taught you how to participate in them?

10 Conclusion

Julia: But they tell me I don't speak Spanish

Julia is a fourth-generation Mexican American from Texas who married a man from Mexico. Her great-grandparents emigrated to Texas from Coahuila. *My great grandma crossed when they put the border there.* Her family were migrant workers who lived in Nebraska part of the year to work in the fields, which is the reason why Julia and her sisters were born here. *When people tell me 'go back where you came from', hello? I'm from here.* As a Mexican American, Julia speaks Chicano varieties of Spanish and English. At school she is a paraprofessional, and part of her job is to help with the English classes that most of the moms in our group attend every week. Her desk is at the back of the room, and during our sessions she follows our conversations while doing her work, but never participates. Over the course of several weeks, I notice an underlying tension because one or two of the moms correct her lexical choices and her pronunciation in Spanish, or criticize her when she code-switches. Because of this, I've made a conscious effort to include her, to share snacks, to chat – and code-switch – with her after every meeting.

Today, the topic of our group discussion was: 'common fears about being bilingual, or living with bilinguals in the same household'. We talked about the fear of discrimination, about the third space, about identity: *Where do I belong? What does it mean to be American? Does one language equal one nation?* After the moms go home, I speak with a school visitor for about ten minutes. Julia waits for me.

You know, those things you said today, about feeling like you don't belong ... This is the beginning of a 45-minute conversation about the very personal, very emotional, very powerful things we had just been discussing. And these are some of the things that Julia shares with me. An hour later, I sit in a café and write as fast as I can, trying not to forget them. The main points, as I remember them: It's annoying and hurtful when the moms in the group correct her. *But you understood what I said, right? So why are you giving me a hard time?* It's annoying when they ask for her help in English and then criticize her Spanish. *Hey, I speak both*, she thinks, but doesn't say. Doesn't want to antagonize. It's annoying when moms accept correction from the Anglo teacher, but not from her. That's in part why she places the dictionary on the desk when they're working on homework. Is she calling on outside authority? For her? For the moms? For both? And then comes the hardest part: *I get their experiences of discrimination, but there's nothing they can tell me that I haven't lived through.* Being called names and being spit at in school when she was a child, and the teacher doing nothing about it. She tells me that's why, as an adult, she taught her children not to discriminate, and to name racism when they see it. *My tortillas are not like yours, but they are MY tortillas.* Not being Mexican enough among Mexicans, not Texan enough in Texas, not Nebraskan enough in Nebraska. Cue inevitable quote of Edward James Olmos playing Selena Quintanilla's father. *Before anything else, we're human.* I invite Julia to talk about this with the rest of the group during one of our workshop sessions. She's not sure. Doesn't want a confrontation, doesn't want conflict. I tell her that it would be an opportunity to learn for all of us. She's not sure.

Two weeks later, as I start to put my things away, Julia asks me to leave my notes about bilingual acquisition and code-switching up on the whiteboard. She says she wants to write them down, that she wants to understand for herself. Earlier this morning I've used our conversations as examples of code-switching skills in action. She was *glued* to what I was saying. *Riveted* to be hearing that there is a theory for what she knows as everyday life. For the first time in all these months, she raised her hand three times to make a comment.

Rarely do the urgent and the important so squarely align. The last pages of this book are written in a political context characterized by a marked animus against many of the families that live in the neighborhoods where the present study was conducted. On 2 August 2017, President Donald J. Trump announced a proposal to reduce the number of immigrants admitted to the country.[1] With this plan, which would designate English proficiency as one of the preferred preconditions for admission, the 45th President of the United States dismisses both the lived experience of the 60.3 million people who as of 2013 spoke a language other than English at home,[2] and the multilingual heritage of this country – a heritage that includes, among millions, Thomas Jefferson (*English, French, Italian, Latin*); Benjamin Franklin (*English, French, Italian*); John Adams (*English, French, Latin*) and James Madison (*English, Greek, Latin, Hebrew*).

On 5 September of the same year, Jefferson Beauregard Sessions III, Attorney General of the United States, stood before the nation to announce the end of the Deferred Action for Childhood Arrivals program. Signed into law by President Barack Obama in 2012, this program granted work permits and temporary respite from deportation to undocumented immigrants brought into the country as children.[3] In his address, Sessions made use of implicature and misstatements[4] to present the thousands of young unauthorized immigrants who have benefited from DACA as criminals, terrorists, and a threat to the freedom, safety, and prosperity of this nation. Not some generalized other, not some fuzzy abstraction that will fade away with the next news cycle, but concrete youths, with names, families, talents, and faces that I see even as I type these lines.

This is a book about the maintenance and loss of a family language in everyday intimate household settings. Is it political? It is, per force. 'Wherever the relevance of speech is at stake, matters become political by definition', writes Hannah Arendt (1958: 4) in *The Human Condition*, 'for speech is what makes man a political being [...] And whatever men do or know or experience can make sense only to the extent that it can be spoken about'. This is also a book that takes a stance, an argument that situates itself within a long tradition of researchers who conceive of the study of language use in US Latino communities as a socially engaged endeavor (Bernal-Enríquez & Hernández Chávez, 2003; Fishman, 1989; García, 1993; Martínez, 2009; Peñalosa, 1981; Zentella, 1995, 2002, 2016). Almost four decades ago, in an essay addressing the theoretical and methodological challenges of the then nascent field of Chicano sociolinguistics, Fernando Peñalosa (1981) argued:

> And because scientific research of any sort affects people, all of us, natural and social scientists alike, must consider the possible effects of our research on the welfare of human beings. Since I subscribe to this viewpoint, I cannot claim complete objectivity, only honesty as I state my biases: a firm commitment to cultural pluralism and a belief in the inherent worth of every human being, ethnic group, and variety of language; further, that sociolinguistic research pertaining to the Chicano must be judged in terms of its potential to benefit or harm the Chicano people. Social research is thus considered inseparable from social action. (Peñalosa, 1981: 3)

The maintenance and transmission of linguistic and cultural resources in Latino communities is indeed of the utmost importance, not as a nostalgic deference to the parents, but as a source for resilience in the children. As Villenas and Moreno (2001: 672) write: 'Mothering that takes place in an ambience of anti-immigrant xenophobia involves the psychological work of teaching cultural dignity and integrity in the midst of cultural assault'. Latino families in this and other New Latino Diaspora communities will endure, survive and thrive once more not in spite of these resources, but in large part because of them – and often because of what Villenas and Moreno (2001: 672) call Latina mothers' 'willful act of imagining and practicing alternative ways of community, family, and nation'. The question is at what cost, and with how much human potential wasted.

In *Historia de un flemón, una mujer y dos hombres* by Argentinian playwright Osvaldo Dragún (1982 [1965]), an impoverished salesman with a tooth abscess and a fever is about to die in the middle of a Buenos Aires subway station because he cannot afford a doctor. Amid the indifference of rush-hour passengers, he shouts at the audience: *Listen to me! I have to matter to you, because when I die, you are going to be missing a piece of yourselves. Listen to me! These three trains only work if they are my blood and they run through my veins! Listen to me! Don't whistle by! It doesn't hurt anymore, yes ..., but my face, doesn't it tell you anything?* (Dragún, 1982 [1965]: 65).[5] And thus, the last paragraph of this book is not about what immigrant households lose when intergenerational language transmission is interrupted, but about the cost to us all, independent of ethnicity and language ability. Inasmuch as we are economically engaged, interdependent social agents, the waste of human potential is an affront to all. This is not, dear reader, a story about *them*. It is not a story about aliens on forgotten exoplanets. It is a story about you and me, about the type and quality of the communities in which we want to live. It is, dare I say it? A story about *us*.

Lincoln, Nebraska, September 2017

Notes

(1)   Bennett, B. (2017) Trump pushes to sharply cut the number of legal immigrants and move to a 'merit based' immigration system. *Los Angeles Times*, 2 August. Online edition. See http://www.latimes.com/politics/washington/la-na-essential-washington-updates-trump-is-pushing-for-a-merit-based-1501681787-htmlstory.html.
(2)   US Census Bureau (2015b) *Detailed Languages Spoken at Home and Ability to Speak English for the Population 5 Years and Over for United States: 2009–2013*. American Community Survey 5-year Estimates. See https://www.census.gov/data/tables/2013/demo/2009-2013-lang-tables.html.
(3)   The Pew Hispanic Research Center estimates that, since its inception, DACA has shielded some 790,000 youths from deportation (Krogstad, 2017). Unauthorized immigrants from Mexico make up more than three-quarters of all DACA recipients. A large number of them are bilingual.
(4)   C-SPAN (2017) Attorney General Sessions on DACA, 5 September. Transcript. See https://www.c-span.org/video/?433616-1/attorney-general-rescinds-daca-program.
(5)   '¡Óiganme, tiene que importarles de mí ..., porque cuando yo muera va a faltarles un pedazo! ¡Óiganme! ¡Estos tres subtes solamente sirven si son mi sangre y corren por mis venas! ¡Óiganme! ¡No pasen silbando a mi lado! Ya no me duele, sí ..., pero mi cara, ¿no les dice nada?' (Dragún, 1982 [1965]: 65).

Appendices

Appendix 1. Factors for Language Vitality Assessment

Vitality measures for Spanish in NLD communities (in gray)

Factor 1: Intergenerational language transmission

5 Safe	4 Unsafe	3 Definitively endangered	2 Severely endangered	1 Critically endangered	0 Extinct
Language used by all ages	Language used by some children in all domains and by all children in some domains	Language used mostly by parent generation and up	Language used mostly by grandparent generation and up	Language used by very few speakers, great-grandparent generation	No speakers

Factor 2: Absolute Number of Speakers (Specific to each community)

Factor 3: Proportion of speakers within the total population

5 Safe	4 Unsafe	3 Definitively endangered	2 Severely endangered	1 Critically endangered	0 Extinct
All speak language	Nearly all speak it	A majority speaks it	A minority speaks it	Very few speak it	No speakers

Factor 4: Trends in existing language domains

5 Universal use	4 Multilingual parity	3 Dwindling domains	2 Limited domains	1 Highly limited domains	0 Extinct
Language used in all domains, all functions	Two or more languages used in most social domains and for most functions	Language used in home domains and for many functions, but dominant language begins to penetrate home domains	Language used in limited social domains and functions	Language used in very restricted domains, very few functions	Language not used in any domain or function

Factor 5: Response to new domains and media

5 Dynamic	4 Robust	3 Receptive	2 Coping	1 Minimal	0 Inactive
Language used in all new domains	Language used in most new domains	Language used in many domains	Language used in some new domains	Language used in few new domains	Language not used in new domains

Factor 6: Materials for language education and literacy

5	4	3 → → →	← ← ← 2	1 Minimal	0
Writing used in administration and education	Children are developing literacy Writing not used in administration	Children may be exposed to written form at school Literacy not promoted through media	Literacy not part of school curriculum Written materials only useful for some members of community	Practical orthography Some written material	No orthography

Source: Adapted from Brenzinger *et al.* (2003).

Appendix 2. Adult Instrument

Place and date of interview: _____

Interviewee ID # _____   Interviewer: _____

Part 1. Demographic information

Number of household members: Adults: _____   Ages: _____   Gender: _____

                                Children: _____   Ages: _____   Gender: _____

Languages spoken in household: _____

(1) About the respondent

Gender: _____   Age: _____   Languages spoken: _____   Occupation: _____

Years of residence in the US/NE: _____   Place of origin: _____

Years of schooling in Spanish: _____   In English: _____   Type of schooling in English: _____

(2) About the respondent's partner

Gender: _____   Age: _____   Languages spoken: _____   Occupation: _____

Years of residence in the US/NE: _____   Place of origin: _____

Years of schooling in Spanish: _____   In English: _____   Type of schooling in English: _____

(3) About the respondent's children [listed from eldest to youngest]

Child 1: Gender: _____ Age: _____ Languages spoken: _____

Place of birth: _____

Years of schooling in Spanish: _____ Type of schooling in Spanish: _____

Years of schooling in English: _____ Type of schooling in English: _____

Child 2: Gender: _____ Age: _____ Languages spoken: _____

Place of birth: _____

Years of schooling in Spanish: _____ Type of schooling in Spanish: _____

Years of schooling in English: _____ Type of schooling in English: _____

Child 3: Gender: _____ Age: _____ Languages spoken: _____

Place of birth: _____

Years of schooling in Spanish: _____ Type of schooling in Spanish: _____

Years of schooling in English: _____ Type of schooling in English: _____

Child 4: Gender: _____ Age: _____ Languages spoken: _____

Place of birth: _____

Years of schooling in Spanish: _____ Type of schooling in Spanish: _____

Years of schooling in English: _____ Type of schooling in English: _____

[Use additional pages if needed.]

Part 2. Respondent's social network

Antes de que empecemos a platicar sobre el desarrollo del español y del inglés en sus niños, le voy a preguntar algunas cosas sobre su experiencia personal. Le voy a pedir que piense en las personas que usted considere más cercanas a usted, pero que no vivan en su casa. No tiene que decirme sus nombres, puede decirme nada más 'mi hermano menor', 'mi amiga L', 'mi vecina', etc. ¿Ya? ¿Quiénes son?

[Before talking about the development in Spanish and English in your children, I'm going to ask you a few things about your personal experience. I'm going to ask you to think about the people whom you consider closest to you, that do not live in your household. You don't have to tell me their names, you can just say 'my youngest brother', 'my friend L', 'my neighbor', etc. Ready? Who are they?]

Persona	¿Dónde vive?	¿En qué idioma(s) habla mayormente con él/ella?
1.		
2.		
3.		
4.		
5.		

[Use additional pages if needed.]

Ahora le voy a pedir que piense en cinco personas que usted ve más de tres veces en una semana normal y que no viven en su casa. ¿Ya? ¿Quiénes son?

[Now I'm going to ask you to think about five people whom you see more than three times in a normal week, and who do not live in your household. Ready? Who are they?]

Persona	¿Dónde vive?	¿En qué idioma(s) habla mayormente con él/ella?
1.		
2.		
3.		
4.		
5.		

[Use additional pages if needed.]

Part 3. Perceived language competence

En esta parte le voy a pedir que escoja una de las siguientes respuestas, o alguna otra, si se le hace que describe mejor su situación. ¿Lista?
[In this part, I'm going to ask you to choose one of the following answers, or any other, if you feel that it better describes your situation. Ready?]

(a) ¿Qué tan fácil o difícil se le hace ...?
    [For you, how easy or how hard is it to ...]

	Muy fácil [very easy]	Más o menos fácil [Somewhat easy]	Más o menos difícil [Somewhat hard]	Muy difícil [very hard]	Otro [Other]
Hablar el español [Speaking Spanish]					
Entender el español [Understanding Spanish]					
Leer en español [Reading in Spanish]					
Escribir en español [Writing in Spanish]					
Hablar el inglés [Speaking English]					
Entender el inglés [Understanding English]					
Leer en inglés [Reading in English]					
Escribir en inglés [Writing in English]					

Ahora le voy a pedir que haga un poco de memoria ...
[Now, I'm going to ask you to remember a few things ...]

(b) ¿Se acuerda? [Do you remember ...]

   ¿Cuáles son las últimas tres cosas que leyó en español? _____
   [What are the last three things you read in Spanish?]

   ¿Cuáles son las últimas tres cosas que escribió en español? _____
   [What are the last three things you wrote in Spanish?]

¿Cuáles son las últimas tres cosas que leyó en inglés? _____
[What are the last three things you read in English?]

¿Cuáles son las últimas tres cosas que escribió en inglés? _____
[What are the last three things you wrote in English?]

Fuera de las personas que viven en su casa y sin contarme a mí, ¿cuando
fue la última vez que habló en español? ¿Con quién? _____
[Other than the people who live in your home, and without counting
me, when was the last time you spoke Spanish? With whom?]

Fuera de las personas que viven en su casa y sin contarme a mí, ¿cuando
fue la última vez que habló en inglés? ¿Con quién? _____
[Other than the people who live in your home, and without counting
me, when was the last time you spoke English? With whom?]

Part 4. Patterns of household language use

(a) [See additional form]

(b) En una semana normal … ¿Con quién hablan español sus hijos? ¿Con
quién hablan inglés?
[In a normal week … with whom do your children speak Spanish/
English?]

(c) En una semana normal … ¿Sus niños ven televisión en español?
(ejemplos)
[In a normal week … do your children watch TV in Spanish?
(examples)]

(d) En una semana normal … ¿Sus niños oyen música en español?
(ejemplos)
[In a normal week … do your children listen to music in Spanish?
(examples)]

(e) ¿Sus niños saben leer en español? Si saben ¿cómo aprendieron?
[Do your children know how to read in Spanish? If they do, how did
they learn?]

(f) ¿Sus niños saben escribir en español? Si saben ¿cómo aprendieron?
[Do your children know how to write in Spanish? If they do, how did
they learn?]

Part 5. Parental understandings of bilingualism, maintenance

(a) En su opinión …
[In your opinion …]

¿Cuáles son algunas cosas buenas de hablar español?
[What are some good things about speaking Spanish?]

¿Cuáles son algunas cosas malas de hablar español?
[What are some bad things about speaking Spanish?]

¿Cuáles son algunas cosas buenas de hablar inglés?
[What are some good things about speaking English?]

¿Cuáles son algunas cosas malas de hablar inglés?
[What are some bad things about speaking English?]

(b) ¿Qué tan importante es ...?
[How important is it ...]

	Muy importante	Más o menos importante	Poco importante	No es importante
... para usted? [for you to ...]				
Poder entender el español [understand Spanish]				
Poder hablar en español [speak Spanish]				
Poder leer en español [read Spanish]				
Poder escribir en español [write Spanish]				
... que sus hijos? [that your children ...]				
Puedan entender el español [understand Spanish]				
Puedan hablar en español [speak Spanish]				
Puedan leer en español [read Spanish]				
Puedan escribir en español [write Spanish]				
Sean bilingües [are bilingual]				
... para usted? [for you to ...]				
Poder entender el inglés [understand English]				
Poder hablar en inglés [speak English]				
Poder leer en inglés [read English]				
Poder escribir en inglés [write English]				
... que sus hijos? [that your children ...]				
Puedan entender el inglés [understand English]				
Puedan hablar en inglés [speak English]				
Puedan leer en inglés [read English]				
Puedan escribir en inglés [write English]				

(c) En su opinión ... [In your opinion ...]

¿Qué características identifican a una persona bien educada?
[What characteristics identify a well-educated person?]

¿Cómo sabe usted que una persona es bien educada?
[How do you know when a person is well-educated?]

¿Cuáles de estas características le gustaría fomentar en sus hijos (si es que le gustaría fomentar alguna)?
[Which of these characteristics, if any, would you like to foster in your children?]

¿Cree usted que es necesario saber hablar español para ser una persona bien educada?
[Do you think that it's necessary to speak Spanish to be a well educated person?]

¿Cree usted que es necesario saber hablar inglés para ser una persona bien educada?
[Do you think that it's necessary to speak English to be a well educated person?]

Part 6. Attitudes regarding language use and transmission

En esta parte voy a leerle algunas frases, y le voy a pedir que me haga favor de decirme para cada frase que yo le lea si usted está muy de acuerdo, más o menos de acuerdo, más o menos en desacuerdo, o totalmente en desacuerdo. ¿Lista?

[In this section I'm going to read you several phrases, and I'm going to ask you to tell me, for each phrase I read, If you agree, somewhat agree, somewhat disagree, or completely disagree. Ready?]

1. La gente que se viene a vivir a los Estados Unidos debe aprender inglés y olvidarse del español. [People who come to the United States to live should learn English and forget their Spanish.]				
Completamente de acuerdo [Fully agree]	Más o menos de acuerdo [Somewhat agree]	Me da igual/no sé [Either way/I don't know]	Más o menos en desacuerdo [Somewhat disagree]	Completamente en desacuerdo [Fully disagree]

2. Por más que hagan sus padres, los niños latinos que viven en Estados Unidos van a olvidar el español. [No matter what their parents do, Latino children living in the United States will forget Spanish.]				
Completamente de acuerdo [Fully agree]	Más o menos de acuerdo [Somewhat agree]	Me da igual/no sé [Either way/I don't know]	Más o menos en desacuerdo [Somewhat disagree]	Completamente en desacuerdo [Fully disagree]

3. Cuando les ayudan a sus niños a mantener el español, los padres les hacen un regalo muy valioso. [When they help their children to maintain their Spanish, parents are giving them a very valuable gift.]				
Completamente de acuerdo [Fully agree]	Más o menos de acuerdo [Somewhat agree]	Me da igual/no sé [Either way/I don't know]	Más o menos en desacuerdo [Somewhat disagree]	Completamente en desacuerdo [Fully disagree]

4. Hablarles en dos idiomas confunde a los niños. [Speaking two languages to children can be confusing for them.]				
Completamente de acuerdo [Fully agree]	Más o menos de acuerdo [Somewhat agree]	Me da igual/no sé [Either way/I don't know]	Más o menos en desacuerdo [Somewhat disagree]	Completamente en desacuerdo [Fully disagree]

5. Si los niños no quieren aprender español no hay que forzarlos.
[If children don't want to learn Spanish you shouldn't force them.]

Completamente de acuerdo [Fully agree]	Más o menos de acuerdo [Somewhat agree]	Me da igual/no sé [Either way/I don't know]	Más o menos en desacuerdo [Somewhat disagree]	Completamente en desacuerdo [Fully disagree]

6. Es importante que mi(s) hij(a/o)(s) valore(n) y se sienta(n) cómodos en sus dos culturas.
[It's important that my child(ren) value(s) and feel(s) comfortable in her/his/their two cultures.]

Completamente de acuerdo [Fully agree]	Más o menos de acuerdo [Somewhat agree]	Me da igual/no sé [Either way/I don't know]	Más o menos en desacuerdo [Somewhat disagree]	Completamente en desacuerdo [Fully disagree]

7. No hablo buen español, así que no puedo enseñarle(s) a mis hijos.
[I don't speak good Spanish, so I can't teach it to my child(ren).]

Completamente de acuerdo [Fully agree]	Más o menos de acuerdo [Somewhat agree]	Me da igual/no sé [Either way/I don't know]	Más o menos en desacuerdo [Somewhat disagree]	Completamente en desacuerdo [Fully disagree]

8. No enseñarles español a los niños mexicanos/mexicanoamericanos/latinos es negarles parte de su cultura.
[Not teaching Spanish to Mexican/Mexican American/Latino children is to deny them a part of their culture.]

Completamente de acuerdo [Fully agree]	Más o menos de acuerdo [Somewhat agree]	Me da igual/no sé [Either way/I don't know]	Más o menos en desacuerdo [Somewhat disagree]	Completamente en desacuerdo [Fully disagree]

9. Mis hijos saben que ser bilingüe es importante.
[My children know that being bilingual is important.]

Completamente de acuerdo [Fully agree]	Más o menos de acuerdo [Somewhat agree]	Me da igual/no sé [Either way/I don't know]	Más o menos en desacuerdo [Somewhat disagree]	Completamente en desacuerdo [Fully disagree]

10. No necesito enseñarle español a mi(s) hij(a/o)(s) porque vivo en Estados Unidos.
[I don't need to teach Spanish to my child(ren) because I live in the United States.]

Completamente de acuerdo [Fully agree]	Más o menos de acuerdo [Somewhat agree]	Me da igual/no sé [Either way/I don't know]	Más o menos en desacuerdo [Somewhat disagree]	Completamente en desacuerdo [Fully disagree]

11. Los padres mexicanos/mexicanoamericanos/latinos tienen la obligación de enseñarle a sus hijos español.
[Mexican/Mexican American/Latino parents have the obligation to teach Spanish to their children.]

Completamente de acuerdo [Fully agree]	Más o menos de acuerdo [Somewhat agree]	Me da igual/no sé [Either way/I don't know]	Más o menos en desacuerdo [Somewhat disagree]	Completamente en desacuerdo [Fully disagree]

12. Cuando les hablan en español, mexicanos/mexicanoamericanos/latinos les hacen un daños a sus hijos.
[When they speak to them in Spanish, Mexican/Mexican American/Latino parents harm their children.]

Completamente de acuerdo [Fully agree]	Más o menos de acuerdo [Somewhat agree]	Me da igual/no sé [Either way/I don't know]	Más o menos en desacuerdo [Somewhat disagree]	Completamente en desacuerdo [Fully disagree]

Part 7. Parental motivations to use and transmit the language

En esta parte le voy a pedir que me dé su opinión sobre varios temas relacionados.

[In this section I'm going to ask your opinion on several related topics.]

1. ¿Qué tan importante es saber hablar español para conseguir un buen trabajo?
[How important is it to know Spanish to get a good job?]

2. ¿Qué idioma o idiomas hablan las personas exitosas aquí en Lincoln?
[Here in Lincoln, what language(s) do successful people use?]

3. ¿Le parece que saber español es una ventaja en el trabajo?
[Do you think there's an advantage at work if you know Spanish?]

4. ¿Usted reza? Si reza, ¿en qué idioma?
[Do you pray? If you do, in what language?]

5. ¿Usted asiste a la iglesia/templo? Si lo hace, ¿en qué idioma prefiere la misa o el servicio?
[Do you attend church/temple? If you do, in what language do you prefer the mass or service?]

6. Si usted es una persona religiosa, ¿qué idioma o qué idiomas usa para hablar con Dios?
[If you are a religious person, what language do you use to speak with God?]

7. ¿Qué tan importante es para usted poder hablar español con su familia?
[How important is it for you to be able to speak Spanish with your family?]

8. ¿Qué tan importante es para usted poder hablar español con sus amigos?
[How important is it for you to be able to speak Spanish with your friends?]

9. ¿Qué tan importante es para usted poder hablar español con sus hijos?
[How important is it for you to be able to speak Spanish with your children?]

10. En un día normal, ¿qué tanto necesita el español para comunicarse con otras personas?
[On a normal day, how necessary is it for you to use Spanish to communicate with other persons?]

11. ¿Alguna vez le ha dado miedo que no le den un trabajo porque habla inglés con acento?
[Have you ever been afraid of not getting a job because you speak English with an accent?]

12. En su opinión, ¿Cuáles son algunas ventajas y desventajas de hablarle español a sus hijos?
[In your opinion, what are some advantages and disadvantages of speaking Spanish to your children?]

13. 15. ¿Para qué le sirve a sus hijos saber español aquí en Estados Unidos?
[What purpose does your children's speaking Spanish serve here in the United States?]

14. ¿Qué tan importante es para usted que sus hijos hablen español con su familia?
[How important is it for you that your children speak Spanish with your family?]

15. En su opinión, ¿Qué idioma(s) van a necesitar sus hijos para tener un buen futuro?
[In your opinion, what language(s) will your children need to have a good future?]

16 ¿Qué tan cierta es esta frase para usted: 'El español abre puertas'?
[How true is this phrase for you: 'Spanish opens doors'?]

17. ¿Qué tan cierta es esta frase para usted: 'No me gusta que mis hijos hablen español en la escuela porque siento que los pueden hacer menos'?
[How true is this phrase for you: 'I don't like my children speaking Spanish in school because I feel they might be discriminated against'?]

18. Imagínese que un día usted está en el super con sus hijos y mientras usted está pagando ellos están hablando en español. La persona que está atrás de ustedes hace un comentario desagradable en inglés. ¿Usted qué hace?
[Imagine that you are with your children at the supermarket, and while you are paying, they are speaking Spanish to someone else. The person standing behind you in line makes a rude comment. What do you do?]

19. ¿Qué tan importante es para usted que sus hijos tengan amigos que hablen español? [How important is it for you that your children have friends who speak Spanish?]
20. ¿Por qué les habla español a sus hijos? [Why do you speak Spanish to your children?]
21. Si usted reza con sus hijos por la noche, ¿en qué idioma dicen sus oraciones? [If you pray with your children at night, in what language do you say your prayers?]
22. ¿Para usted qué tan importante es que sus hijos reciban o hayan recibido su educación religiosa en español? [How important is it for you that your children receive/have received religious education in Spanish?]
23. ¿Qué idioma o idiomas van a hablar sus nietos? [What language or languages will your grandchildren speak?]
24. ¿Se puede enseñarle a los niños su cultura sin hablar español? [Can you teach children about your culture without using Spanish?]

Part 8. Parent's perceived role in their children's linguistic and academic development

En esta parte le voy a pedir otra vez que escoja una de las siguientes respuestas, o alguna otra, si se le hace que describe mejor su situación. Puede marcar más de una respuesta si gusta ¿Lista?

[In this part, I'm going to ask you again to choose one of the following answers, or any other, if you feel that it better describes your situation. You may chose more than one answer if you'd like. Ready?]

a. ¿Qué tanto depende de usted que sus niños usen el español?
[How much does it depend on you that your children use Spanish?]

Depende completamente de mí [It depends completely on me]	Depende de mi esposo/mi pareja y de mí [It depends on my husband/partner and me]	Depende de mis hijos y de mí [It depends on my children and me]	Depende de toda la familia [It depends on the whole family]	Depende de la escuela [It depends on the school]	Depende de la familia y la comunidad [It depends on the family and the community]	No sé/Otro [I don't know/Other]

¿Por qué?

b. ¿Qué tanto depende de usted que sus niños aprendan el inglés?
[How much does it depend on you that your children learn English?]

Depende completamente de mí	Depende de mi esposo/mi pareja y de mí	Depende de mis hijos y de mí	Depende de toda la familia	Depende de la escuela	Depende de la familia y la comunidad	No sé/Otro

¿Por qué?

c. ¿Qué tanto depende de usted que sus niños vayan bien en la escuela?
[How much does it depend on you that your children are successful in school?]

Depende completamente de mí	Depende de mi esposo/mi pareja y de mí	Depende de mis hijos y de mí	Depende de toda la familia	Depende de la escuela	Depende de la familia y la comunidad	No sé/Otro

¿Por qué?

d. ¿Qué tanto depende de usted que sus niños estén bien educados?
[How much does it depend on you that your children are well-educated?]

Depende completamente de mí	Depende de mi esposo/mi pareja y de mí	Depende de mis hijos y de mí	Depende de toda la familia	Depende de la escuela	Depende de la familia y la comunidad	No sé/Otro

¿Por qué?

e. ¿Qué tanto depende de su esposo/su pareja que sus niños usen el español? [How much does it depend on your husband/partner that your children use Spanish?]

Depende completamente de él/ella [It depends completely on him/her]	Depende de mi esposo/mi pareja y de mí [It depends on my husband/partner and me]	Depende de mis hijos y de mi esposo/mi pareja [It depends on my children, my husband/partner and me]	Depende de toda la familia [It depends on the whole family]	Depende de la escuela [It depends on the school]	Depende de la familia y la comunidad [It depends on the family and the community]	No sé/Otro [I don't know/Other]

¿Por qué?

f. ¿Qué tanto depende de su esposo/su pareja que sus niños aprendan el inglés? [How much does it depend on your husband/partner that your children learn English?]

Depende completamente de él/ella	Depende de mi esposo/mi pareja y de mí	Depende de mis hijos y de mi esposo/mi pareja	Depende de toda la familia	Depende de la escuela	Depende de la familia y la comunidad	No sé/Otro

¿Por qué?

g. ¿Qué tanto depende de su esposo/su pareja que sus niños vayan bien en la escuela? [How much does it depend on your husband/partner that your children are successful in school?]

Depende completamente de él/ella	Depende de mi esposo/mi pareja y de mí	Depende de mis hijos y de mi esposo/mi pareja	Depende de toda la familia	Depende de la escuela	Depende de la familia y la comunidad	No sé/Otro

¿Por qué?

h. ¿Qué tanto depende de su esposo/su pareja que sus niños estén bien educados? [How much does it depend on your husband/partner that your children are well-educated?]

Depende completamente de él/ella	Depende de mi esposo/mi pareja y de mí	Depende de mis hijos y de mi esposo/mi pareja	Depende de toda la familia	Depende de la escuela	Depende de la familia y la comunidad	No sé/Otro

¿Por qué?

i. ¿Qué tanto depende de la escuela que sus niños usen el español?
[How much does it depend on the school that your children use Spanish?]

Depende completamente de la escuela [It depends completely on the school]	Depende de la escuela y de mí [It depends on the school and on me]	Depende de la escuela, de mi esposo/mi pareja y de mí [It depends on the school, my husband/partner and me]	Depende de la escuela y de toda la familia [It depends on the school and the whole family]	Depende de la familia, la escuela y la comunidad [It depends on the family, the school and the community]	No depende de la escuela [It doesn't depend on the school]	No sé/Otro [I don't know/Other]

¿Por qué?

j. ¿Qué tanto depende de la escuela que sus niños aprendan el inglés?
[How much does it depend on the school that your children learn English?]

Depende completamente de la escuela	Depende de la escuela y de mí	Depende de la escuela, de mi esposo/mi pareja y de mí	Depende de la escuela y de toda la familia	Depende de la familia, la escuela y la comunidad	No depende de la escuela	No sé/Otro

¿Por qué?

k. ¿Qué tanto depende de la escuela que sus niños vayan bien en la escuela?
[How much does it depend on the school that your children do well in school?]

Depende completamente de la escuela	Depende de la escuela y de mí	Depende de la escuela, de mi esposo/mi pareja y de mí	Depende de la escuela y de toda la familia	Depende de la familia, la escuela y la comunidad	No depende de la escuela	No sé/Otro

¿Por qué?

l. ¿Qué tanto depende de la escuela que sus niños estén bien educados?
[How much does it depend on the school that your children are well-educated?]

Depende completamente de la escuela	Depende de la escuela y de mí	Depende de la escuela, de mi esposo/mi pareja y de mí	Depende de la escuela y de toda la familia	Depende de la familia, la escuela y la comunidad	No depende de la escuela	No sé/Otro

¿Por qué?

m. ¿Cuáles son tres cosas que usted hace normalmente que le ayudan a sus hijos a mantener el español?
[What three things that you normally do help your children maintain Spanish?]

n. ¿Cuáles son tres cosas que su esposo/su pareja hace normalmente que le ayudan a sus hijos a mantener el español?
[What three things that your husband/partner normally does help your children maintain Spanish?]

o. Se acuerda usted de algo que pase cada semana en su casa o en la comunidad que hace que sus hijos tengan que usar el español?
[Can you remember anything that happens every week in your home or in the community that makes your children have to use Spanish?]

p. ¿Es importante para usted que sus hijos hablen español?
[Is it important to you that your children speak Spanish?]

q. ¿Qué se le hace más difícil de hacer que sus hijos hablen español en la casa?
[What is the hardest part for you to make your children speak Spanish at home?]

r. ¿En la escuela?
[In school?]

s. ¿En la comunidad?
[In the community?]

t. ¿Cree usted que mantener el español le va a ayudar a sus hijos a desarrollar el inglés?
[Do you think that maintaining Spanish will help your children develop their English?]

u. ¿Cree usted que mantener el español le va a impedir a sus hijos a desarrollar el inglés?
[Do you think that maintaining Spanish will keep your children from developing their English?]

v. ¿Cree usted que desarrollar el inglés le va a ayudar a sus hijos a desarrollar el español?
[Do you think that developing their English will help your children develop their Spanish?]

w. ¿Cree usted que desarrollar el inglés le va a impedir a sus hijos a desarrollar el español?
[Do you think that developing their English will keep your children from developing their Spanish?]

x. ¿Cree usted que es posible para sus niños desarrollar el español y el inglés al mismo nivel? ¿Por qué?
[Do you think it's possible for your children to develop their Spanish and their English at the same level? Why?]

y. ¿Qué se necesita para que suceda?
[What is necessary for this to happen?]

Part 9. Home strategies for maintenance

Aquí llegamos a la parte final de nuestra conversación. Ahora le voy a preguntar acerca de las estrategias que usted y su familia usan en la casa que tienen que ver con el uso del español y del inglés. Le voy a leer varias frases y después de leérselas le voy a pedir que escoja la que se parezca más a lo que sucede en su casa. Si ustedes no hacen nada de lo que le voy a decir, o si hacen otra cosa completamente diferente, me dice, por favor.

[And so, we arrive at the end of our conversation. Now I'm going to ask you about strategies that your family and you use at home, and that are related to the use of Spanish and English. I'm going to read several phrases to you, and I'm going to ask you to choose those that more closely resemble what goes on in your household. If your family doesn't do any of the things I'm describing, or if you do something different, please tell me.]

1. El inglés lo van a aprender en la escuela, así que en la casa les hablamos español a nuestros hijos. [They're going to learn English in school, so at home we speak Spanish to our children.]	
2. Hablamos inglés para que mis hijos lo practiquen. [We speak in English so the children can practice it.]	
3. Hablamos español para que lo aprendan/para que no lo olviden. [We speak in Spanish so they can learn it/don't forget it.]	
4. Hablamos los dos porque somos una familia bilingüe. [We speak both languages because we are a bilingual family.]	
5. Hablo inglés con mis hijos, porque estoy aprendiendo y necesito practicar. [I speak English with my children because I'm learning and I need to practice.]	
6. Los pongo a leer o a escribir en español para que practiquen. [I make my children practice their reading or writing in Spanish.]	
7. Mi esposo/pareja les habla en un idioma y yo en el otro. [My husband/partner speaks to my children in one language and I speak to them in another.]	
8. Le pedimos a los familiares y amigos adultos que les hablen en español. [We ask adult family members and friends to speak to our children in Spanish.]	
9. Le pedimos a los familiares y amigos adultos que les hablen en inglés. [We ask adult family members and friends to speak to our children in English.]	

Notes

Appendix 3. Patterns of Reported Household Language Use

Place and date of interview: _____   Respondent ID #_____   Interviewer_____

Household size: _____   Home languages: _____

	Lang I use most often with:				Child most often speaks to me:				My spouse/partner speaks to child:				Child most often speaks to spouse/partner:				Total
	Child 1	Child 2	Child 3	Child 4	Child 1	Child 2	Child 3	Child 4	Child 1	Child 2	Child 3	Child 4	Child 1	Child 2	Child 3	Child 4	
To scold																	
To console																	
To tell a secret																	
To ask for money/favor																	
To play/have fun																	
To pray together																	
To sing together																	
To read for fun																	
To do homework/teach something																	
To tell a joke																	
To tell a story																	
To warn																	
To express affection																	
To express anger																	
To give information																	
Total																	

Code: Spanish 2; Mixed or both 1; English 0.   [Use another form for additional children or adults in household, use back of this form for notes]

Dominant language of interaction by household: _____

Dominant language of interaction by child: _____

Dominant language of interaction by parent: _____

Source: Adapted from Velázquez (2008).

Appendix 4. Child Instrument

Place and date of interview: ————————————————————

Interviewee ID # ———————————— Interviewer: ——————

Part 1. Listening skills

Hola, ————————. ¿Cómo estás? ¿Te acuerdas de mí? Yo me llamo ———————— y trabajo en la Universidad de Nebraska. La semana pasada te conté que estoy haciendo un estudio sobre las personas que saben hablar español e inglés aquí en Lincoln, y te pregunté si querías platicar conmigo, ¿te acuerdas? ¿Te puedo hacer algunas preguntas? ¿Podemos platicar?

[Hi ———————— How are you? Do you remember me? My name is ————————, and I work for the University of Nebraska. Last week I told you that I'm studying people who know how to speak Spanish and English here in Lincoln, and I asked you if you wanted to speak with me, remember? Can I ask you a few questions? Can we talk?]

[Child says no, interview ends. Child says yes, proceed with next part.]

¡Muy bien! Entonces vamos a comenzar. Voy a prender mi grabadora para que cuando llegue a mi casa, no se me olvide lo que platicamos. ¿Está bien? Si te pregunto algo que no entiendes, me puedes preguntar. Y si te pregunto algo que no quieres contestar, o si te cansas, puedes decirme que no quieres contestar, o puedes decirme que paremos, ¿ok?

[Very well! Let's start. I'm going to turn on my recorder, so when I get home, I don't forget any of the things we talked about, ok? If I ask you something that you don't understand, you can ask me. And if I ask you something you don't want to answer, or if you get tired, you can tell me that you don't want to answer. Or you can tell me you want us to stop. Ok?]

Bueno, primero te voy a preguntar unas cosas muy fáciles. ¿Estás lista/o?

1. ¿Cómo te llamas?

2. ¿Cuántos años tienes?

3. ¿Vas a la escuela? ¿En qué grado estás?

[Well, first I'm going to ask you a couple of very easy questions. Ready?

1. What is your name?

2. How old are you?

3. Do you go to school? What grade are you in?]

[If child doesn't go to school, ask questions a, b, c, d, skip questions 4, 5, 6, 7, and proceed to question 8.]

    a.   ¿Y hasta cuando vas a ir a la escuela? ¿El año que viene, o todavía falta mucho?
        [When will you go to school? Next year, or a long time from now?]

    b.   ¿Tú crees que te va a gustar la escuela?
        [Do you think you will like school?]

    c.   ¿Vas a ir a la misma escuela que tus [hermanos/amigos/primos/vecinos]?
        [Are you going to the same school as your brothers and sisters/friends/cousins/neighbors?]

    d.   ¿Tu escuela va a ser in inglés o en español, o en los dos?
        [Are you going to a school where they speak English, Spanish, or both?]

4. ¿Tu escuela es fácil o difícil? ¿Te gusta?
   [Is your school easy or hard? Do you like it?]

5. ¿Qué hacen en tu salón?
   [What do you do in class?]

6. ¿Te dejan mucha tarea, o poca?
   [Do you get a lot of homework, or not a lot?]

7. Y fuera de la escuela, ¿qué te gusta hacer?
   [And outside of school, what do you like to do?]

8. ¿A qué te gusta jugar?
   [What do you like to play?]

9. ¿A tus amigos les gusta jugar a lo mismo?
   [Do your friends like to play the same things?]

10. ¿Tus amigos van a la misma escuela que tú? ¿en qué año están?
    [Are your friends in the same school as you? In what grades?]

11. ¿Saben español?
    [Do they know how to speak Spanish?]

12. ¿Saben inglés?
    [Do they know how to speak English?]

13. ¿En qué hablan cuando están jugando?
    [What do you speak when you're playing with them?]

14. Oye, y cuando juegas con tus hermanos, ¿en qué hablan?
    Listen, and when you play with your brothers/sisters, what do you speak?]

15. ¿Y cuando hablas con tu mamá, le hablas en español o en inglés? ¿Y ella en qué te habla a ti?
[And when you speak with your mom, do you speak to her in Spanish or in English?]

16. ¿Y tu papá, en qué le hablas? ¿Y él en qué te habla a ti?
[And your dad? Do you speak to him in Spanish or in English? And in what does he talk to you?]

17. ¿Algunas veces hablas español con otros niños? ¿Con quién?
[Do you sometimes speak Spanish with other kids? With whom?]

18. ¿Quiénes son algunos adultos que tú conoces que saben hablar español?
Who are some adults that you know, that can speak Spanish?]

19. ¿Cuál es tu color favorito? ¿El *[name of color mentioned by child]*?
Ah, sí, ese es un color muy bonito. Pero no es mi color favorito. ¿Sabes cuál es mi color favorito? A ver, adivina … *[Researcher makes a pause to let child guess.]* No, ese no es. Adivina … Ok, te voy a dar una pista. Por mucha atención … ¿Listo/a? en este cuarto hay una cosa que es de mi color favorito. Es una cosa cuadrada, que sirve para …

[What is your favorite color? *[name of color mentioned by child]*? Ah, yes, that's a very pretty color. But it's not my favorite color. Do you know what's my favorite color? Let's see, guess … No, it's not that one. Ok. I'm going to give you a hint. Pay close attention … Ready? In this room there's a thing that is the same color as my favorite color. It's a square thing that you use to …]

[After child guesses the researcher's favorite color, the researcher says that the guess is incorrect, and that she will give the child a hint. The researcher proceeds to describe an object by size, weight, spatial location and function. Then tells the child: Guess what is my favorite color? If the child is correct, the researcher says so, and praises the correct answer. Then she asks the child to stand up and touch the object she was describing to verify that they are talking about the same object. If the child guesses correctly and follows instructions, the researcher will praise the child. If the child is unable to guess or does not understand/follow instructions in Spanish, the researcher will provide the answer and go on with the next part of the interview. If child was able to guess and follow instructions correctly, researcher asks him/her if he/she would like to trade places. The child describes an object and the researcher must guess what it is.]

Part 2. Narrative production

[At the beginning of the interview, researcher places two picture books within sight, but away from where she and the child will be sitting.]

Bueno, ahora quiero enseñarte dos libros que traje. ¿Me los pasas? Son esos dos que están allá.

[Well, now I want to show you two books that I brought with me. Can you hand them to me? They're the ones over there.]

[Child reaches for the books.]

Sí, ésos, muy bien. Mira, este es sobre un niño que tiene una rana y se le pierde, y éste es sobre el mismo niño, pero además de la rana, en este libro el niño tiene un perro.

[Yeah, those two, great. Look, this is about a boy that has a frog and the frog gets lost. And this one is about the same boy, but in this book the boy has the frog plus a dog.]

[Researcher pauses for a moment to allow child to view the books.]

Primero vamos a trabajar con este libro de aquí. Si te fijas, éste es un libro que no tiene palabras. Te voy a pedir que te imagines qué está pasando en cada página y que me cuentes la historia en español. ¿Sale? ¿Me puedes contar toda esta historia en español? Ok, adelante, estoy lista …

[First we're going to work with this book here. As you can see, this book has no words. I'm going to ask you to imagine what's happening on every page, and that you tell me the story in Spanish. Cool? Can you tell me this story in Spanish? Ok, go ahead, I'm ready …]

[Child narrates story in Spanish.]

¡Muy bien, lo hiciste muy bien, buen trabajo! Ahora vamos a trabajar con este otro libro. ¿Me puedes contar esta historia en inglés? *[Researcher switches to English]* Can you tell me what happens in this story using only English? You can? Ok. Ready? Go …

[Great! You did it very well, good job! Now we're working with this book. Can you tell me this story in English? *[Researcher switches to English]* Can you tell me what happens in this story using only English? You can? Ok. Ready? Go …]

[Child narrates story in Spanish] Great job! Well done. *[Researcher switches to Spanish]* ¡Lo hiciste muy bien! ¿Cómo estás? Ya te cansaste, o podemos seguir platicando?

[Great job! Well done. *[Researcher switches to Spanish]* You did it very well. How are you feeling? Are you tired, or can we keep talking?]

[Researcher pauses, and allows child to verify if he/she wants to continue with the conversation.]

Part 3. Attitudes toward speaking Spanish, speaking English, bilingualism

Muy bien, ahora vamos a seguir con nuestras preguntas. Ya casi terminamos … Te quería preguntar …

[Very well, now we are going to continue with our questions. We are almost done … I wanted to ask you …]

20. ¿Algunas veces hablas español con otros niños? ¿Con quién?
[Do you sometimes speak Spanish with other children? With whom?]
21. ¿Algunas veces hablas inglés con otros niños? ¿Con quién?
[Do you sometimes speak English with other children? With whom?]

22. ¿Quiénes son algunos adultos que tú conoces que saben hablar los dos?
[Who are some adults that you know that know how to speak both?]

23. ¿Cuáles son algunas cosas buenas de saber hablar español?
[What are some good things about knowing Spanish?]

24. ¿Cuáles son algunas cosas buenas de saber hablar inglés?
[What are some good things about knowing English?]

25. ¿Hay cosas malas de saber hablar español?
[Are there bad things about knowing how to speak Spanish?]

26. ¿Hay cosas malas de saber hablar inglés?
[Are there bad things about knowing how to speak English?]

27. ¿Te gusta saber español?
[Do you like knowing how to speak Spanish?]

28. ¿Te gusta saber inglés?
[Do you like knowing how to speak English?]

¡Uf! ¿Pues qué crees?, ya terminamos. Antes de que apague mi grabadora, ¿hay algo que quieras decirme que yo no te he preguntado?

[Uf! Guess what? We're done. Before I turn off my recorder, is there something that you want to tell me that I haven't asked you?]

[Researcher pauses.]

¡Muchas gracias!
[Thank you!]

Appendix 5. Youth Instrument

Place and date of interview: _____

Interviewee ID # _____ Interviewer: _____

Part 1. Listening skills

Hola, _____. ¿Cómo estás? ¿Te acuerdas de mí? Yo me llamo _____ y trabajo en la Universidad de Nebraska. La semana pasada te conté que estoy visitando varias familias que hablan español e inglés aquí en Lincoln, porque quiero conocer más sobre su experiencia como familias bilingües. Ya conozco un poco sobre la experiencia de tus papás y tu hermanos, pero me interesa platicar contigo porque tú ya eres adolescente, y quizá tengas otra perspectiva. ¿Tienes tiempo? ¿Podemos platicar? ¿Te puedo hacer algunas preguntas?

[Hi _____ How are you? Do you remember me? My name is _____, and I work for the University of Nebraska. Last week I told you that I'm visiting several families who speak Spanish and English here in Lincoln, because I want to learn more about their experience as bilingual families. Now I know a little bit about your parents' and siblings' experience, but I'm interested in speaking with you because you're a teenager, and perhaps you have a different perspective. Do you have time? Can we talk? Can I ask you a few questions?]

[Respondent says no, interview ends. Respondent says yes, proceed with next part.]

¡Muy bien! Entonces vamos a comenzar. Voy a prender mi grabadora. ¿Está bien? Si te pregunto algo que no entiendes, me puedes preguntar. Y si te pregunto algo que no quieres contestar, o si te cansas, puedes decirme que no quieres contestar, o puedes decirme que paremos, ¿ok?

[Very well! Let's start. I'm going to turn on my recorder. Ok? If I ask you something that you don't understand, you can ask me. And if I ask you something you don't want to answer, or if you get tired, you can tell me that you don't want to answer. Or you can tell me you want us to stop. Ok?]

Bueno, primero te voy a preguntar algunas cosas muy generales. ¿Estás lista/o?
[Well, first I'm going to ask you some very general things. Ready?]

1. ¿Cuántos años tienes?
   [How old are you?]

2. ¿Vas a la escuela? ¿En qué grado estás?
   [Do you go to school? What grade are you in?]

3. ¿Cuál es tu mejor clase en la escuela? ¿Por qué?
   [What is your best class in school? Why?]

4. ¿Qué te gusta hacer en tu tiempo libre?
   [What do you like to do in your spare time?]

5. ¿Trabajas? ¿En qué?
   [Do you work? What do you do?]

6. ¿Qué te gustaría hacer después de graduarte de high school?
   [What would you like to do after you graduate from high school?]

7. ¿Cuál sería tu trabajo ideal?
   [What would your ideal job be?]

8. ¿Tus amigos van a la misma escuela que tú? ¿en qué año están?
   [Are your friends in the same school as you? What grade are they in?]

9. ¿Saben español?
   [Do they know how to speak Spanish?]

10. ¿Saben inglés?
    [Do they know how to speak English?]

11. ¿Te sientes más cómodo hablando con ellos en inglés o en español?
    [Do you feel more comfortable speaking with them in English or in Spanish?]

12. ¿Hay alguna situación en la que te sientas cómodo hablando en español con tus amigos?
    [Is there ever a situation in which you feel comfortable speaking to your friends in Spanish?]

13. Oye, y cuando hablas con tus hermanos, ¿en qué hablan? ¿por qué?
    [Listen, and when you talk with your brothers/sisters, what do you speak? Why?]

14. ¿Y cuando hablas con tu mamá, le hablas en español o en inglés? ¿Y ella en qué te habla a ti?
    [And when you speak with your mom, do you speak to her in Spanish or in English? Why?]

15. ¿Y tu papá, en qué le hablas? ¿Y él en qué te habla a ti?
    [And your dad? Do you speak to him in Spanish or in English? And in what does he talk to you?]

16. Además de tus papás, ¿quiénes son algunos adultos que tú conoces que sepan hablar español?
    [Aside from your parents, who are some adults that you know, that know how to speak Spanish?]

17. ¿Cuántas personas de tu familia saben hablar los dos idiomas?
    [How many people in your family speak both languages?]

18. ¿Cuántas personas de tu escuela saben hablar los dos idiomas?
[How many people in your school speak both languages?]

19. ¿Cuántos de tus amigos hablan los dos idiomas?
[How many of your friends speak both languages?]

Part 2. Reported proficiency

Ahora quisiera preguntarte acerca de tu experiencia con el español y el inglés. No hay respuestas correctas o incorrectas, estamos hablando de tu experiencia, de lo que tú piensas, ok?

[Now I'd like to ask you about your experience with Spanish and English. There are no right or wrong answers, we're talking about your experience, about what you think, ok?]

¿Qué tan fácil o difícil se te hace ...?
[For you, how easy or how hard is it to ...]

	Muy fácil [very easy]	Más o menos fácil [Somewhat easy]	Más o menos difícil [Somewhat hard]	Muy difícil [very hard]	Otro [Other]
Hablar el español [Speaking Spanish]					
Entender el español [Understanding Spanish]					
Leer en español [Reading in Spanish]					
Escribir en español [Writing in Spanish]					
Hablar el inglés [Speaking English]					
Entender el inglés [Understanding English]					
Leer en inglés [Reading in English]					
Escribir en inglés [Writing in English]					

Part 3. Narrative production

Bueno, ahora quiero pedirte que te acuerdes de algún viaje que hayas hecho. ¿Ya? ¿A dónde fuiste ¿Quién iba contigo? Cuéntame cómo fue el viaje y qué hiciste.

¿Pasó algo chistoso/triste/emocionante?

¿Te hubiera gustado X?

¿Qué fue lo que más te gusto/te dió miedo/te interesó/se te quedó grabado?

¿Te gustaría hacer otro viaje?

¿A dónde te gustaría ir?

¿Qué lugar te gustaría conocer?

Si tuvieras el permiso de tus papás y mucho dinero, ¿a quién invitarías al viaje? ¿Por qué?

Qué interesante. A mí también me gustaría/no me gustaría conocer X.

[Well, now I want to ask you to remember any trip that you've taken. Done? Where did you go? Who went with you? Tell me about that trip, and what you did. Did something funny/sad/exciting happen? Would you have liked to X? What did you like most/scare you/interest you/do you remember most? Would you like to take another trip? Where would you like to go? Where would you like to visit? If you had your parents' permission and a lot of money, whom would you take on that trip? Why? That's interesting. I would/wouldn't like to visit X.]

Part 4. Attitudes toward speaking Spanish, speaking English, bilingualism

Muy bien, ahora vamos a seguir con nuestras preguntas. Ya casi terminamos … Te quería preguntar …
[Very well, now we are going to continue with our questions. We are almost done … I wanted to ask you …]

20. En tu opinión, ¿quién es, o qué sabe hacer una persona bilingüe?
    [In your opinion, who is a bilingual person, what does a bilingual person know?]

21. ¿Eres una persona bilingüe?
    [Are you a bilingual person?]

22. ¿Quiénes son tres adultos que tú conozcas que sepan hablar muy bien el inglés y el español?
    [Who are three adults that you know that know how to speak English and Spanish very well?]

23. ¿Te gusta hablar español?
    [Do you like to speak Spanish?]

24. ¿Te gusta hablar inglés?
    [Do you like to speak English?]

25. ¿Para qué les sirve a las personas hablar español?
    [How do people benefit from speaking Spanish?]

¿Pues qué crees?, ya terminamos. Antes de que apague mi grabadora, ¿hay algo que quieras decirme que yo no te he preguntado?

[Guess what? We're done. Before I turn off my recorder, is there something that you want to tell me that I haven't asked you?]

[Researcher pauses.]

¡Muchas gracias!
[Thank you!]

Appendix 6. Example of Travel Anecdotes Elicited from Teens

FAM #1 Youth, story, Iteration #1

Participant: (F01) Female, 16

Researcher:	Bueno. Ahora quiero que me pid- que me cuentes sobre algún viaje (1) que hayas hecho
F01:	[XXX Unintelligible due to background noise]
Researcher:	Bueno, ¿a dónde fuiste?
F01:	A México
Researcher:	¿Y con quién ibas?
F01:	Con: mis hermanas
Researcher:	¿Con tus hermanos?
F01:	Con mis hermanas
Researcher:	[Oh, okay
F01:	Con Marilú: su- bueno, y su esposo (1) y luego con ella también [points at sister in the room]
Researcher:	Okay, so cuatro personas
F01:	Ey
Researcher:	Okay. Bueno, ¿cómo fue el viaje que hiciste? (3) ¿Cuánto tiempo estuviste?
F01:	[XXX como: un mes
Researcher:	[clears throat] Okay. Okay
F01:	[Algo así
Researcher:	(3) ¿Cómo fue?
F01:	Pues fue bien, divertido. (Visité) toda la familia [giggles] Yeah
Researcher:	Okay. ¿Qué tipo de cosas hiciste? ¿Qué actividades?
F01:	Pues: salimos a la plaza
Researcher:	Uh huh
F01:	A comer, a (1) los cines, en la calle no más [giggles]
Researcher:	Ah, okay
F01:	En los ranchos así, que tenemos ahí
Researcher:	[Uh huh (1) ¿Y hace cuánto fue, el viaje? (2) ¿Hace bastante?
F01:	Sí hace como tres años yo creo
Researcher:	Oooh bastante. Bueno, ¿paso algo: chistoso?
F01:	[laughter] Yeah, muchas cosas
Researcher:	¿Cómo qué, por ejemplo?
F01:	[laughter] Pues eeh (2) XXX [laughter]
Researcher:	¿Es cómo? [giggles] ¿Cómo?
F01:	Es tan- (tan) es asqueroso [laughter]
Researcher:	No importa, no importa
F01:	Mi prima se (gomitó) de comer tantas chucherías, que salimos un día y ya XXX
Researcher:	Uh huh okay (2) Eso es XXX [giggles]
F01:	[giggles]
Researcher:	Eeemm, ¿algo triste pasó?
F01:	(2) No

Researcher:	¿Y algo emocionante?
F01:	(2) Pues todo el viaje [giggles]
Researcher:	Sí claro. Okay. ¿Te hubiera gustado que: (3) alguien más hubiera venido o que algo fuera- hubiera sido diferente?
F01:	No, (todo) estuvo bien
Researcher:	Okay. Bueno, ¿qué fue lo que más te gustó (2) o que se te quedó grabado del viaje? O sea, de lo que más te acuerdas
F01:	Estar entre toda la familia
Researcher:	Okay. ¿Algo que te dio miedo?
F01:	No
Researcher:	No (2) ¿Y: algo que te pareció muy interesante?
F01:	Este: (3) Pues no sé [laughter] A mí todo se me hace- todo
Researcher:	[Pues XXX sí pues sí
F01:	Eehh
Researcher:	Bueno, ¿te gustaría hacer otro viaje?
F01:	Sí
Researcher:	¿Y a dónde te gustaría ir?
F01:	Al:: ¿cómo se llama? (4) Este: ¿Rome?
Researcher:	Uh huh Italia
F01:	[Roma
Researcher:	Roma Uh huh uh huh
F01:	Sí
Researcher:	Sí, ¿y por qué Roma?
F01:	Porque tienen muchas cosas así como antigüas (1) so (1) se ve interesante
Researcher:	[Uh huh uh huh sí es super interesante. Claro que- no vayas en verano porque hay demasiada gente (1) y hace demasiado calor
F01:	[giggles]
Researcher:	Yo estuve una vez (3) pero bueno (3) igual
F01:	[Ya lo tengo en mente [giggles]
Researcher:	Sí, sí, sí, sí. Vale la pena. Vale muchísimo la pena. Bueno y si tuvieras eehh- el permiso de tus papás y mucho dinero, ¿a quién invitarías a Roma?
F01:	A mis amigos. A dos de mis amigos
Researcher:	¿A dos?
F01:	Yeah
Researcher:	¿Y por qué a tus amigos?
F01:	¿Por qué? Porque están XXX [laughter]

Appendix 7. Calques in Children's Stories

Calques. Iteration #1

F12 (8)	Fell down in a pond **[PHRASAL VERB]**	*Se cayó en un estanque*
F15 (9)	The boy saw the jar empty **[ADJ]**	*El niño vio el frasco vacío*
F17 (7)	Y atraparon al perro en vez [ADV]	*And they caught the dog instead*
F19 (9)	Está buscando en hoyos [PREP] Se cayó en un río con su perro [PREP] Está preocupado de la rana [PREP]	*He is looking in holes???* *He fell in a river with his dog* *He's worried about the frog*
F22 (9)	Y se cayeron en el agua [PREP]	*And they fell in the water*
F23 (6)	Entonces las abejas estaban [DETERMINER] Encontró su rana porque estaban dos ranas [SER/ESTAR]	*Then ø bees [generic] were …* *He found his frog because there were two frogs*
F24 (5)	La llamó en un agujero [PREP] Y usó sus ojos para ver el niño [OTHER] The boy fell out to the water **[P. VERB]** The dog was having the frog in his head **[V]** [PREP]	*He called him in/through a hole ???* *And he used his eyes to see the boy* *El niño se cayó al agua* *El niño tenía la rana en la cabeza???*
F25 (7)	Su rana se quería ir afuera [ADV] Cualquiera parte a encontrar su rana [ADV] Y quería quitarse esa cosa afuera [ADV] Estaba llamando para su rana [PREP] Dos ranas con unos chiquitos bebés [ADJ] Tenían una grande familia [ADJ]	*His frog wanted to go out* *Everywhere to find his frog* *And he wanted to take that thing out* *He was calling for his frog* *Two frogs with some small babies* *They had a big family*

Calques. Iteration #2

F17 (7)	Un gigante splash [ADJ] They shouted through a hole **[P.VERB]**	*A giant splash* *(Le) Gritaron por un hoyo*
F19 (9)	Arriba de una grande roca [ADJ]	*On top of a big rock*
F22 (9)	Ellos miraron en todos lugares El fin [OTHER]	*They looked in every place/* *everywhere???* *The end*
F23 (6)	And the dog got on the bathtub **[P. VERB]**	*Y el perro se metió en la tina.*
F24 (5)	El niño está buscando por una rana [PREP] El perro puso sus dos patas afuera [OTHER]	*The boy is looking for a frog* *The dog put/stuck his two legs out*
F25 (7)	Se cayó abajo (2 tokens) [ADV]	*Fell down*

Appendix 8. Extension, Circumlocution, Metaphor and Metonym in Children's Stories (Tokens)

[Original version included an image of a boy and a frog here]	[Original version included an image of a deer here]	[Original version included an image of a beehive here]
Lexical item: Male and female frogs	Lexical item: Deer	Lexical item: Beehive
(A) METAPHOR Anthropomorphization: 'Y ahí estaba la mujer rana y el hombre' 'Y tenían bebés y el niño se llevó una bebé para la casa' 'Y encontraron la rana y tenía una familia' 'Porque la rana tuvo una mamá y los hijos' 'Y luego su papá y su mamá y sus hermanos tenían una grande familia' 'Y la rana tenía una esposa y tenía niños' 'Tenían una gran familia con todas las ranas chiquitas' 'Vio la rana y un esposo' 'Ahí están, está su mama' 'Y también había bebés' 'Un rana con otra rana y tenían bebés'	**(B) SEMANTIC EXTENSION** Four-legged animal, same family: 'Y luego lo asustó un venado' 'Llegó un reno' 'Y encontró un venado, a deer' 'Lo tiró el mus y su perro también.' Four-legged animal, different family: 'Se encontró con un burro'	**(C) CIRCUMLOCUTION** 'Se salieron como abejas' 'Trantando de alcanzar donde están las abejas' **METAPHOR** 'La casa de las abejas' 'La casa de la bee' **METONYM** 'Y luego se cayó la miel y se cayeron las abejas' 'Y estaba buscando en la miel'
Some examples in English		
'The frog's family' 'And saw the baby frogs (...) all the frogs were happy' 'They found two frogs (...) and then they found the babies' 'They found a frog and frog babies' 'There were two frogs and the babies'	'The moose' 'He didn't see the horns of a deer' 'The moose, the reindeer got him'	'Beehive' 'The hive' 'The bees fell down (...) they were sliding towards the dog'

Appendix 9. Results for Narrative Organization in Children's Stories

Storytelling task in Spanish. Iteration #1

	5		6		7		8	9			10
Age:	F11	F24	F20	F23	F25	F17	F12	F15	F19	F22	F21
Narrative organization											
Abstract or summary	0	0	1	0	0	0	0	0	0	0	0
Orientation	1	1	1	1	1	1	1	1	1	1	1
Complicating action	1	1	1	1	1	1	1	1	1	1	1
Suspension	0	1	0	0	0	1	0	0	0	0	0
Evaluation	1	1	1	0	0	1	0	1	0	0	1
Resolution	1	1	1	0	1	1	1	1	1	1	1
Coda	1	1	0	0	0	1	0	1	0	0	1
Action is detailed and clear; has evaluation or resolution (8)		6				6					
Action detailed and clear; some evaluation or resolution (7)	5							5	5		
Minimal detail, clarity, evaluation, resolution (6)			4								
Action borders on minimal					3		3			3	
Narrative coherence											
More than two past-tense events, highpoint, resolution (8)	8	8				8		8	8	8	8
More than two past-tense events, highpoint, no resolution (7)			7	7	7		7				
More than two past-tense events, highpoint, resolution in chronological sequence, no evaluation or highpoint (6)											
More than two past-tense events, not in chronological sequence (5)											
Only two past-tense events (4)											
Only one past-tense event (3)											
Present-tense description of immediate activity (2)											
No narrative interaction (1)											

Source: Adapted from Schecter and Bayley (2002); Wishard Guerra (2008).

Appendix 10. Instrument for Analysis of Verb Forms

Iteration #1/Spanish story
FXX (age X)

Total verbs:	Spanish:	English:	Hybrid:
Agreement			
Person agreement (+1 point)			
Number agreement (+1 point)			
Tense			
Events narrated in logical temporal sequence (+1 point) (i.e. consistently in the past or in the present)			
Aspect			
Preterite to encode past perfective aspect (+1 point)			
Imperfect to encode past imperfect aspect (+1 point)			
Estar + gerund to encode progressive events (+1 point)			
Modal verb + participle (+1 point)			
Mood			
Subjunctive to encode irrealis clauses (+1 point)			
Other			
Total			X/X

References

Alarcón Alarcón, A. and Parella Rubio, S. (2013) Linguistic integration of the descendants of foreign immigrants in Catalonia. *Migraciones Internacionales* 7 (1).

Aliaga Linares, L. and Cogua-Lopez, J. (2016) *Latinos and the Economic Downturn in Nebraska: Demographic and Socioeconomic Trends 2005–2013/2014*. Omaha, NE: Office of Latino/Latin American Studies (OLLAS) at the University of Nebraska at Omaha.

Arendt, H. (1958) *The Human Condition*. Chicago, IL: University of Chicago Press.

Baker, C. (1992) *Attitudes and Language*. Clevedon: Multilingual Matters.

Baker, C. (2005) Psycho-sociological analysis in language policy research. In T. Ricento (ed.) *An Introduction to Language Policy: Theory and Method* (pp. 210–228). Malden, MA: Blackwell.

Baker, C. (2014) *A Parents' and Teachers' Guide to Bilingualism* (4th edn). Bristol: Multilingual Matters.

Baldauf, R.B. (1994) [Unplanned] language policy and planning. *Annual Review of Applied Linguistics* 14, 82–89.

Bankston, C.L., III (2004) Social capital, cultural values, immigration, and academic achievement: The host country context and contradictory consequences. *Sociology of Education* 77 (2), 176–179.

Baron, D.E. (1992) *The English-only Question: An Official Language for Americans?* New Haven, CT: Yale University Press.

Barron-Hauwaert, S. (2010) *Bilingual Siblings: Language Use in Families*. Bristol: Multilingual Matters.

Beaudrie, S.M. (2012) A corpus-based study on the misspellings of Spanish heritage learners and their implications for teaching. *Linguistics and Education* 23 (1), 135–144.

Bergin, N. (2014) Nebraska takes cattle-feeding crown. *Lincoln Journal Star*, 25 February. See https://journalstar.com/news/state-and-regional/nebraska/nebraska-takes-cattle-feeding-crown/article_9a9d44bf-ea40-5e8e-ae82-e3a0c4b20453.html.

Berman, R.A. and Slobin, D.I. (1987) *Five Ways of Learning How to Talk about Events: A Crosslinguistic Study of Children's Narratives*. Cognitive Science Program, Institute of Cognitive Studies: University of California at Berkeley.

Bernal-Enríquez, Y. and Chávez, E.H. (2003) La enseñanza del español en Nuevo México. In A. Roca and M.C. Colombi (eds) *Mi lengua: Spanish as a Heritage Language in the United States* (pp. 96–119). Washington, DC: Georgetown University Press.

Bissoonauth, A. (2018) Language practices and attitudes of Australian children of Indian descent in a primary education setting. *International Journal of Multilingualism* 15 (1), 54–71.

Bojczyk, K.E., Davis, A.E. and Rana, V. (2016) Mother–child interaction quality in shared book reading: Relation to child vocabulary and readiness to read. *Early Childhood Research Quarterly* 36, 404–414.

Bourgogne, A. (2013) *Be Bilingual. Practical Ideas for Multilingual Families* (Kindle edn). Amazon.com.

Bourhis, R.Y., Giles, H. and Rosenthal, D. (1981) Notes on the construction of a 'subjective vitality questionnaire' for ethnolinguistic groups. *Journal of Multilingual and Multicultural Development* 2 (2), 145–155.
Brannon, E.M. and Van de Walle, G.A. (2001) The development of ordinal numerical competence in young children. *Cognitive Psychology* 43 (1), 53–81.
Brenzinger, M., Yamamoto, A., Aikawa, N., Koundiouba, D., Minasyan, A., Dwyer, A. et al. (2003) Language vitality and endangerment. *Paris: UNESCO Intangible Cultural Unit, Safeguarding Endangered Languages*. http://www. unesco. org/culture/ich/doc/src/00120-en. pdf. (last accessed 1, July 2010).
Caer el veinte (n.d.) In *Diccionario de Mexicanismos*. Academia Mexicana de la Lengua. See https://www.academia.org.mx/obras/obras-de-consulta-en-linea/diccionario-de-mexicanismos.
Carranza, M.A., Gouveia, L., Cogua, J. and Ondracek-Sayers, K. (2002) *The Integration of the Hispanic/Latino Immigrant Workforce*. Report to the Nebraska Mexican American Commission and the Legislative Task Force on the Productive Integration of the Immigrant Workforce Population.
Cashman, H.R. (2006) Mexican Spanish. In A.R. Cayton, R. Sisson and C. Zacher (eds) *The American Midwest: An Interpretive Encyclopedia* (pp. 344–346). Bloomington, IN: Indiana University Press.
Cayton, A.R., Sisson, R. and Zacher, C. (eds) (2006) *The American Midwest: An Interpretive Encyclopedia*. Bloomington, IN: Indiana University Press.
Cenoz, J. (2001) The effect of linguistic distance, L2 status and age on cross-linguistic influence in third language acquisition. *Cross-linguistic Influence in Third Language Acquisition: Psycholinguistic Perspectives* 111 (45), 8–20.
Cho, G. (2000) The role of heritage language in social interactions and relationships: Reflections from a language minority group. *Bilingual Research Journal* 24 (4), 369–384.
Crawford, J. (ed.) (1992) *Language Loyalties: A Source Book on the Official English Controversy*. Chicago, IL: University of Chicago Press.
Cummins, J. (2000) *Language, Power, and Pedagogy: Bilingual Children in the Crossfire*. Clevedon: Multilingual Matters.
Davis, R.P. (2002) Latinos along the Platte: The Hispanic experience in central Nebraska. *Great Plains Research* 12 (1), 27–50.
Deckner, D.F., Adamson, L.B. and Bakeman, R. (2006) Child and maternal contributions to shared reading: Effects on language and literacy development. *Journal of Applied Developmental Psychology* 27 (1), 31–41.
De Houwer, A. (1999) Environmental factors in early bilingual development: The role of parental beliefs and attitudes. In G. Extra (ed.) *Bilingualism and Migration* (pp. 75-96). Berlin: Mouton de Gruyter.
Del Valle, J. (2006) US Latinos, la hispanofonía, and the language ideologies of high modernity. In C. Mar-Molinero and M. Stewart (eds) *Globalization and Language in the Spanish-speaking World* (pp. 27–46). London: Palgrave Macmillan.
Dragún, O. and Márquez, R.L. (1965; 1982) *Historias para ser contadas*. Ottawa: Girol Books.
Durand, T.M. (2010) Latina mothers' school preparation activities and their relation to children's literacy skills. *Journal of Latinos and Education* 9 (7), 207–222.
Eckert, P. and McConnell-Ginet, S. (1992) Communities of practice: Where language, gender and power all live. In K. Hall, M. Bucholtz and B. Moonwomon (eds) *Locating Power: Proceedings of the Second Berkeley Women and Language Conference, Vol. 1* (pp. 89–99). Berkeley, CA: Berkeley University.
Edwards, J. (2009) *Language and Identity: An Introduction*. Cambridge: Cambridge University Press.
Endo, R. (2013) Realities, rewards, and risks of heritage-language education: Perspectives from Japanese immigrant parents in a Midwestern community. *Bilingual Research Journal* 36 (3), 278–294.

Faulstich Orellana, M. (2003) Responsibilities of children in Latino immigrant homes. *New Directions for Student Leadership* 100, 25–39.

Faulstich Orellana, M. (2009) *Translating Childhoods: Immigrant Youth, Language, and Culture*. New Brunswick, NJ: Rutgers University Press.

Feagans, L. (1982) The development and importance of narratives for school adaptation. In L. Vernon-Feagans and D.C. Farran (eds) *The Language of Children Reared in Poverty: Implications for Evaluation and Intervention* (pp. 95–116). Academic Pr.

Fernández, C. and Ortiz, A. (2008) La evolución del pensamiento ordinal en los escolares de 3 a 6 años. *Infancia y aprendizaje* 31 (1), 107–130.

Fishman, J.A. (1972) *The Sociology of Language* (pp. 55–106). Rowley, MA: Newbury House.

Fishman, J.A. (1989) *Language and Ethnicity in Minority Sociolinguistic Perspective*. Clevedon: Multilingual Matters.

Fishman, J.A. (1991) *Reversing Language Shift: Theoretical and Empirical Foundations of Assistance to Threatened Languages*. Clevedon: Multilingual Matters.

Fishman, J.A. (ed.) (2001) *Can Threatened Languages Be Saved? Reversing Language Shift, Revisited*. Clevedon: Multilingual Matters.

Gallo, S. (2017) *Mi Padre: Mexican Immigrant Fathers and their Children's Education*. New York: Teachers College Press.

García, J.R. (1996) *Mexicans in the Midwest, 1900–1932*. Tucson, AZ: University of Arizona Press.

García, O. (1993) From Goya portraits to Goya beans: Elite traditions and popular streams in US Spanish language policy. *Southwest Journal of Linguistics* 12, 69–86.

García, O. and Torres-Guevara, R. (2009) Monoglossic ideologies and language policies in the education of US Latinas/os. In E.G. Murillo, S.A. Villenas, R. Trinidad Galván, J. Sánchez Muñoz, C. Martínez and M. Machado-Casas (eds) *Handbook of Latinos and Education: Theory, Research, and Practice* (pp. 182–193). New York: Routledge.

Garza, J.A. (2009) The long history of Mexican immigration to the rural Midwest. *Journal of the West* 48 (4), 88–95.

Gerena, L. (2011) Parental voice and involvement in cultural context: Understanding rationales, values, and motivational constructs in a dual immersion setting. *Urban Education* 46 (3), 342–370.

Giacchino-Baker, R. and Piller, B. (2006) Parental motivation, attitudes, support, and commitment in a southern Californian two-way immersion program. *Journal of Latinos and Education* 5 (1), 5–28.

Giles, H., Bourhis, R.Y. and Taylor, D. (1977) Towards a theory of language in ethnic group relations. In H. Giles (ed.) *Language, Ethnicity and Intergroup Relations* (pp. 307–348). New York: Academic Press.

Gonzales, M.G. (2009) *Mexicanos: A History of Mexicans in the United States*. Bloomington, IN: Indiana University Press.

González, N., Moll, L.C. and Amanti, C. (eds) (2006) *Funds of Knowledge: Theorizing Practices in Households, Communities, and Classrooms*. New York: Routledge.

Gouveia, L. (1994) Global strategies and local linkages: The case of the US meatpacking industry. In A. Bonanno, L. Busch, W.H. Friedland, L. Gouveia and E. Mingione (eds) *From Columbus to ConAgra: The Globalization of Agriculture and Food* (pp. 125–148). Lawrence, KS: University Press of Kansas.

Gouveia, L. and Powell, M.A. (2007) Second-generation Latinos in Nebraska: A first look. *Migration Information Source*, 16-18.

Gouveia, L. and Stull, D.D. (1996) Latino Immigrants, Meatpacking Work, and Rural Communities: A Nebraska Case Study. Unpublished Manuscript.

Grajeda, R.F. (1998) Mexicans in Nebraska. In R.F. Grajeda (ed.) *Our Treasures. A Celebration of Nebraska's Mexican Heritage. Nuestros Tesoros. Una celebración de la herencia Mexicana de Nebraska* (pp. 15–18). Lincoln: Nebraska State Historical Society.

Granovetter, M.S. (1973) The strength of weak ties. *American Journal of Sociology* 78 (6), 1360–1380.

Great Plains Research 12 (Spring 2001): 27-50 © Copyright by the Center for Great Plains Studies

Guardado, M. (2008) Language, identity, and cultural awareness in Spanish-speaking families. *Canadian Ethnic Studies* 40 (3), 171–181.

Guardado, M. (2009) Speaking Spanish like a boy scout: Language socialization, resistance, and reproduction in a heritage language scout troop. *Canadian Modern Language Review* 66 (1), 101–129.

Gumperz, J.J. (1964) Linguistic and social interaction in two communities. *American Anthropologist* 66 (6, Part 2), 137–153.

Guitérrez-Clellen, V.F. and Kreiter, J. (2003) Understanding child bilingual acquisition using parent and teacher reports. *Applied Psycholinguistics* 24 (2), 267–288.

Gutiérrez-Clellen, V.F. and Goldstein, B. (2004) Narrative development and disorders in bilingual children. In B.A. Goldstein (ed.) *Bilingual Language Development and Disorders in Spanish-English Speakers* (pp. 235–256). Baltimore, MD: Brookes.

Halliday, M.A. (1985) *An Introduction to Functional Linguistics*. London: Edward Arnold.

Hamann, E.T. and Zúñiga, V. (2011) Schooling and the everyday ruptures transnational children encounter in the United States and Mexico. Faculty Publication, Department of Teaching, Learning and Teacher Education, University of Nebraska-Lincoln.

Hawe, P., Webster, C. and Shiell, A. (2004) A glossary of terms for navigating the field of social network analysis. *Journal of Epidemiology and Community Health* 58 (12), 971–975.

Hedberg, N.L. and Westby, C.E. (1993) *Analyzing Storytelling Skills: Theory to Practice*. Communication Skill Builders.

Hernández Gutiérrez, E. (2013) El aprendizaje del número natural en un contexto ordinal en la Educación Infantil. *Edma 0–6: Educación Matemática en la Infancia* 2 (1), 41–56.

Hill, J.H. (1998) Language, race, and white public space. *American Anthropologist* 100 (3), 680–689.

Hult, F.M. (2014) Drive-thru linguistic landscaping: Constructing a linguistically dominant place in a bilingual space. *International Journal of Bilingualism* 18 (5), 507–523.

Husband, C. and Saifullah Khan, V. (1982) The viability of ethnolinguistic vitality: Some creative doubts. *Journal of Multilingual and Multicultural Development* 3, 193–205.

Johansson, V. (2009) Lexical diversity and lexical density in speech and writing: A developmental perspective. *Working Papers in Linguistics* 53, 61–79.

Johnson, D.C., Lynch, S. and Stephens, C. (2016) Educational language policy and the new Latino diaspora in Iowa. *Proceedings of the 14th Annual Conference Latinos in the Heartland: Shaping the Future: Leadership for Inclusive Communities* (pp. 55–59). Columbia, MO: Cambio Center at the University of Missouri.

Kao, S.M. (2015) Narrative development of children. In S.M. Kao (ed.) *Narrative Development of School Children* (pp. 33–51). Singapore: Springer.

Kaplan, R.B. and Baldauf, R.B. (1997) *Language Planning from Practice to Theory*. Clevedon: Multilingual Matters.

Karahan, F. (2004) Ethnolinguistic vitality, attitudes, social network and code-switching: The case of Bosnian-Turks living in Sakarya, Turkey. *International Journal of the Sociology of Language* 165, 59–92.

Karan, M.E. (1996) The dynamics of language spread: A study of the motivations and the social determinants of the spread of Sango in the Republic of Central Africa. Ph.D. dissertation. University of Pennsylvania.

Karan, M.E. (2000) Motivations: Language vitality assessments using the perceived benefit model of language shift. In G. Kindell and M.P. Lewis (eds) *Assessing Ethnolinguistic Vitality: Theory and Practice* (pp. 65–77). Dallas: SIL International.

Karan, M.E. (2011) Understanding and forecasting ethnolinguistic vitality. *Journal of Multilingual and Multicultural Development* 32 (2), 137–149.

Kayitsinga, J. (2015) *A Socioeconomic Profile of Latino/Hispanic Population*. JSRI Demography Report No. DR.07. East Lansing, MI: Julian Samora Research Institute, Michigan State University.

Kindell, G. and Lewis, M.P. (eds) (2000) *Assessing Ethnolinguistic Vitality: Theory and Practice: Selected Papers from the Third International Language Assessment Conference*. Dallas, TX: SIL International.

King, K.A. and Mackey, A. (2007) *The Bilingual Edge: Why, When, and How to Teach your Child a Second Language*. New York: Collins.

King, K., Fogle, L. and Logan-Terry, A. (2008) Family language policy. *Language and Linguistics Compass* 2 (5), 907–922.

Kremser, M.C. (2011) Frog, where are you? Doctoral dissertation, University of Vienna.

Krogstad, J.M. (2017) DACA has shielded nearly 790,000 young unauthorized immigrants from deportation. *FactTank*, 1 September. See http://www.pewresearch.org/fact-tank/2017/09/01/unauthorized-immigrants-covered-by-daca-face-uncertain-future/.

Labov, W. (1972) *Language in the Inner City: Studies in the Black English Vernacular*. Philadelphia, PA: University of Pennsylvania Press.

Labov, W. (1974) The art of sounding and signifying. *Language in its Social Setting* (pp. 84–116). Washington, DC: Anthropological Society of Washington.

Labov, W. and Waletzky, J. (1967) Narrative analysis. Essays on the verbal and visual arts. In *Proceedings of the 1966 Spring Meeting of the American Ethnological Society*. Seattle: University of Washington Press.

Lanza, E. (2007) Multilingualism and the family. In P. Auer and L. Wei (eds) *Handbook of Multilingualism and Multilingual Communication* (pp. 45–67). Berlin: Mouton de Gruyter.

Lapresta-Rey, C., Huguet, Á. and Fernández-Costales, A. (2017) Language attitudes, family language and generational cohort in Catalonia: New contributions from a multivariate analysis. *Language and Intercultural Communication* 17 (2), 135–149.

Lincoln Public Schools (2011) Ethnic distribution of Lincoln Public School students by grade level. *LPS 2011–2012 Annual Statistical Handbook*. See https://docushare.lps.org/docushare/dsweb/Get/Document-990912/Student%20Section.pdf.

Lo Bianco, J. (2008a) Organizing for multilingualism: Ecological and sociological perspectives. In *Keeping Language Diversity Alive: A TESOL Symposium* (pp. 1–18). Alexandria, VA: Teachers of English to Speakers of Other Languages.

Lo Bianco, J. (2008b) Policy activity for heritage languages: Connections with representation and citizenship. In D.M. Brinton, O. Kagan and S. Bauckus (eds) *Heritage Language Education: A New Field Emerging* (pp. 53–69). New York: Routledge.

Lo Bianco, J. and Kreeft Peyton, J. (2013) Vitality of heritage languages in the United States: The role of capacity, opportunity, and desire. *Heritage Language Journal* 10 (3), i–viii.

López, M.M. (2013) Mothers choose: Reasons for enrolling their children in a two-way immersion program. *Bilingual Research Journal* 36 (2), 208–227.

Lunden, M. and Silven, M. (2011) Balanced communication in mid-infancy promotes early vocabulary development: Effects of play with mother and father in mono- and bilingual families. *International Journal of Bilingualism* 15 (4), 535–559.

Maldonado, M. and Licona, A. (2007) Re-thinking integration as reciprocal and spatialized process. *Journal of Latino/Latin American Studies* 2 (4), 128–143.

Mann, C.C. (2000) Reviewing ethnolinguistic vitality: The case of Anglo-Nigerian Pidgin. *Journal of Sociolinguistics* 4 (3), 458–474.

Mar-Molinero, C. and Paffey, D. (2011) Linguistic imperialism: Who owns global Spanish? In M. Diaz-Campos (ed.) *The Handbook of Hispanic Sociolinguistics* (pp. 747–764). Oxford: Wiley-Blackwell.

Martínez, G.A. (2006) *Mexican Americans and language: Del dicho al hecho*. University of Arizona Press.

Martínez, G.A. (2009) Hacia una sociolingüística de la esperanza: El mantenimiento intergeneracional del español y el desarrollo de comunidades hispanohablantes en el sudoeste de los Estados Unidos. *Spanish in Context* 6 (1), 127–137.
Martinez, R., Buntin, J.T. and Escalante, W. (2012) The policy dimensions of the context of reception for immigrants (and Latinos) in the Midwest. In *Cambio de Colores: Latinos in the Heartland: Migration and Shifting Human Landscapes. Proceedings of the 10th Annual Conference, Kansas City, 8–10 June 2011*. Columbia, MO: Cambio Center, University of Missouri.
Martinez, R., Kayitsinga, J., Vélez Ortiz, D. and Horner, P. (2015) *Latinos 2025: A Needs Assessment of Latino Communities in Southeast Michigan*. East Lansing, MI: Julian Samora Research Institute, Michigan State University. See http://jsri.msu.edu.
Mayer, M. (1967) *A Boy, a Dog, and a Frog*. New York: Dial Press.
Mayer, M. (1969) *Frog, Where Are You?* New York: Dial Press.
McGroarty, M. (2008) The political matrix of linguistic ideologies. In B. Spolsky and F.M. Hult (eds) *The Handbook of Educational Linguistics* (pp. 98–112). Malden, MA: Blackwell.
Miller, C.P. (2000) Modifying language beliefs: A role for mother-tongue advocates? In G. Kindell and M. P. Lewis (eds) *Assessing Ethnolinguistic Vitality: Theory and Practice* (pp. 167-187). Dallas: SIL International.
Milroy, L. (1987) *Language and Social Networks* (2nd edn). Oxford: Blackwell.
Milroy, L. (2002) Introduction: Mobility, contact and language change-Working with contemporary speech communities. *Journal of Sociolinguistics* 6 (1), 3–15.
Milroy, L. and Li, W. (1995) *A Social Network Approach to Code-switching*. Cambridge: Cambridge University Press.
Milroy, L. and Milroy, J. (1992) Social network and social class: Toward an integrated sociolinguistic model. *Language in Society* 21 (1), 1–26.
Montrul, S. (2002) Incomplete acquisition and attrition of Spanish tense/aspect distinctions in adult bilinguals. *Bilingualism: Language and Cognition* 5 (1), 39–68.
Muñoz, M.L., Gillam, R.B., Peña, E.D. and Gulley-Faehnle, A. (2003) Measures of language development in fictional narratives of Latino children. *Language, Speech, and Hearing Services in Schools* 34 (4), 332–342.
New American Economy (2016) *The Contributions of New Americans in Nebraska*. August. New York: New American Economy. See www.renewoureconomy.org.
Okita, T. (2002) *Invisible Work. Bilingualism, Language Choice and Childrearing in Intermarried Families*. Amsterdam: John Benjamins.
Oladejo, J. (2010) Parents' attitudes towards bilingual education policy in Taiwan. *Bilingual Research Journal* 30 (1), 147–170; doi:10.1080/15235882.2006.10162870.
Olendzki, A. (2012) No-Self 2.0 [Review of Bruce Hood's *The Self Illusion: How the Social Brain Creates Identity*]. *Shambhala Sun*, November, pp. 81–82.
Park, S.M. and Sarkar, M. (2007) Parents' attitudes toward heritage language maintenance for their children and their efforts to help their children maintain the heritage language: A case study of Korean-Canadian immigrants. *Language, Culture and Curriculum* 20 (3), 223–235.
Pearson, B.Z. (2002) Narrative competence among monolingual and bilingual school children in Miami. In D.K. Oller and R.E. Eilers (eds) *Language and Literacy in Bilingual Children* (pp. 135–174). Clevedon: Multilingual Matters.
Pearson, B.Z. (2008) *Raising a Bilingual Child*. New York: Living Language.
Peñalosa, F. (1981) Some issues in Chicano sociolinguistics. In R.P. Durán (ed.) *Latino Language and Communicative Behavior* (pp. 3–18). Norwood, NJ: Ablex.
Peterson, C. and McCabe, A. (1992) Parental styles of narrative elicitation: Effect on children's narrative structure and content. *First Language* 12 (36), 299–321.
Pew Hispanic Research Center (2014) Demographic profile of Hispanics in Nebraska, 2014. See http://www.pewhispanic.org/states/state/ne/.

Phinney, J.S., Romero, I., Nava, M. and Huang, D. (2001) The role of language, parents, and peers in ethnic identity among adolescents in immigrant families. *Journal of Youth and Adolescence* 30 (2), 135–153.

Potowski, K. (2004) Spanish language shift in Chicago. *Southwest Journal of Linguistics* 23 (1), 87–116.

Potowski, K. (2008) I was raised talking like my mom. The influence of mothers in the development of MexiRicans' phonological and lexical features. In M. Niño-Murcia and J. Rothman (eds) *Bilingualism and Identity* (pp. 201–220). Spanish at the crossroads with other languages.

Quiroz, B.G., Snow, C.E. and Zhao, J. (2010) Vocabulary skills of Spanish–English bilinguals: Impact of mother–child language interactions and home language and literacy support. *International Journal of Bilingualism* 14 (4), 379–399.

Reese, E. and Cox, A. (1999) Quality of adult book reading affects children's emergent literacy. *Developmental Psychology* 35 (1), 20.

Reilly, J., Losh, M., Bellugi, U. and Wulfeck, B. (2004) 'Frog, where are you?' Narratives in children with specific language impairment, early focal brain injury, and Williams syndrome. *Brain and Language* 88 (2), 229–247.

Reyes, I. and Moll, L.C. (2008) Bilingual and biliterate practices at home and school. In B. Spolsky and F.M. Hult (eds) *The Handbook of Educational Linguistics* (pp. 147–160). Malden, MA: Blackwell.

Ricento, T. (2006) Language policy: Theory and practice – an introduction. In T. Ricento (ed.) *An Introduction to Language Policy: Theory and Method* (pp. 10–23). Malden, MA: Blackwell.

Rochín, R.I. (2000) Introduction: Latinos on the Great Plains: An overview. *Great Plains Research* 10 (2), 243–252.

Rochin, R.I., Siles, M.E. and Gomez, J. (1996) Latinos in Nebraska: A Socio-Historical Profile. JSRI Statistical Brief No. 9.

Rodríguez, E., Sunderman, G. and Wood, C. (2017) The relationship between parental language dominance of heritage Spanish-speaking children and child performance in normative language assessments. *Heritage Language Journal* 14 (3), 264–287.

Saenz, R. and Cready, C.M. (1997) *The Southwest-Midwest Mexican American Migration Flows, 1985–1990* (No. 20). Julian Samora Research Institute: Michigan State University.

Santillan, R. (1989) Rosita the Riveter: Midwest Mexican American Women During World War II, 1941–1945. *Perspectives in Mexican American Studies.*

Schecter, S.R. and Bayley, R.J. (2002) *Language as Cultural Practice: Mexicanos en el Norte.* Mahwah, NJ: Lawrence Erlbaum.

Schecter, S.R., Sharken-Taboada, D. and Bayley, R. (2013) Bilingual by choice: Latino parents' rationales and strategies for raising children with two languages. *Bilingual Research Journal* 20 (2), 261–281; doi:10.1080/15235882.1996.10668630.

Shannon, S. and Milian, M. (2002) Parents choose dual language programs in Colorado: A survey. *Bilingual Research Journal* 26 (3), 681–696; doi:10.1080/15235882.2002.1 0162584.

Silva-Corvalán, C. (2014) *Bilingual Language Acquisition: Spanish and English in the First Six Years.* Cambridge: Cambridge University Press.

Simons, G.F. and Fennig, C.D. (eds) (2018) *Ethnologue: Languages of the World* (21st edn). Dallas, TX: SIL International. See http://www.ethnologue.com.

Sittig, A.L. and González, M.F. (2016) *The Mayans among us: Migrant Women and Meatpacking on the Great Plains.* Lincoln, NE: University of Nebraska Press.

Skibbe, L.E., Justice, L.M., Zucker, T.A. and McGinty, A.S. (2008) Relations among maternal literacy beliefs, home literacy practices, and the emergent literacy skills of preschoolers with specific language impairment. *Early Education and Development* 19 (1), 68–88.

Snow, C. (1983) Literacy and language: Relationships during the preschool years. *Harvard Educational Review* 53 (2), 165–189.

Snow, C.E. and Dickinson, D.K. (1990) Social sources of narrative skills at home and at school. *First Language* 10 (29), 87–103.

Spolsky, B. (2009) *Language Management*. Cambridge: Cambridge University Press.

Steinfield, C., Ellison, N.B. and Lampe, C. (2008) Social capital, self-esteem, and use of online social network sites: A longitudinal analysis. *Journal of Applied Developmental Psychology* 29 (6), 434–445.

Takemoto, M. (2010, May) Bilingual children's codeswitching in storytelling activities in Japanese and English. In M.T. Prior, Y. Watanabe and S.-K. Lee (eds) *Selected Proceedings of the 2008 Second Language Research Forum* (pp. 229–245). Somerville, MA: Cascadilla.

Tannenbaum, M. and Howie, P. (2002) The association between language maintenance and family relations: Chinese immigrant children in Australia. *Journal of Multilingual and Multicultural Development* 23 (5), 408–424.

Tollefson, J.W. (1991) *Planning Language, Planning Inequality: Language Policy in the Community*. London: Addison-Wesley Longman.

Touminen, A. (1999) Who decides the home language? A look at multilingual families. *International Journal of the Sociology of Language* 140, 59–76.

Tse, L. (1995) Language brokering among Latino adolescents: Prevalence, attitudes, and school performance. *Hispanic Journal of Behavioral Sciences* 17 (2), 180–193; doi:10.1177/07399863950172003.

Uccelli, P. and Páez, M.M. (2007) Narrative and vocabulary development of bilingual children from kindergarten to first grade: Developmental changes and associations among English and Spanish skills. *Language, Speech, and Hearing Services in Schools* 38 (3), 225–236.

UNESCO (2003) *Language Vitality and Endangerment*. Report from Ad Hoc Expert Group on Endangered Languages. See http://www.unesco.org/new/fileadmin/MULTIMEDIA/HQ/CLT/pdf/Language_vitality_and_endangerment_EN.pdf.

Urciuoli, B. (1996) Exposing Prejudice: Puerto Rican Experiences of Language, Race, and Culture.

Ure, J. and Ellis, J. (1977) Register in descriptive linguistics and linguistic sociology. In O. Uribe-Villas (ed.) *Issues in Sociolinguistics* (pp. 197–243). The Hague: Mouton.

US Census Bureau (2013) *State and County Quick Facts 2013*. See https://www.census.gov/quickfacts/fact/table/US/PST045217.

US Census Bureau (2015a) *Language Spoken at Home*. American Community Survey 1-year Estimates. See https://factfinder.census.gov/faces/tableservices/jsf/pages/productview.xhtml?pid=ACS_15_1YR_S1601&prodType=table.

US Census Bureau (2015b) *Detailed Languages Spoken at Home and Ability to Speak English for the Population 5 Years and Over for United States: 2009–2013*. American Community Survey 5-year Estimates. See https://www.census.gov/data/tables/2013/demo/2009-2013-lang-tables.html.

US Department of Agriculture (2014) January–October 2014 Export Data. See http://usda.mannlib.cornell.edu/MannUsda/viewDocumentInfo.do?documentID=1488 (last accessed 8 August 2018).

Vega, A., Martínez, R. and Stevens, T. (2011) Cosas politicas: Politics, attitudes, and perceptions by region. In R.O. Martínez (ed.) *Latinos in the Midwest* (pp. 57–86). East Lansing, MI: Michigan State University Press.

Vargas, Z. (1991) Armies in the fields and factories: the mexican working classes in the Midwest in the 1920s. *Mexican Studies/Estudios Mexicanos* 7 (1), 47–71.

Velázquez, I. (2008) *Intergenerational Spanish Language Transmission: Attitudes, Motivations and Linguistic Practices in 2 Mexican American Communities*. ProQuest.

Velázquez, I. (2009) Intergenerational Spanish transmission in El Paso, Texas: Parental perceptions of cost/benefit. *Spanish in Context* 6 (1), 69–84.

Velázquez, I. (2012) Mother's social network and family language maintenance. *Journal of Multilingual and Multicultural Development* 34 (2), 189–202.

Velázquez, I. (2014a) Maternal attitudes toward Spanish transmission in the US Midwest: A necessary but insufficient condition for success. *Sociolinguistic Studies* 7 (3), 225–248.

Velázquez, I. (2014b) Maternal perceptions of agency in intergenerational transmission of Spanish: The case of Latinos in the US Midwest. *Journal of Language, Identity & Education* 13 (3), 135–152.

Velázquez, I., Garrido, M. and Millán, M. (2015) Heritage speakers of Spanish in the US Midwest: Reported interlocutors as a measure of family language relevance. *Journal of Multilingual and Multicultural Development* 36 (3), 1–18.

Villenas, S. (2001) Latina mothers and small-town racisms: Creating narratives of dignity and moral education in North Carolina. *Anthropology & Education Quarterly* 32 (1), 3–28.

Villenas, S. and Moreno, M. (2001) To valerse por si misma between race, capitalism, and patriarchy: Latina mother–daughter pedagogies in North Carolina. *International Journal of Qualitative Studies in Education* 14 (5), 671–687.

Vogt, R.J., Cantrell, R.L., Carranza, M.A., Johnson, B.B. and Tomkins, A.J. (2006) Perceptions of Latin American immigration among rural Nebraskans. *Publications from the Center for Applied Rural Innovation (CARI)*, 47, 1–25.

Weigel, D.J., Martin, S.S. and Bennett, K.K. (2006) Contributions of the home literacy environment to preschool-aged children's emerging literacy and language skills. *Early Child Development and Care* 176 (3–4), 357–378.

Wiley, T.G. (1995) Language planning and policy. In S.L. McKay and N.H. Hornberger (eds) *Sociolinguistics and Language Teaching* (pp. 103–148). New York: Cambridge University Press. Published online in July 2006.

Williams, R. (1961) *The Long Revolution*. London: Chatto & Windus.

Williamson, G. (2009) Mean length of utterance. *Speech and language therapy Information (SLTinfo)*. See http://www.sltinfo.com/wp-content/uploads/2014/01/mean-length-of-utterance.pdf.

Williamson, G. (2014) Lexical density. *Speech and language therapy Information (SLTinfo)*. See http://www.sltinfo.com/lexical-density/.

Wimmer, A. (2009) Herder's heritage and the boundary-making approach: Studying ethnicity in immigrant societies. *Sociological Theory* 27 (3), 244–270.

Wishard Guerra, A. (2008) The intersection of language and culture among Mexican-heritage children 3 to 7 years old. In A. McCabe, A.L. Bailey and G. Melzi (eds) *Spanish-language Narration and Literacy: Culture, Cognition, and Emotion*, (pp. 146–174). Cambridge: Cambridge University Press.

Woolard, K.A. and Schieffelin, B.B. (1994) Language ideology. *Annual Review of Anthropology* 23 (1), 55–82.

Wortham, S., Murillo, E. and Hamann, E.T. (eds) (2002) *Education in the New Latino Diaspora. Policy and the Politics of Identity*. Westport, CT: Ablex.

Worthy, J. and Rodríguez-Galindo, A. (2006) 'Mi hija vale dos personas': Latino immigrant parents' perspectives about their children's bilingualism. *Bilingual Research Journal* 30 (2), 579–601.

Yagmur, K. and Ehala, M. (2011) Tradition and innovation in the Ethnolinguistic Vitality theory. *Journal of Multilingual and Multicultural Development* 32 (2), 101–110.

Young, R.L. and Tran, M.T. (2013) Vietnamese parent attitudes toward bilingual education. *Bilingual Research Journal* 23 (2–3), 225–233; doi:10.1080/15235882.1999.10668688.

Yu, B. (2013) Issues in bilingualism and heritage language maintenance: Perspectives of minority-language mothers of children with autism spectrum disorders. *American Journal of Speech-Language Pathology* 22 (1), 10–24.

Zentella, A.C. (1995) The 'Chiquitafication' of US Latinos and their languages, OR why we need an anthropolitical linguistics. In *SALSA III: Proceedings of a Symposium on Language and Society, Austin, TX, 5–7 April 1995*.

Zentella, A.C. (1997) *Growing up Bilingual: Puerto Rican Children in New York*. New York: Wiley-Blackwell.

Zentella, A.C. (2002) Latin languages and identities. In M. Suárez-Orozco and M. Páez (eds) *Latinos: Remaking America* (pp. 321–338). Berkeley: University of California Press.

Zentella, A.C. (2016) Language politics versus el habla del pueblo. In R.E. Guzzardo Tamargo, C.M. Mazak and M. Carmen Parafita Couto (eds) *Spanish-English Codeswitching in the Caribbean and the US* (pp. 11–35). Amsterdam: John Benjamins.

Zhang, A. (2015) *Profile of the Minority Population in Nebraska*. State of Nebraska Health Disparities Report. Lincoln, NE: Nebraska Department of Health and Human Services.

Zhang, D. and Slaughter-Defoe, D.T. (2009) Language attitudes and heritage language maintenance among Chinese immigrant families in the USA. *Language, Culture and Curriculum* 22 (2), 77–93.

Zhang, J. (2009) Mandarin maintenance among immigrant children from the People's Republic of China: An examination of individual networks of linguistic contact. *Language, Culture and Curriculum* 22 (3), 195–213; doi:10.1080/07908310903308279.

Zúñiga, V., Hamann, E.T. and Sánchez García, J. (2016) Students we share are also in Puebla, Mexico: Preliminary findings from a 2009–2010 survey. In H. Romo and O. Mogollón-Lopez (eds) *Mexican Migration to the United States: Perspectives from Both Sides of the Border* (pp. 248–264). Austin, TX: University of Texas Press.

Author Index

Subject Index

www.ingramcontent.com/pod-product-compliance
Ingram Content Group UK Ltd.
Pitfield, Milton Keynes, MK11 3LW, UK
UKHW030427181224
452686UK00026B/521

9 781788 928687